The Repository of Mysteries

The epic mystical poem of Junun

The Repository of Mysteries

The epic mystical poem of Junun

Introduction and translation
by
Jamshid Fanaian

Wollongong, Australia

Copyright © Jamshid Fanaian 2017
Australia

ISBN-13: 978-0-909991-10-4

Cover design by Yvonne I. Woźniak and Michael W. Thomas
Background: adapted detail from an abstract painting by Yvonne I. Woźniak.

The following work is dedicated to the author of the epic verses that have been translated in Part II of this book—a great and courageous man, and a dedicated Bahá'í, whose soul was filled with mystic light and whose heart was filled with loving-kindness—my beloved grandfather, Jináb-i-Mírzá Faraj'u'lláh Faná'ián, writing under the pen-name "Junun".

Acknowledgements

First and foremost I wish to acknowledge and thank my dearly beloved wife, Mahnaz, for her continual, loving support and encouragement in all my writing endeavours. I also wish to express my gratitude to Yvonne I. Woźniak for her many hours of editing, metrical and rhyming adaptation, and other suggestions for the improvement of the text of *The Repository of Mysteries*. Lastly, I thank her husband, Michael W. Thomas, for his exacting work in finalizing the editing, formatting, adding a bibliography and preparing the book for publication.

Contents

Preface xi

Part I:
Introduction

Mysticism in brief 3
   The Hidden Treasure 3
   Mysticism in traditional religions 6
   Following the mystic path 7
   The mystic path and the New World Order 8
   The "verities of the unseen world" 10
   A spiritual path to saving the world 12
   Bringing us closer to Bahá'u'lláh 13
   Two levels of consciousness 16
   Junun's verses 19

The poet—Junun 23
   Origins 23
   "May my life be a sacrifice unto Thee!" 25
   Stories about Junun's love for humanity 27
   Second sight 28
   Seeing into the future 29
   Healer and friend of all 30
   His passing 31
   His continuing influence 33

Junun and his poem 35

Part II:
Translated text of
The Repository of Mysteries
by
Junun

Overture	41
The First Valley	
THE VALLEY OF SEARCH	53
The Second Valley	
THE VALLEY OF LOVE	65
The Third Valley	
THE VALLEY OF KNOWLEDGE	77
The Fourth Valley	
THE VALLEY OF UNITY	117
The Fifth Valley	
THE VALLEY OF CONTENTMENT	159
The Sixth Valley	
THE VALLEY OF WONDERMENT	175
The Seventh Valley	
THE VALLEY OF TRUE POVERTY AND ABSOLUTE NOTHINGNESS	199
Appendix	209
Bibliography	211

Preface

Within the pages of this book are contained my humble efforts to translate the epic verses from the Persian tongue of the masterpiece, *"The Repository of Mysteries"*, composed by my beloved grandfather, Jinab-i-Mirza Faraju'llah Fanaian,[1] designated Junun, who was a great Bahá'í poet and mystic of recent times.

According to the *Encyclopaedia Iranica*, "Junun left behind 70,000 verses of poetry and a few essays. His best known work, *Majma'u'l-Asrár* [*The Repository of Mysteries*] treats, in more than 3,000 verses, man's spiritual journey through the seven valleys (*haft vádí*) to attain reunion with his Creator."[2]

The Universal House of Justice, which is the supreme governing institution of the Bahá'í Faith, has praised the merits *of "The Repository of Mysteries"*. When they realized that I was planning to translate Junun's epic poem into English, that Supreme Body addressed a letter to me, dated 22 September 2010, referring thus to the translation: "The Universal House of Justice hopes that you may be rendered successful in this undertaking and that you may adorn the Bahá'í publications in English with a work that is befitting of Jináb-i-Junún's enormous poetic talents and literary creativity."

The translation of *"The Repository of Mysteries"* has undergone several revisions in the attempt to achieve a result "… that is befitting of Jináb-i-Junún's enormous poetic talents and literary creativity." The magnitude of the task has been staggering and the difficulties manifold.

Translation is never simply a matter of rendering the words and syntax from one language into another because language is so much more than its grammar and vocabulary. Language enshrines the culture—even the very soul—of its people. Between the Persian tongue and the English lies an enormous, seemingly unnegotiable gulf. On the one hand are the elaborately embellished and emotionally charged idioms typical of the languages of the Orient; on the other, the coolly rationalistic and precise phraseology of the Anglo-Saxon West.

Despite the difficulties in the translation of prose from Persian to English, wonderful examples exist in the work of Shoghi Effendi (1897–

---

[1] Jináb-i-Mírzá Faraj'u'lláh Faná'ián. Jináb-i-Mírzá is a title meaning "His excellence, Sir …". The meaning of Mírzá is "son of a prince". The designation "Junun" (Junún), was the pen-name that my grandfather chose for his authorship.

[2] *Encyclopaedia Iranica*, vol. IX, p. 206–207.

1957), appointed Guardian of the Bahá'í Faith and authorized interpreter of its Teachings, whose translations of the Bahá'í Writings are a model of the balance that can be created between poetic beauty and doctrinal clarity. His wife, Rúḥíyyih Khánum, neé Mary Sutherland Maxwell (1910–2000), wrote in her biography of her beloved husband:

> The supreme importance of Shoghi Effendi's English translations and communications can never be sufficiently stressed because of his function as sole and authoritative interpreter of the Sacred Writings, appointed as such by 'Abdu'l-Bahá in His Will. There are many instances when, owing to the looseness of construction in Persian sentences, there could be an ambiguity in the mind of the reader regarding the meaning. Careful and correct English, not lending itself to ambiguity in the first place, became, when coupled with Shoghi Effendi's brilliant mind and his power as interpreter of the Holy Word, what we might well call the crystallizing vehicle of the teachings.[1]

In the case of *"The Repository of Mysteries"*, translation is further complicated by the attempt to render the interpretation within the structure of rhyme and metre to match the original, without significantly altering the meaning or stepping beyond the limits of each couplet. With such restrictions, some translated lines may appear contrived or clumsy. I think it would be impossible to fully reflect the mastery of Junun's poetry in any translation. One is ever left with the feeling that this is still a work in progress.

Notwithstanding the general problems of translation already delineated, there is a further aspect of Junun's masterpiece, *"The Repository of Mysteries"*, that poses the greatest challenge to any translator, however fluent in both languages he or she may be, and however skilled in the art of versification. Any book on mysticism touches on themes for which there are no words or phrases in any language. Mysticism explores realms of being that cannot be expressed by any syllable or sound—where communication is on the level of heart-to-heart and soul-to-soul. Therefore, the vision of the mystic can only be shared in writing through allegory and enigma, through parable and paradox.

As regards, *"The Repository of Mysteries"* it is no ordinary treatise on mysticism. Junun's vision opens onto the highest realms, while at the same time plunging into unfathomable depths of unexplored domains, delving into mystery within mystery. He penetrates into the various layers of the world of being that are beyond the grasp of the keenest mind. He soars to an atmosphere higher than any intellectual concept

---

[1] Rúḥíyyih Khánum Rabbani, *The Priceless Pearl*, p. 202.

can follow. Junun ventures to probe into the meaning of the creation and Creator. He explores the intrinsic essence of the cosmos.

A translator must grasp the inner meanings of a work in order to render it into another language. I most humbly admit my limitations. Such elevated spheres as those through which my beloved grandfather was able to soar are as far beyond my own spiritual experience as they are beyond any intellectual concept.

Another point that should be made is that in Persian, as in many other languages, there is no distinction between the male and female pronoun in the third person, the same word being used for both 'he' and 'she'. Therefore, theoretically, when referring to God, the Persian pronoun could be translated into English as 'He' or 'She'. Although traditionally God is referred to as 'He', we know that God has no gender; therefore in allegorical writing there should be no difference whether one uses the male or female pronoun—and using them interchangeably should not be seen as anthropomorphism or pantheism. In "*The Repository of Mysteries*", I found that there were many allegories that refer to God using feminine terms such as: sweetheart, loved one, heart-charmer, enchanter, with long hair, scented locks, musk-laden tresses, charming eyes, attractive stature, a face covered by a veil, etc. Here I considered that the use of the female pronoun 'She' was more appropriate than 'He'. To use the pronoun, 'He' for the symbolic Presence of God, described in feminine terms would have been inconsistent with the context. In fact, in the following line, Junun clearly demonstrates that God can be addressed allegorically as either male or female:

Sometimes we call Him He-God, sometimes She-Beloved.

However, we have to bear in mind that in the Arabic language, as in English, both male and female pronouns exist. Also, generally, in the Bahá'í Writings, whether they are translated from Arabic or Persian, the pronoun 'He' has been used for God as indeed has been the case in traditional scriptures.

While we are referring to feminine allegories for the Presence of God, it should be noted that those Christian readers, who have been brought up with the notion that celibacy is more consistent with saintliness than marital love, may find some of Junun's allegories surprisingly erotic. It might help them to remember the fact that the sexual expression of love between a husband and wife was the creation of God for the procreation of the human race. Not only is it not sinful but it should be treated with respect and gratitude. The requirement for celibacy in the priesthood was a later construct of the Roman Catholic Church, and the notion arose from an erroneous assumption that Jesus was unmarried because of His sanctity rather than because of His homelessness. In the early Christian church, marriage was not forbidden to the priesthood. In his second epistle to Timothy, Saint Paul wrote:

> A bishop then must be blameless, **the husband of one wife**,[1] vigilant, sober, of good behaviour, given to hospitality, apt to teach; Not given to wine, no striker, not greedy of filthy lucre; but patient, not a brawler, not covetous; One that ruleth well his own house, having his children in subjection with all gravity; (For if a man know not how to rule his own house, how shall he take care of the church of God?)[2]

In fact many of the writings of mystics—even Christian mystics—have contained allusions to sexual love. For, how better to describe to the uninitiated the overwhelming desire that a true seeker on the path of reunion with God feels than by comparing it to the feeling that all adult human beings will experience at some time in their passionate yearning for their beloved one—and the transportations of joy experienced when that desire is fulfilled.

Both the Old and the New Testaments of the Holy Bible use the metaphor of the coming of a bride when referring to a new revelation from God. The following example from the Deuterocanonical Apocrypha of the Old Testament states explicitly in reference to the first coming of Christ:

> Behold, the time shall come, that these tokens which I have told thee shall come to pass, and the bride shall appear, and she coming forth shall be seen, that now is withdrawn from the earth.[3]

In the New Testament appears the following passage from the Revelation of St John, the "new Jerusalem", which means the new Law of God revealed for our present age, is also described as a bride:

> And I John saw the holy city, new Jerusalem, coming down from God out of heaven, prepared as a bride adorned for her husband.[4]

Bahá'u'lláh also makes allusions to erotic love in His mystical Writings. For example the image of the unveiling of the bride symbolizes the unveiling of the new Revelation as well as being an

---

[1] The present author's emphasis.
[2] 2 Timothy 3:2–6 (KJB)
[3] Esdras 2 (Ezra 4) (KJB)
[4] Revelation 21:2 (KJB)

expression of the ecstasy of Bahá'u'lláh's own spiritual experience.

> *The mystic and wondrous Bride, hidden ere this beneath the veiling of utterance (Bayan), hath now, by the grace of God and His divine favour, been made manifest even as the resplendent light shed by the beauty of the Beloved.* 1

In another Tablet, Bahá'u'lláh makes mention of a Maiden, who is

> *... the embodiment of the remembrance of the name of my Lord. ... So rejoiced was she in her very soul that her countenance shone with the ornament of the good-pleasure of God, and her cheeks glowed with the brightness of the all-Merciful. Betwixt earth and heaven she was raising a call which captivated the hearts and minds of men. She was imparting to both My inward and outward being tidings which rejoiced my soul, and the souls of God's honoured servants.* 2

There are other Writings, yet to be officially translated, in which Bahá'u'lláh enthrals the reader with His aesthetically erotic and enchanting depiction of yearning love, only to shatter the illusion with the tragic images of the heartbreak of betrayal and death.[3] So, following the same tradition, Junun also uses erotic imagery to describe the indescribable.

In rendering Junun's poetry into English, I regretfully admit that it was not possible for me to preserve all the beauty, the rhythmic effect, the music of the words, the ornate style and the subtleties of the original language. Neither was it possible for me to preserve the beauty of mystical terms that have no equivalent in the English language.

There is an enormous difference between the structure and syntax of the Persian and English languages. Moreover, the mystic experience of the author is beyond intellectual concept, while the music of his poetry touches the soul and the heart with a sense that rises far beyond the literal meaning of his words. So, it has required much effort to render Junun's depictions into English with any degree of accuracy and poetic beauty.

Junun strives to elevate us to another realm of the world of being, which is light upon light, where we soar in an atmosphere which is full of joy and bliss. To find words that express a realm higher than this material world is not easy in any language. Words have been created to convey human experiences; yet experience of the higher realm is not a

---

1 Bahá'u'lláh, *The Hidden Words*, Persian epilogue
2 Bahá'u'lláh, *Súratu'l-Haykal*, cited by Shoghi Effendi in *God Passes By*, p. 101.
3 See http://bahai-library.com/walbridge_erotic_allegory

common human experience. However, Junun has an uncommon command of language. It is as if he has been able to download the necessary phrases to express his inner meanings through some secret, spiritual channel. Dr Iman, a Persian Bahá'í scholar, once commented: "Junun has an amazing command of words. The words are like wax in his hand; he can shape them in any way he wants."

In the process of translating, I had to assure myself of the exact meaning of every word that Junun used. It happened that sometimes I needed to consult *Mo'ín's Persian Dictionary*, which consists of six thick volumes. Although it is the largest monolingual dictionary in the Persian language, consisting of a total of 5,594 pages of words, I could not find in it some of the words that Junun used. Those words could only be found in *Dehkhoda's Dictionary*, a sixteen volume encyclopaedic dictionary.[1] I was amazed at my grandfather's erudition. My dear grandfather had not entered any school and had no academic qualifications. In fact he had only been taught to recognize the Persian alphabet. Yet his choice of words was most accurate and professional. Certainly he had not consulted *Dehkhoda's Dictionary* as it was not published until half a century after Junun had left this mortal realm.

Despite all the above-mentioned difficulties, I have made every attempt to render the mystic vision of Junun as accurately as possible into English. My determination to do so has stemmed from the deep love that I have felt for my grandfather since my earliest childhood, to which was later added my awed admiration for his achievements.

The other driving force for my translation of *"The Repository of Mysteries"* has been the desire to introduce Junun's mystic work to the West. The hope is that perhaps from the present English version it will be possible to translate this important and beautiful work into other languages. Thus its mystic melodies might become available to all people who wish to turn their vision away from the material world, to explore other more glorious horizons and discover realms of reality far beyond anything they have ever imagined could possibly exist.

The theme of *"The Repository of Mysteries"* is concerned with bringing out the innate potential—the potential to grow the seed of divinity—that lies at the core of each soul. The spiritual wayfarer succeeds in transcending the limited self and gains access to heights beyond his utmost aspiration. He will undergo a second birth, being reborn into the realm of spirit. He becomes the citizen of a universe immeasurably greater than he could ever imagine, even in his wildest dreams.

---

[1] Compiled by lexicographer, Ali Akbar Dehkhoda *et alia*, published posthumously in 1999.

Preface

Thus *"The Repository of Mysteries"* can be described as a mystic manual to guide the seeker in the search for the Beloved. The soul yearns to return to its spiritual source. Although the soul starts its existence at the moment of the conception of the human embryo, its creation comes from the celestial realm, which is its natural home. It, therefore, longs to break its earthly fetters and attain the bliss and rapture of that heavenly sphere.

In the following pages of the *Introduction*, we will discuss the role of mysticism in religion and especially the emphasis placed in the Bahá'í Faith on the importance of spiritual development and the search for mystic understanding.

We will also present some biographical details of the life of Junun, who was stirred by the love of Bahá'u'lláh from a tender age, thus becoming a channel of inspiration not only to all who knew him personally but also to generations of potential readers of his writings now and in the future.

Part I

Introduction

Mysticism in brief
The Hidden Treasure

The world of creation is the proof of the existence of a Creator. In his epistle to the Romans, St Paul states that "... the invisible things of him from the creation of the world are clearly seen, being understood by the things that are made, even his eternal power and Godhead ...."[1] St Paul adds that, therefore, there is no excuse for man not to recognize, worship and obey God.

Bahá'u'lláh reveals another element to our understanding of God's creation—the fact that creation is the emanation of God's Love:

> O SON OF MAN! I loved thy creation, hence I created thee. Wherefore, do thou love Me, that I may name thy name and fill thy soul with the spirit of life.[2]

According to a well-known Islamic tradition, the reason that God called creation into being was because He was the Hidden Treasure Who wished to make Himself known. This tradition is affirmed repeatedly in the Bahá'í Writings. For example, in His *Prayers and Meditations*, Bahá'u'lláh wrote:

> Lauded be Thy name, O Lord my God! I testify that Thou wast a hidden Treasure wrapped within Thine immemorial Being and an impenetrable Mystery enshrined in Thine own Essence. Wishing to reveal Thyself, Thou didst call into being the Greater and the Lesser Worlds, and didst choose Man above all Thy creatures, and didst make Him a sign of both of these worlds, O Thou Who art our Lord, the Most Compassionate!

> Thou didst raise Him up to occupy Thy throne before all the people of Thy creation. Thou didst enable Him to unravel Thy mysteries, and to shine with the lights of Thine inspiration and Thy Revelation, and to manifest Thy names and Thine attributes. Through Him Thou didst adorn the preamble of the book of Thy creation, O Thou Who art the Ruler of the universe Thou hast fashioned![3]

In this prayer, the word *"Man"* refers to the Manifestations of God—the Prophets or Messengers Who are sent by God in every age to reveal

---

[1] Romans 1: 20 (KJB)
[2] Bahá'u'lláh, *The Hidden Words*, Arabic No. 4.
[3] *Prayers and Meditations by Bahá'u'lláh*, No. XXXVIII, p. 48.

1 THE REPOSITORY OF MYSTERIES: INTRODUCTION

in Themselves the Divine Attributes of God, educate the people in the Way of God and advance human civilization to consecutively higher levels. At Bahá'u'lláh's own request, His Son, 'Abdu'l-Bahá, who was only an adolescent boy at the time, explained to an enquirer the meaning of the tradition, *"I was the Hidden Treasure and I wished to be made known"* in the following commentary: [1]

> *O wayfarer in the path of the Beloved! Know thou that the main purpose of this holy tradition is to make mention of the stages of God's concealment and manifestation within the Embodiments of Truth, They who are the Dawning-places of His All-Glorious Being. For example, before the flame of the undying Fire is lit and manifest, it existeth by itself within itself in the hidden identity of the universal Manifestations, and this is the stage of the "Hidden Treasure". And when the blessed Tree is kindled by itself within itself, and that Divine Fire burneth by its essence within its essence, this is the stage of "I wished to be made known". And when it shineth forth from the Horizon of the universe with infinite Divine Names and Attributes upon the contingent and placeless worlds, this constituteth the emergence of a new and wondrous creation which correspondeth to the stage of "Thus I called creation into being". And when the sanctified souls rend asunder the veils of all earthly attachments and worldly conditions, and hasten to the stage of gazing on the beauty of the Divine Presence and are honoured by recognizing the Manifestation and are able to witness the splendour of God's Most Great Sign in their hearts, then will the purpose of creation, which is the knowledge of Him Who is the Eternal Truth, become manifest.* [2]

There are several important truths contained within this commentary. Firstly, 'Abdu'l-Bahá makes it clear that:

- The *"Hidden Treasure"* is the concealment of God's Divine Names and Attributes in the *"Embodiments of Truth"*—the Universal Manifestations—before Their emergence.
- When God wishes *"to be made known"*, He activates through the Holy Spirit His Chosen Messenger for the age, to arise in His Cause and reveal the Word of God that has been sent down to Him.
- The Word of God revealed for the age instigates "the emergence of a new and wondrous creation", which is the stage of "Thus I called creation into being".

Therefore we realize that the word "creation" in the Islamic tradition does not refer to the physical Universe and all that it contains,

---

[1] Adib Taherzadeh, *The Covenant of Bahá'u'lláh*, p. 24.
[2] *The Kitáb-i-Aqdas*, Notes, p. 175.

which has always existed in some form. If the creation had a beginning in time it would imply that God has not always been the Creator. Yet there can never have been a time when God, the Pre-Existent and Unchangeable, was not the Creator.

From 'Abdu'l-Bahá's commentary, it is clear that God makes Himself known to man through the *"Embodiments of Truth"*, the Manifestations of God; and that *"sanctified souls"* can become acquainted with *"the purpose of creation"* when they:

- rend asunder the veils of all earthly attachments and worldly conditions;
- hasten to the stage of gazing on the beauty of the Divine Presence;
- are honoured by recognizing the Manifestation; and
- are able to witness the splendour of God's Most Great Sign in their hearts.

When the seeker has fulfilled the above requirements, he or she will understand that *"the purpose of creation"* is *"the knowledge of Him Who is the Eternal Truth, become manifest"*—in other words, the Manifestation of God. Otherwise the knowledge and the love of God cannot be developed to the fullest extent that is possible within the limits of the human heart and soul. It cannot be achieved by the logic of the mind or worldly comprehension, no matter how sophisticated. Rather it requires the seeker to emerge into the Divine Light of the Manifestation of God. The Divine Light sheds radiance on the hidden reality and makes it visible to the inner eye. On their own, neither the study of the physical sciences nor the delving into philosophy can ever lead the human to the higher realm and its glorious mysteries.

From the above it is clear that, from the Bahá'í point of view, whenever we use the terms:

- God
- recognition of God
- attaining the presence of God
- having a vision of God,

we mean the inner reality of the Manifestation of God in the seen and unseen worlds. To tread the mystic path means to tread the path towards the Manifestation of God. Shoghi Effendi says:

> There is, therefore, only one way to God and that is through the realization of his Manifestation or Prophet in that age. ... Anyhow it is only through these that we can know God. These manifest the divine attributes and therefore by knowing them we can know God. The mystic path that the traveller should

I THE REPOSITORY OF MYSTERIES: INTRODUCTION

follow is therefore to the Prophet.[1]

Mysticism in traditional religions

The role of religion has ever been to promote the spiritual development of individual believers and to cultivate their heavenly potential. Unfortunately, in every faith, the upsurge of an ambitious and power-hungry religious hierarchy has led to the stunting of the spiritual development of their lowly followers. Instead of uplifting and inspiring the souls of their congregations, the priestly classes have indoctrinated them with their own interpretations of the scriptures, and aroused their religious ardour with their man-made rituals and ceremonies. At times they have even incited hatred within their flock for any individual or group that does not accept the dogmas of their particular religious brand.

Nevertheless, there have been saintly men and women in every faith and culture who have striven to achieve a closer relationship with Transcendent Reality—union with God. In the past, only a select few—most often members of monastic orders who had access to the scriptures and time for contemplation—were empowered to make this aspect of religion their main aim. Such mystics and free-thinkers often trod a dangerous path, always at risk of excommunication, with the attendant horrors of being branded as heretics.

Although in the western democratic world, religious persecution is no longer tolerated, the mystic path remains the domain of but a few. There are over 50,000 sects of Christianity, most of which have a professional clergy who organize church services in accordance with the accepted standards and doctrines of that particular denomination. The greatest majority of the congregations are "spoon-fed" with the church's interpretations of the Scriptures and strongly discouraged from independent thought. For instance, bible study classes are based on a particular textbook with set questions and answers. There is only one right answer, and no time is allowed for discussion around different understandings.

One of the few Christian sects, which, to some degree, has encouraged independent search along the mystic path, is the Society of Friends (Quakers), a Christian movement founded in the mid-17th century by a religious free-thinker, the saintly George Fox. A central principle of the Quaker faith is the concept of the 'Inner Light', which refers to Christ's direct working in the soul. The Society of Friends has no clergy as such. A meeting for worship consists mostly of silent meditation unless a member of the meeting is inspired by the Holy

---

[1] Shoghi Effendi in *Lights of Guidance*, p. 511.

Spirit to speak by way of ministry. Although initially the Quakers rejected all set forms of worship, sacraments and rituals, today a large percentage of Quakers, particularly in the United States of America, belong to splinter groups of so-called "evangelical Quakers". The evangelical Quakers appoint pastors to lead programmed services, in which readings from the bible and hymn singing break the silent worship.

In synagogues and mosques, the services are led by the rabbis and imams, respectively, with set responses from the congregation. Judaism has a tradition of ancient mystical teachings known as the Kabbalah, which was taught only to those who were already versed in the Torah and Talmud, and often not until the believer was over 40 years of age. As often happens when sacred scriptures are restricted to an elect minority, the Kabbalah and its teachings have been distorted by some so-called mystics and occultists who have applied them to their own agendas.

Similarly, the teachings of Islam have been set aside by some Sufi mystics who claim that its religious laws are only intended for the common man and not for spiritual masters such as themselves. The well-known and loved mystic, Jalálu'd-Dín Rúmí, however, was a true follower of Muḥammad and a shining example of Islamic mysticism. Rúmí's spiritual insights are expressed in his allegorical stories and poetry, which were articulated in the highest classical style of Persian literature. These were beyond the understanding of some of the Mullas (Muslim priests) who rejected him out of ignorance.

Although daily prayer is a requirement of every religion, there has generally been no encouragement for the common folk to engage in meditation or contemplation. That is what has been missing in the spiritual experience of the majority of devout adherents of the world's traditional religions.

As the spiritually starved drifted away from the traditional churches, many dropped religion altogether and created a new deity for themselves in the "golden calf" of materialism. Others have taken up one or other of the modes of meditation taught by various gurus of the ancient Hindu and Buddhist traditions; or those who adhere to so-called "New Age" practices. As such transcendental meditation groups have been increasing in popularity, they have been perceived by the churchmen as a greater threat than mere materialism. Mystic leaders are seen as competing for the souls of the congregation.

Following the mystic path

True mysticism is not a competitive rival to religion; rather, it is an essential element of every true faith. It should be regarded as a pathway or a method of practice through which the believer can experience the beauty of religion, discovering its fathomless mysteries and experiencing the bliss of union with God. Following the mystic path enhances the spiritual development of the believers and cultivates the inner reality of their lives.

In recent times, science and technology have flourished exponentially. The resulting developments have been greeted with much enthusiasm by the majority of people. However, while society changed rapidly, the traditional religions remained lingering behind the times; they could not cope with the fast progress seen in every branch of human knowledge and the new ethical questions that were arising as a result. The social teachings of the former religions could not meet the requirements of the time; they became a stumbling block along the way of social and scientific progress. The conflict already existing between science and religion was exacerbated. To some it seemed that science could solve all problems, satisfy the needs of the time and take the place of outdated religion.

However, scientific advances have not brought complete satisfaction to the souls of mankind as human existence is not confined to the experience of the material world. Mystic intuition is not foreign to the nature of man. In fact, mysticism can be described as a "total experience". In their search for inner meaning, spiritual thinkers and sages in every age and from every faith were already gaining an understanding of the physical realm that has only been uncovered by science in recent decades. Spiritually revealed truth has often proved to be more reliable than any experiment in the scientific laboratory or deduction of reason. At the same time, Divine Revelation has had the most profound influence on the individual and collective life of the mankind throughout the ages. The appearance of every Manifestation[1] of God has propelled humanity onto another stage of an advancing civilization.

The mystic path and the New World Order

The Revelation of Bahá'u'lláh has enormously impacted the souls and minds of the inhabitants of the world, although most of them do not realize whence their inspiration has originated. There is an inclination towards the spiritual. It is gradually becoming the aspiration of the human species to disentangle itself from the chains of materialism. There is a growing disgust for the old pattern of life—shallow, greedy, exploitative and selfish. Like a blossom budding in the springtime after winter snows have thawed, the human world is ready to acknowledge: "That's enough. It's time to grow." But there is only one source of the

---

[1] See Note 4 in the Appendix.

light and energy that can provide humanity with the impetus for that growth.

In the words of Shoghi Effendi:

> What else ... but the unreserved acceptance of the Divine Programme enunciated ... by Bahá'u'lláh, embodying in its essentials God's divinely-appointed scheme for the unification of mankind in this age, coupled with an indomitable conviction in the unfailing efficacy of each and all of its provisions, is eventually capable of withstanding the forces of internal disintegration which, if unchecked, must needs continue to eat into the vitals of a despairing society. It is towards this goal—the goal of a new World Order, Divine in origin, all-embracing in scope, equitable in principle, challenging in its features—that a harassed humanity must strive. [1]

All previous Revelations have contributed towards the recognition and development of man's inner spiritual potential. The virtues have been taught in the scriptures of every faith. Even in pagan civilizations, whatever has been moral and ethical has stemmed from a Divine Teacher of an ancient, forgotten time. However, the latest Divine Revelation of God, which occurred in the middle of the nineteenth century, not only offers a more elevated standard of spiritual development, but has also released mysterious forces that can assist human beings to manifest their deepest intellectual and spiritual reality. All that was previously hidden must now become manifest.

In this new age, the mystic quest is to be everyone's concern. Bahá'u'lláh calls this day, **"the Day whereon the Finger of majesty and power hath opened the seal of the Wine of Reunion, and called all who are in the heavens and all who are on the earth."**[2]

The "verities of the unseen world"

In the Bahá'í Faith, the pursuit of mystic perception, which brings one to a realization of the Presence of God through union with the Beloved Revealer for the age, is central to the religious practices of the whole community. This is something that has not been encouraged in world religions in the past, where rapturous union with God has been treated with suspicion even amongst the priestly or monastic classes. Therefore, the generality of the people, even devout believers, have not been aware of the inner realm or experienced it as a reality.

---

[1] Shoghi Effendi, The Goal of the New World Order, *The Compilation of Compilations* vol. II, p. 175.
[2] *Gleanings from the Writings of Bahá'u'lláh*, p. 28.

I   The Repository of Mysteries: Introduction

Bahá'u'lláh writes, **"Ascend unto My heaven, that thou mayest obtain the joy of reunion."** [1] Man's ultimate realization comes from the experience of union with God, which is the goal of the mystic journey. Again Bahá'u'lláh prays:

> Cast upon this poor and desolate creature, O my Lord, the glance of Thy wealth, and flood his heart with the beams of Thy knowledge, that he may apprehend the verities of the unseen world, and discover the mysteries of Thy heavenly realm, and perceive the signs and tokens of Thy kingdom, and behold the manifold revelations of this earthly life all set forth before the face of Him Who is the Revealer of Thine own Self. [2]

In this prayer, Bahá'u'lláh supplicates that what the seeker experiences on the mystic path should **"be set forth before the face of Him Who is the Revealer of Thine own Self"**—in other words: the seeker's path should be illumined by the light of the Manifestation of God. It is important for us to remember that, when we are meditating, it is difficult for us to distinguish the **"verities of the unseen world"** from the visions that are created in our imaginations by our own egos—visions that may be powerful enough to even be mistaken for the Ultimate Reality, Who is in fact the Unknowable and the Inaccessible. The only way that we can ensure the authenticity of our experience is to turn towards the Manifestation of God for our age, the Christ Spirit, returned in "the Glory of God"—the "new name" promised in both the Old and the New Testament of the Bible. The title "Bahá'u'lláh" is Arabic for "The Glory of God" or "The Glory of the Lord".

In referring to this age, Isaiah wrote: "And the Gentiles shall see thy righteousness, and all kings thy glory: and thou shalt be called by a new name, which the mouth of the LORD shall name." [3] This is affirmed by St John of Patmos in his Book of Revelation:

> Him that overcometh will I make a pillar in the temple of my God, and he shall go no more out: and I will write upon him the name of my God, and the name of the city of my God, which is new Jerusalem, which cometh down out of heaven from my God: and I will write upon him my new name. [4]

The following words of Bahá'u'lláh are matchless in describing the role of the prophets, and unique in the entire body of sacred Scriptures of the world in defining the subtleties of the nature of the

---

[1]   Bahá'u'lláh, *The Hidden Words*, Arabic No. 61.
[2]   *Prayers and Meditations of Bahá'u'lláh*, No, XXXVII, p. 52.
[3]   Isaiah, 62:2 (KJB)
[4]   Revelation, 3:12 (KJB)

Manifestations of God.

> The door of the knowledge of the Ancient of Days being thus closed in the face of all beings, the Source of infinite grace ... hath caused those luminous Gems of Holiness to appear out of the realm of the spirit, in the noble form of the human temple, and be made manifest unto all men, that they may impart unto the world the mysteries of the unchangeable Being, and tell of the subtleties of His imperishable Essence.
>
> These sanctified Mirrors, these Day Springs of ancient glory, are, one and all, the Exponents on earth of Him Who is the central Orb of the universe, its Essence and ultimate Purpose. From Him proceed their knowledge and power; from Him is derived their sovereignty. The beauty of their countenance is but a reflection of His image, and their revelation a sign of His deathless glory. They are the Treasuries of Divine knowledge, and the Repositories of celestial wisdom. Through them is transmitted a grace that is infinite, and by them is revealed the Light that can never fade.... These Tabernacles of Holiness, these Primal Mirrors, which reflect the light of unfading glory, are but expressions of Him Who is the Invisible of the Invisibles. By the revelation of these Gems of Divine virtue all the names and attributes of God, such as knowledge and power, sovereignty and dominion, mercy and wisdom, glory, bounty, and grace, are made manifest. [1]

Thus God reveals Himself through the Manifestation of God. It is only by this grace and bounty that man is not totally deprived of the vision of the beauty and the dazzling glory of God. Without illumination from the rays of the Divine Sun, the heart is narrow and dark like a miser's porch. Such a heart does not expand, nor do doors open within it to the vastness of the spiritual realms. Being empty of the Loving God's sweet savour, it is like being in a sepulchre.

A spiritual path to saving the world

With the appearance of the Manifestation of God on earth, the Timeless has entered into time. The Revelation of Bahá'u'lláh has created a balance between the outer and inner life. Although mystic in its essence, the Bahá'í Faith has a mission to save the planet, and to establish a new world order, which is divinely revealed and unique in the annals of human governing systems. That is why Bahá'u'lláh has prohibited His followers from turning their back on society. Rather, every Bahá'í is obliged to devote his or her life to the transformation of humanity. So, while a Bahá'í has an ardent longing to become closer to

---

[1] *Gleanings from the Writings of Bahá'u'lláh*, pp. 47-48.

I The Repository of Mysteries: Introduction

God and to enter into His Presence, this inner journey does not render him neglectful of his outer duties in his daily life. On the contrary, it transforms his life to that of service to humankind. The purpose of spiritual training is to partake of the available spiritual powers that inspire and energize the seeker in his or her work so as to be of practical benefit to the world.

The Bahá'í Faith discourages a theoretical discussion about deity that does not have a practical aim, or result in the betterment of the world. Instead, the Bahá'í believers are encouraged to draw regularly on the energies of the celestial source, which is only accessible through the Manifestation of God, Bahá'u'lláh. It is much more productive and beneficial to turn directly to the Mediator than to become involved in arguments about theories that might cause disunity or may lead one into a labyrinth of fancy and superstition.

The Bahá'í Writings give us the guidelines on how to take practical steps along the path of spiritual development, which means acquiring the virtues that have been at the foundation of every religion. However, it is not enough to have a mere knowledge about the spiritual virtues. We must also practice them to the extent that they become internalized, thus becoming part of who we are. To become illumined is a vital and real experience; reading alone cannot replace the actual experience. Just to read a text book about driving a vehicle does not make one a proficient driver. One must have practice in driving. In the same way, no matter how much time and devotion we expend in reading the guidelines of the Holy Writings, we must still devote the time to practice them. Without practicing we cannot realize their true significance. The Bahá'í teachings can demonstrate their efficacy and transforming effect only when they are applied to our daily life; for to practice the virtues when we are in easy circumstances and amongst loving friends does not prove that they are truly ingrained into our souls. It is when we are tested by difficult encounters, and the trials and tribulations of life, that we can prove ourselves. 'Abdu'l-Bahá states:

> Likewise, an expert student prepareth and memorizeth his lessons and exercises with the utmost effort, and in the day of examination he appeareth with infinite joy before the master. Likewise, the pure gold shineth radiantly in the fire of test. [1]

The dynamic possibilities encoded in each one of us must be explored and exploited. We have to recognize, orchestrate and develop all the positive potentialities within us. In so doing we will learn to cast aside our petty, selfish egos, leaving the way clear for the discovery of

---

[1] 'Abdu'l-Bahá in *Baha'i World Faith*, p. 371.

the divine Self within—the portion of divinity that lies enshrined in the innermost reality of our souls In some, this process can be fast and explosive; in others it might be slow and steady. Whatever stage of spiritual development one achieves, one cannot 'rest on one's laurels', imagining that one has done enough. We are like the concert pianist who must continue the daily practice of scales, arpeggios and other tiresome finger exercises in order to maintain his skills at the highest level. One has to be determined, and exert the utmost efforts for the continual unfolding of one's inner light.

Our efforts are rewarded a hundredfold through the release of the inner energies that give strength to our character. As we discover our divine reality, we experience the joy of leading a richer and more fruitful life. Rather than suffering the disappointments encountered in self-centered goals, we can participate in work of a world-embracing vision. At the same time, we are sustained in our struggles through our prayers and our contemplation of the Beauty of God as manifested in His Chosen One for this age—Bahá'u'lláh, the Glory of God. Thus we have entered upon the mystic path of union with the Beloved. *"The Repository of Mysteries"* of Junun covers this theme thoroughly and powerfully.

Bringing us closer to Bahá'u'lláh

In the same way that Rúmí remained humbly faithful to Muḥammad and the laws of Islam, so the poet and mystic, Junun, remained submissive to the Law of God, as revealed by Bahá'u'lláh, and did not deviate as much as a hairsbreadth from it. Thus, through *"The Repository of Mysteries"* the seeker can safely share something of Junun's experience of his spiritual journey to the Beloved. Seen through Junun's eyes, the mystic path leads to a complete transformation, a spiritual rebirth through which the seeker gains entry into the presence of God, to experience a vision of the Beauty of God as manifested in Bahá'u'lláh. This level of consciousness goes beyond the limits of the mind; it is a blissful mystic experience. To have a glimpse of the Divine is sufficient to intoxicate one for the rest of one's life. It brings immeasurable joy and rapture.

As *"The Repository of Mysteries"* of Junun is based on *"**The Seven Valleys**"* of Bahá'u'lláh, it is appropriate to say a few words about the position and the role of *"**The Seven Valleys**"* in sacred literature. Shoghi Effendi has hailed *"**The Seven Valleys**"* of Bahá'u'lláh as a **"treatise that may well be regarded as His greatest mystical composition ... in which He describes the seven stages which the soul of the seeker must needs traverse ere it can attain the object** of its existence."[1]

Bahá'u'lláh wrote *"The Seven Valleys"* in reply to the challenges and questions of a certain mystic, Shaykh Muḥiyu'd-Dín, the Qáḍí of Khániqayn. In this treatise, Bahá'u'lláh used the traditional seven-step Sufi concept of man's spiritual journey through varying levels of detachment from the physical world in order to achieve knowledge of the numinous—but His depiction of each of these stages is unique in its transcendence. Starting out on his or her odyssey with the first valley, "the Valley of Search", the seeker then passes through the valleys of Love, Knowledge, Unity, Contentment and Wonderment. Of the sixth valley Bahá'u'lláh states:

> *Now is he struck dumb with the beauty of the All-Glorious; again is he wearied out with his own life. How many a mystic tree hath this whirlwind of wonderment snatched by the roots, how many a soul hath it exhausted. For in this Valley the traveller is flung into confusion, albeit, in the eye of him who hath attained, such marvels are esteemed and well beloved. At every moment he beholdeth a wondrous world, a new creation, and goeth from astonishment to astonishment, and is lost in awe at the works of the Lord of Oneness.* [2]

Finally, the spiritual wayfarer reaches the Valley of True Poverty and Absolute Nothingness (*Faná'*). When the seeker reaches the Valley of *Faná'*, it does not mean that he literally becomes nothing; rather he has died to the "self"—to that ego that tends to interfere and obstruct the seeker upon the mystic path. In the words of Bahá'u'lláh:

> *This station is the dying from self and the living in God, the being poor in self and rich in the Desired One. Poverty as here referred to signifieth being poor in the things of the created world, rich in the things of God's world. For when the true lover and devoted friend reacheth to the presence of the Beloved, the sparkling beauty of the Loved One and the fire of the lover's heart will kindle a blaze and burn away all veils and wrappings. Yea, all he hath, from heart to skin, will be set aflame, so that nothing will remain save the Friend.*
>
> ...
>
> *He who hath attained this station is sanctified from all that pertaineth to the world. Wherefore, if those who have come to the sea of His presence are found to possess none of the limited things of this perishable world, whether it be outer wealth or personal*

---

[1] Shoghi Effendi, *God Passes By*, p. 140.
[2] Bahá'u'lláh, *The Seven Valleys and The Four Valleys*, p. 31.

opinions, it mattereth not. *For whatever the creatures have is limited by their own limits, and whatever the True One hath is sanctified therefrom; this utterance must be deeply pondered that its purport may be clear.* [1]

Thus freed, the wayfarer gains access to innate powers through which spiritual miracles are manifested. He develops an awareness of the inner realm that hitherto has lain dormant. He acquires the ability to integrate different states of earthly and celestial awareness. It is as if he is breathing in a pure atmosphere of uncontaminated air that raises him to a new level of consciousness, where nothing remains save the Supreme Being. Such an expression of a seeker's inner potential is impossible to achieve without the annihilation of the lower self.

Junun invites the reader to join him in the quest of God:

If thou art in quest of God, step up onto this Path;
So that of God's mysteries some inkling thou might have.
At the start of the journey, if I speak of love and yearning,
It means that our Lord's Face is hidden, not for our discerning.
Ere long He removes the veils from His hidden Countenance;
Then shines He forth brightly, haloed in dazzling radiance.

Junun's epic poem uplifts the reader to an atmosphere of pure light beyond the turmoil and agitation of a troubled age. He conveys a level of mystic experience that few people might ever enjoy. He has burned away the veils that shut man out from the most beauteous Countenance of God through the countenance of Bahá'u'lláh. It is a breath-taking moment to enter into the Presence of God. In the ecstatic spiritual experience of seeing the Beauty of God, the Source of all beauty, mystery and truth has been revealed to him. Thus *"The Repository of Mysteries"* of Junun reveals, in many ways, how one can connect to one's higher Self and the infinite consciousness, and become awakened and joyful. When one realizes the mystery of one's higher Self, one sees the world, oneself, and all other people with new eyes. One develops a strong desire to serve one's fellow man and work for the good of every aspect of God's creation simply for the love of the Creator.

Rúmí says:

The divine essence, the divine light is like a pot of musk. This material world and its delights are the scent of the musk, so everything that you love and adore and delight in, everything that you see is the scent of the musk …. Whatever gladdens the mind is the scent of my beloved; Whatever enraptures the heart

---

[1] Bahá'u'lláh, *The Seven Valleys and The Four Valleys*, p. 35.

I THE REPOSITORY OF MYSTERIES: INTRODUCTION

is a ray from my Friend.[1]

Bahá'u'lláh has written:

> I am well aware, O my Lord, that I have been so carried away by the clear tokens of Thy loving-kindness, and so completely inebriated with the wine of Thine utterance, that whatever I behold I readily discover that it maketh Thee known unto me, and it remindeth me of Thy signs, and of Thy tokens, and of Thy testimonies. By Thy glory! Every time I lift up mine eyes unto Thy heaven, I call to mind Thy highness and Thy loftiness, and Thine incomparable glory and greatness; and every time I turn my gaze to Thine earth, I am made to recognize the evidences of Thy power and the tokens of Thy bounty. And when I behold the sea, I find that it speaketh to me of Thy majesty, and of the potency of Thy might, and of Thy sovereignty and Thy grandeur. And at whatever time I contemplate the mountains, I am led to discover the ensigns of Thy victory and the standards of Thine omnipotence.
>
> I swear by Thy might, O Thou in Whose grasp are the reins of all mankind, and the destinies of the nations! I am so inflamed by my love for Thee, and so inebriated with the wine of Thy oneness, that I can hear from the whisper of the winds the sound of Thy glorification and praise, and can recognize in the murmur of the waters the voice that proclaimeth Thy virtues and Thine attributes, and can apprehend from the rustling of the leaves the mysteries that have been irrevocably ordained by Thee in Thy realm.[2]

Bahá'u'lláh also enjoins upon us to reflect on creation:

> Look at the world and ponder a while upon it. It unveileth the book of its own self before thine eyes and revealeth that which the Pen of thy Lord, the Fashioner, the All-Informed, hath inscribed therein. It will acquaint thee with that which is within it and upon it and will give thee such clear explanations as to make thee independent of every eloquent expounder.[3]

Two levels of consciousness

Without the fire of love of God our hearts are frigid; our lives are machine-like and soulless. The entire world seems callous and cold; and that is how we respond to it. In the Tablet of Fire, Bahá'u'lláh says, **"Coldness hath gripped all mankind: Where is the warmth of Thy**

---

[1] Rúmí in *The way of Passion*, chapter 10.
[2] Bahá'u'lláh, *Prayers and Meditations*, No. CLXXVI, pp. 271–2.
[3] *Tablets of Bahá'u'lláh*, p. 142.

love, O Fire of the worlds?" [1] Reaching to the Presence of the Beloved enkindles a fire in the heart of the lover that gives warmth to his life and he, in turn, transfers it to others. Junun is attempting to share the fire, the heat and rapture of divine consciousness through his poetry. Bahá'u'lláh describes the effects of a ***"mystic transformation"*** thus:

> *Then will the manifold favours and outpouring grace of the holy and everlasting Spirit confer such new life upon the seeker that he will find himself endowed with a new eye, a new ear, a new heart, and a new mind. He will contemplate the manifest signs of the universe, and will penetrate the hidden mysteries of the soul.* [2]

In the following passage, Junun refers clearly to his direct vision of the higher realms, and the Beauty of God manifested in Bahá'u'lláh:

> *Thou gazed upon God's Beauty astounded and enthralled;*
> *While the secrets of creation He did for thee unfold.*
> *Nought remained concealed to thee, not least the smallest atom;*
> *Love's rapture elevated thee to His divine asylum.*
> *Through His compassion's bounty was thine inner eye unsealed;*
> *The universal mysteries were thus to thee revealed.*

The nature of *"The Repository of Mysteries"* is as an experience of the joy that the Blessed Beauty transmits from the unseen spiritual reservoir to the seen world. Thus the ultimate purpose of Junun's epic poem is for the reader to recognize the inner essence of Bahá'u'lláh and to learn to love Him; the reader comes into unity with Him and gains access to His ultimate reality.

Junun lives on two levels of consciousness—in two realms: terrestrial and celestial. He is well-aware that his experience is beyond the grasp of any intellectual concept. He tries to suppress his powers of expression; for how can he fully portray the higher realm that he is soaring through:

> *O Junun! Where from, cometh thine unearthly dialect?*
> *Thy words are far beyond the grasp of human intellect.*
> *Tell us only things that lie within our comprehension;*
> *No mind can grasp what lieth outside its limitation.*
> *It is the mental limit to see only the effect;*
> *Till wonderment flashed; all vanished, left nothing to detect.*
> *Which direction hast thou taken? Come back from that beyond;*
> *Return to matters earthly, which will not our minds confound.*

---

[1] Bahá'u'lláh in *Bahá'í Prayers* (US), p. 216.
[2] Bahá'u'lláh, *The Kitáb-i-Íqán*, p. 196.

I The Repository of Mysteries: Introduction

The following passage is from a Tablet revealed by Bahá'u'lláh in honour of Jináb-i-Junun Sangsarí[1] when he was an obscure 18-year-old boy; it was revealed without any previous communication. A provisional translation of this Tablet reads:

> ... The sun is proclaiming that the All-Bountiful hath come. The moon is circling round the Most Great Beauty. If one were to listen attentively with the inner ear one would hear the voice of all created things uttering these blessed words: 'The Lord of mankind hath appeared.' This is the Day of God and the fragrance of divine grace is diffused throughout the world. Blessed is the soul that is not debarred by the doubts and whisperings of the people from taking its portion of the sealed wine in this Day ....
>
> Give thanks and gratitude unto the Desire of the world and the Lord of Eternity that thy deeds and services have been adorned with the ornament of His acceptance. Shouldst thou taste the sweetness of these words thou wilt cry out until the last breath of thine earthly life: 'May my life be a sacrifice unto Thee.' Verily He telleth the truth and showeth the right path. He is the Omnipotent, the Almighty, the Most Beauteous.

As the reader will notice, this Tablet contains profound mystic meanings. It is thought-provoking that Bahá'u'lláh should address a humble teenager with such profound references to the greatness of His revelation. We can deduce, without any doubt, that Bahá'u'lláh was well aware that this youth was to become a great mystic of the Bahá'í Era.

In addition to the fact that Junun was so blessed as to receive a Tablet from Bahá'u'lláh as a youth, another indication of his mystic prowess was an experience that he later confided to a relative. His words to her were: "O my daughter! The worlds that the prophets soar through—I had a glimpse of the vision of those realms; but do not disclose this matter to anyone." In obedience to his instruction, that lady treasured the words of Junun close to her heart and, for many years, spoke to no one about what he had confided to her. However, as she became advanced in years, feeling that she might soon pass away, she wished to share Junun's statement with just one trusted person

---

[1] Persian names often include an adjectival form of the town or district from which they come. In Junun's case, "Sangsarí" refers to the town of Sangsar where he was born. See Note 1 in the Appendix.

before leaving this world; and I was the one to whom she entrusted this secret. What she then told me, however, did not seem to be such a hidden secret; to me, it was no surprise because the vision of the higher realms flickers throughout Junun's poetry. Junun opens the door leading to hidden mysteries. He writes:

> I wish to uncover the hidden secrets and speak of these;
> I desire to entirely disclose the ancient mysteries.

Junun's verses

The spiritual journey that Junun refers to with rapture, confidence and knowledge is the central journey of the soul. We are called upon to take a journey to the presence of the Divine. The Divine can act through us; aiding us in our transformation and, thus, enabling us to work towards ending the miseries of the world and saving the planet. Rúmí says:

> You are the guardians of God's light.
> You are the talisman
> You were born of the rays of God's majesty.

Junun's inner reality had become pure and clean like a hollow reed through which spiritual inspiration could flow. Indeed, 'Abdu'l-Bahá affirms that a ray from the Holy Spirit, which manifests in the reality of the Prophet, may be reflected in the hearts of believers who are in a state of purity. Junun's spiritual and mystic poetry demonstrates that he was connected to a heavenly reservoir of inspiration. So pure in heart was he that a ray of the Holy Spirit is reflected in his verses. Junun lived in the time of Manifestation of God, as well as the Centre of the Covenant and the Sign of God on earth. His poetry expresses in beautiful and powerful images how the Timeless was breaking through into time during his life

Junun had become well versed in the Bahá'í Holy Writings as well as in Persian classical literature. However, the theme of his verses did not come from study or research; nor did it come from his own speculative thoughts. He testifies that whatever he composes is a pure inspiration. Junun writes:

> I am not the one who is communicating with thee;
> It is He Who is telling me what I should say to thee.
> He is behind the mirror; like a parrot I repeat what He says!
> Whether He orders me to be silent or to speak, the words are His.
> My heart hath turned into a reed into which doth blow the Flautist;
> He is behind the mirror; it is His voice you hear in echoes!

Apart from the reference to Junun in the *Encyclopedia Iranica* quoted earlier, here is a translation of the words of Ni'mat'u'lláh

1 The Repository of Mysteries: Introduction

Dhukai-i-Baydai, the author of *"An Anthology of the Poets of the First Century of the Baha'i Era"* who writes: "Jinab-i-Junun ... has composed about 70,000 verses, in all forms of poetry, mostly in the style similar to Mawlana Jalaluddin Rumi. I have seen many of his poems. I found in his works, one and all, the pure rapture, the essence of ardour and a totality of faith and devotion to God." [1]

In total, Junun has composed almost 100,000 verses. The stirring warmth of his emotions; the amazing spiritual insight; the ever-flowing love for the Central Figures of the Faith and for Shoghi Effendi, the beloved Guardian of the Faith; and the overwhelming mystic discoveries expressed in his works, will prove him to be an immortal poet and mystic of the Bahá'í Era.

A Bahá'í who was pioneering for the Faith in Italy once told me that the biography, *"The Priceless Pearl"* written by Rúḥíyyih Khánum, the wife of Shoghi Effendi, brings us close to the Guardian. In the same way, *"The Repository of Mysteries"* of Junun brings us close to Bahá'u'lláh, because he was spiritually very close to the Ancient Beauty. [2]

There are numerous verses in the Writings of Bahá'u'lláh and 'Abdu'l-Bahá urging every believer to try to draw spiritually near to Bahá'u'lláh. For example, in Bahá'u'lláh's **"Hidden Words"** you find His loving summons couched in beautiful phrases such as: **"Thy heart is My home"**; **"Thy spirit is My place of revelation"**; **"Put thy hand into My bosom ..."**; **"Ascend unto My heaven ..."**; while **"The Summons of the Lord of Hosts"** records Bahá'u'lláh's injunction:

> Seek the court of His presence, for God hath verily granted you leave to approach it, as a token of His grace unto all mankind. [3]

To approach Bahá'u'lláh may seem to us to be an impossible goal. Yet, in reading *"The Repository of Mysteries"*, we can clearly see that Junun has achieved exactly this goal, and his achievement inspires us with the hope that it is also a possibility for each one of us.

Junun's epic verse is not simply a theory of spiritual development; neither is it a mental exercise. It is a practical guide for spiritual development by a mystic who has successfully achieved such a high and seemingly inaccessible level. The author has passed through all these stages and he wants to help his readers to tread the spiritual path step by step and stage by stage.

---

[1] *Tadhkirih-i-Shuara-i-Qarn-i-Avval-i-Baha'i*
تذکرۀ شعرای قرن اوّل بهائ, تألیف نعمت الله ذکائ بیدائ

[2] One of the titles of Bahá'u'lláh.

[3] Bahá'u'lláh, *The Summons of the Lord of Hosts*, p. 30.

Junun explains what the reader will find in **"The Repository of Mysteries"**:

This book of rhyming couplets is a fountain, flowing love;
The more its waters are consumed, the more it gusheth forth.
May God assist thee each moment that thou dost peruse this book,
To see in it a surging sea and not just a babbling brook.
God opened for us the door to the hidden mystery;
No one is able to close this door because of jealousy.
I beseech God that He showers upon thee His confirmations and
    favour,
That the door leading to ancient secrets is opened wide to thine
    endeavour.

And:

"The Repository of Mysteries" is a gate to the world of love;
In this book are portrayed the traits of true lovers along their questing
    path.
If thine heart doth beat with love and thou art a perceptive person,
To the melodies of "The Repository of Mysteries" hearken.

Dynamic love motivates us to perform a spiritual flight from self-centeredness to self-transcendence. It is an ennobling elevation raising us above our degrading selfness to be absorbed in the elevating celestial realm. It is the life force to which French philosopher Henri Bergson refers as *élan vital*, in his book *"Creative Evolution"*, in which he addresses the question of self-organisation and spontaneous morphogenesis of things in an increasingly complex manner.

Rúmí writes:

Be Jubilant O our triumphant love
O thou the cure of all the ills of life.
The remedy for our hate and pride
O thou the Plato and the Galen of our life.

"The Repository of Mysteries" portrays an intense spiritual experience and amazing mystic insight—an actualization of spirituality. The ultimate goal is to know God, to love God and to come into union with God. This work is a priceless treasure in the Bahá'í literature.

To grasp the inner meaning of such a spiritual journey requires an effort on the part of the reader. Treading the mystic path is beyond the grasp of normal reasoning and imagining—and beyond the capacity of any words to express them. Junun's phrases have a depth of meaning that one has to probe deeply in order to grasp their inner connotations.

In *"The Repository of Mysteries"*, the treading of a stormy pathway

I THE REPOSITORY OF MYSTERIES: INTRODUCTION

towards the Beloved with its pain and joy of love has been delineated in a beautiful and fascinating poetic language, with its discoveries of the inner reality of the spiritual realm, with its uncovered pearls of wisdom and profound knowledge, and its rapture of unravelling the mysteries. The waves of emotion billow; the uprooting gales of tests bluster and blow; the glimpse of higher realms flashes; and the storms of bewilderment thunder. The pure-hearted soul is equipped with the necessary qualities to tread the pathway of the spiritual journey with all its ups and downs until he reaches the destination—the holy ambiance of blissful joy, a breath-taking beauty and serenity. He will achieve his ultimate goal—to come into union with the Creator.

The poet holds high a shining lamp to shed light along the path that the wayfarer must tread to reach the precincts of his Lord, the Most-Beloved. Junun is sharing the spiritual experience of a Bahá'í mystic—an experience beyond words. He invites the reader to become a co-traveller along the mystic path that he, himself, has already trodden to the end. Junun knows the secrets and pitfalls of the road; thus he can be a great help to the wayfarer. If we tread the path with him then we will not get lost in the labyrinths of an unfamiliar road; we will not go astray as many have done. This book is a celestial voice calling the seekers to elevate themselves, to fly to a realm of light and bliss.

Origins

The poet—Junun

Junun is the penname of Mirza Faraju'llah Fanaian [1] (AD 1871–1945). He was born in Sang-i-Sar (سَنگِسَر), also Romanized as Sangsar, [2]**Error! Bookmark not defined.Error! Reference source not found.** a provincial Persian town of some 10,000 residents, on the day when the flowers were in full bloom in the Northern Hemisphere, and the Bahá'í believers were celebrating the Festival of Flowers (Riḍván Festival).

Before the Islamic revolution, many Bahá'ís had moved to Sangsar to escape the persecution they were suffering in the larger cities. The people of Sangsar were renowned for their bravery. In ancient times they had withstood and repulsed three invasions by enormous forces, which had conquered the rest of Persia.

Junun was the grandson of Mullá Muḥammad Riẓá 'Árif, who was an early follower of the Báb. Mullá Muḥammad 'Árif participated at the Shaykh Ṭabarsí battle where 313 followers of the Báb armed with swords successfully defended themselves for 8 months against 30,000 soldiers from the forces of the Shah of Persia, who were armed with guns and cannons. Shaykh Ṭabarsí was a holy shrine located in the Mazandaran Province of Persia, where the Bábís, following the instructions of the Báb, had taken a stand under the black standard of the Báb, thus fulfilling an Islamic prophecy. There they built defensive fortifications and held out from 10 October 1848 to 10 May 1849 in the face of cannon fire and starvation. As the Shah's army was unable to overcome the Bábís, the Shah resorted to deceit and betrayal, tricking the besieged survivors to leave their fortifications. Most of them were then slaughtered. However, Mullá Muḥammad Riẓá was not martyred, although he suffered a lifelong injury, with one of his arms becoming atrophied as a result of a bullet wound. He was seized to be sold as a slave but, when his brother heard of Mullá Muḥammad Riẓá's predicament, he went to that region and bought his freedom.

At the time of Junun's early adolescence, there was a great Bahá'í teacher, poet, scholar, and philosopher by the name of Nabíl-i-Akbar to whom Bahá'u'lláh had addressed the *"Tablet of Wisdom"*. Many years before, Nabíl-i-Akbar had set out from his town for a teaching trip, leaving in the middle of the night to escape notice. He had not even been able to say good-bye to his sister who had gone into labour. That

---

[1] Mírzá Faraju'lláh Faná'yán (Junún)
[2] See note 1 in the Appendix.

night, she gave birth to a son. By the time Nabíl-i-Akbar returned to his home town from his teaching trip, his nephew, who had been born on the night of his departure, was twenty-one years old.

'Abdu'l-Bahá says:

> Because he [Nabíl] stood steadfast in this holy Faith, because he guided souls and served this Cause and spread its fame, that star, Nabil, will shine forever from the horizon of abiding light. He [Nabíl] brought light to the Qá'in area and converted a great number of people. And when he had become known far and wide by this new name [a follower of the Bahá'í Faith], the clergy, envious and malevolent, arose, and informed against him, sending their calumnies to Ṭihrán, so that Náṣiri'd-Dín Sháh rose up in wrath. He was exposed to danger at all times, always vigilant and on his guard. The Government never gave up its search for him. [1]

Since Nabil-i-Akbar was exposing himself to danger in teaching the Cause, Bahá'u'lláh had recommended that somebody should accompany him on his teaching trips. At the time Nabíl-i-Akbar was passing through Sangsar. When he asked for somebody to volunteer to accompany him on his mission, the fourteen-year-old Junun responded to that call to serve his Lord. Junun then accompanied Nabíl-i-Akbar on his teaching travels throughout Persia. Nabíl-i-Akbar could not travel freely. In order to avoid being recognized, the stalwart workers for the Cause were forced to rest in the daytime at some secure location, and travel at night-time. In the dead silence of night, under the protection of darkness, they cautiously passed through valleys, crossed the hills and trekked along seemingly endless tracks through the desert; Nabíl-i-Akbar on horseback and Junun, his teenage companion, on foot. Thus they travelled thousands of miles to deliver the glad tiding of the new divine Revelation to receptive souls. Whenever they approached a town, word would spread that Nabíl-i-Akbar was close, and the local Bahá'ís would arrange to smuggle him quietly into the town.

For four years, the teenage Junun, forsook all youthful pleasures and pursuits, as well as the safety of his family, friends and birthplace, all for the sake of Bahá'u'lláh. He endured with radiant joy the hardships of the journey and separation from his loved ones in order to serve his Lord. Ofttimes, in moments of privacy he would pray that his service be accepted. The compassionate Lord responded to his prayers. The Tablet, written in Bahá'u'lláh's own handwriting, quoted earlier in part, opened with the following words, *"He hearkens and responds"*.

By starting the Tablet with the words: *"He hearkens and*

---

[1] 'Abdu'l-Bahá, *Memorials of the Faithful*, pp. 2–4.

responds", Bahá'u'lláh assured Junun that his prayers had been heard and his services had been accepted: *"... **thy deeds and services have been adorned with the ornament of His acceptance.**"* There is a vague reference in this Tablet to the fact that Junun would become a poet: *"**Shouldst thou taste the sweetness of these words thou wilt cry out until the last breath of thine earthly life: 'May my life be a sacrifice unto Thee'.**"*

Bahá'u'lláh commissioned the brothers, Nayyer and Sina, two well-known Bahá'í travel-teachers and poets, to find the obscure boy (Junun) to give him the Tablet. Bahá'u'lláh also sent, as a gift, a piece of cloth for Junun to make a shirt for himself, and a kilo of rock sugar for his mother, as a token of congratulations for having given birth to such a meritorious son.

When Nayyer and Sina met a teenage boy in a caravanserai in Tehran where the Sangsarís usually rested on their travels, they felt he might be the youth whom Bahá'u'lláh had sent them to find. Nayyer and Sina asked Junun certain questions, without disclosing their mission, and became assured that he was indeed the one whom Bahá'u'lláh had spoken about. Nayyer and Sina told Junun that they had something to deliver to him, but they did not immediately disclose what it was. Instead they invited him to accompany them to their home on foot; all along the way to their house, they hugged and kissed Junun in turn, repeatedly expressing their wonder with such words as: "O youth! What have you done for God that thy Lord has showered such a favour upon you?" Junun was astonished at the level of Nayyer and Sina's praise of him. In fact neither Nayyer and Sina, nor Junun, were aware of the great potentiality within him that was destined to be manifested later. It seems that it had been ordained that the door to divine mysteries would be opened to Junun's inner eyes, thus making of him a great poet and mystic of the Bahá'í Era. Only the Omniscient Lord knew that Junun was among the chosen ones whose future would so blessed.

"May my life be a sacrifice unto Thee!"

If we could summarize in one sentence the core content of the volumes of Junun's poetry, his writings and his life story, it would be to the effect that they are an echo of the statement of Bahá'u'lláh, **"May my life be a sacrifice unto Thee!"** The fact that the Blessed Beauty would address to a teenager boy a tablet with such profound mystical meanings shows that the latter would become a great mystic of recent times. In the words of Bahá'u'lláh:

> The sun is proclaiming that the All-Bountiful hath come. The moon is circling round the Most Great Beauty. If one were to listen

attentively with the inner ear one would hear the voice of all the created things uttering these blessed words: 'The Lord of mankind hath appeared'.

Junun was destined to explore and expound certain inner mysteries of the new Divine Revelation. Through his praise of the Blessed Perfection (Bahá'u'lláh), the reader can catch a glimpse of the awe-inspiring charm and splendour of the Ancient Beauty. Junun himself testifies to this fact:

Whatever Junun composed, either in verse or in prose,
It was praise unto Abhá, whether voiced or left untold.

It is interesting to note that Junun did not attend any school or undertake any formal course of study. However, his enthusiasm for studying the Bahá'í Holy Writings was exemplary. At an early stage of his life, Junun once borrowed **"Some Answered Questions"** by 'Abdu'l-Bahá. The lender asked him to return the book on the following day. So Junun sat the whole day, and remained awake throughout the night in order to transcribe the entire book; he returned the book to the lender on the following day. But, later on, he arranged with the Bahá'í Publication Trust to have forty copies of each newly released Bahá'í book delivered to him. A relative told me that, every night, a great number of people used to come to his house. They did not spend their time chatting but, rather, Junun engaged them in studying Bahá'í writings. That was the reason he had arranged to receive forty copies of each book to have at home to distribute among those who were present for his 'study circle'. He was also the one person in his small town to regularly receive Bahá'í magazines from the United States, India and Russia.

Another instance demonstrates Junun's enthusiasm for the Bahá'í writings, and the depth to which he probed their inner meanings. One evening he informed his wife that he was planning to read **"The Book of Certitude"** by Bahá'u'lláh. He asked her to fill up the oil lamp, and requested her not to come into his room or to allow anyone else to interrupt him. Then he started reading and continued throughout that night until the morn dawned; still he continued to read until the sun set, and darkness fell. When, on the following night, the oil lamp started to flicker and die, Junun called his wife and asked her why the oil lamp had not been filled according to his request. She gently answered that his wish had not been ignored. He had been so deeply absorbed in his reading that he had not noticed the passage of time.

The example of Junun testifies to what degree the Bahá'í Writings, and the mysterious forces released from this august revelation can bring out the innate human capacity and spur a soul along the spiritual path. Studying the revealed Word of God assists us to access a world of such divine creative forms that our culture is enriched, the impossible becomes possible, and the extraordinary becomes an ordinary everyday occurrence. It was through the spiritual nurturing of the Bahá'í sacred writings that Junun was enabled to uncover the mysteries and create such profound poetry, thus becoming a shining star in the field of spiritual and mystic literature.

Stories about Junun's love for humanity

The door of Junun's house was open from early morning until late at night. All people regardless of their religion, age, social status, and whether they were men or women, could come to visit him; and he bestowed upon all an equally loving welcome. Whenever a person entered his room, Junun would arise and greet them with heart-felt affection.

Junun's genuine and unconditional love for all people, his detachment, his saintly sympathy and helpful attitude towards the needy and heart-broken, made of his personal life a model of a true Bahá'í life. He was the embodiment of Bahá'í virtues and spiritual qualities. It would require a whole volume to delineate the spirit of Junun's selfless services and saintly life.

Many are the stories I have heard about Junun's genuine love and sincere sympathy for people. The following episode told to me by a certain man is just one example. It was a snowy winter, and bitterly cold. The door of Junun's house was open as usual and anyone could enter. Suddenly a teenager boy turned up on the doorstep. His trousers were wet and muddy up to his knees. The soles of his shoes were quite worn out, and mud and slush had penetrated through the holes. As soon as Junun saw the boy, he got up and immediately ushered the boy into the house. After he had removed the shoes and washed his feet, Junun brought the boy into the living room to sit near the heater to get warm. Junun was a skilled shoe maker; so, while the boy refreshed himself on some hot tea and most welcome food, his host fitted the shoes with new soles. Then the unknown boy left the house. Junun had not asked the boy's name, who he was or where he had come from. Every stranger in need was always welcome.

On many occasions, visitors who entered Junun's presence loaded with grief, pain, and despair, would later leave his house unburdened of sorrows and filled, instead, with a feeling of transformation. Even non-Bahá'ís looked on him as a saint. Some openly expressed their impression that his spiritual qualities were of the same rank as those of the high spiritual personages whom they respected and believed in.

A certain Bahá'í stated: "I was fourteen years old and I went to see him. He rose up and hugged me affectionately. I can still feel the warmth of his genuine, spiritual love. Then he told me, 'There is no need your father come to see me. We meet each other in the realm of spirit.'"

Second sight

I heard many first hand stories from people who had observed Junun's ability to see the unseen. One Bahá'í told me that once, when he was a teenage boy, his father and he had gone unannounced to visit Junun at his home. There was no window in Junun's room through which he could have seen whether anyone was coming along the adjoining lane. However, when the boy and his father entered the house they were surprised to see Junun standing in the doorway of his chamber obviously in expectation of their visit.

A certain lady told me that after she had been widowed as a young woman, she met a man, and they fell in love. The people in her small town were extreme fanatics, and were scandalised by any association between a man and a single lady. One day the young widow's older sister came to her house and started accusing her of disgracing their family by being in contact with a single man. As the older sister continued her harangue, the young widow wept copious tears, unable to say a word in her own defence. In the presence of such heart-felt grief, the older sister started to feel sorry for the younger woman. Wishing to ameliorate the situation, she suggested that they both go to Junun's house because anyone could go there at any time. As soon as they arrived, Junun turned to the older sister and said "don't blame this girl so much. Look into her heart. There is a pure genuine love there!" The older sister was astounded that Junun knew how she had been haranguing the younger girl. The widow, however, was not surprised because she was aware that Junun had second-sight. Later she married her new love and spent the rest of her life with him.

Another time a certain woman came to Junun's house, her throat choked with tears, as she expressed her deep distress: "My son has been taken captive by highwaymen. They are going to kill him. He may die at any moment." Junun replied, "Don't be so distressed. Go back to your house; your son might be home by now." The woman could not believe it to be possible. She thought that Junun must have misunderstood the situation. She repeated the story more emphatically. But Junun said again, "Mother! Don't be so despondent. God is helpful. Go home! Your son is there." The woman went away with a heart heavy with sadness and hopelessness. She was absolutely sure that her son was still in danger. Then, when she got home she could not believe her eyes; it was incredible but her son was at home. She returned to Junun and asked him, "Who you are, that you can see the unseen?" But Junun said nothing. He was a paragon of humility. What had actually happened was that some soldiers had tried to catch the highwaymen, who fled. Their young captive was left behind, and rushed home to relieve his mother's anxiety. But how had Junun known this?

Seeing into the future

Dozens of such stories can be narrated to demonstrate that Junun's inner vision could not only penetrate the veil of place but also of time. I would like to narrate only a few stories as examples.

A certain lady by the name of Zahra told me, "Before I was born, a boy was born to our family. My parents went to Junun and asked him to give a name to the boy, which they considered would be a special blessing. To their dismay, the name Junun suggested was 'Zahra', which is an absolutely female name. The parents thought that perhaps Junun had misunderstood them, and did not realize that the new-born was a boy. They repeated, 'God has given us a boy. What should his name be?' But Junun answered, 'Zahra is a good name; it means "splendorous". Why are you not happy with it?' The parents could not ignore his suggestion, but they were worried that, when the boy grew up, people would make fun of him as a man bearing the name of a woman. However, after only four months, the baby boy died and, not much later, I was born. Then my parents passed the name of Zahra to me. They realized that Junun had known that the boy would die and that the next baby would be a girl. He had actually chosen the name for me and not for my brother!"

Another lady told me, "A few days after I had a new baby girl, I went to Junun's house to ask him to give my child a name. Junun said, 'This baby belongs to Zahra; so you go and ask her to choose a name.' [Zahra was a relative, who had moved into Junun's house after the death of his wife to act as his house-keeper.] Junun's words were unexpected and disappointing. I wanted Junun himself to give my baby a name because I believed that would be a special blessing. However, I reluctantly approached Zahra, and she suggested a name for my girl. After twenty years, my daughter got married to Zahra's son and, thus, became Zahra's daughter-in-law. Only then did I realize why Junun had said that my baby belonged to Zahra, who should choose her name." This couple are one of the happiest married couples I have ever seen.

Junun predicted that the Mullás (Muslim priests) would come to power in Iran. A certain relative by the name Muḥammad Taqí told me that he heard Junun several times foreseeing how the Mullás would come to power and, later, be brought low. He depicted the rise and fall of the Mullás in a symbolic way. He said: "Sometimes it happens that the sky is clear when you go to bed; but when you wake up in the morning you see the house-yard is covered with half a meter of snow. It is totally unexpected, and you feel surprised. You go back into the house and get busy. The sun rises and the snow melts and disappears. In the late afternoon you go out and you see no snow. You are again surprised and ask yourself where has all that snow gone? In the same way the Mullás will come to power suddenly and unexpectedly. Wherever you look you will see Mullás and turbans. Then they will disappear as if they have never existed. You will be surprised and will ask yourself 'where have they gone?'"

The following verse was composed over ninety five years ago. Science had not yet split the atom to find out that there is a system similar to the solar system in the microcosm of every atom. Thus, it had not been yet discovered that in a rock you can see the universe. Junun writes:

> *Lo! Behold the mysteries of an ocean in a drop of water;*
> *When you look at a drop you can see the quality of a sea.*
> *If you split apart the innate core of any tiny atom,*
> *You see clearly a solar system in its inmost reality.*

The most amazing prediction of Junun regards a technological innovation. He foresaw an important invention decades in advance. When I was a teenage boy, many times I heard people say that they had heard Junun envisage a time in the future when your friends are in the West eating their supper and you are in the East; yet you can see them and talk to them. He would say, "Your friends will invite you 'join us and eat'; and you will answer them, 'thank you, and *bon appetite!*'" His prediction has been fulfilled now that Skype has made it possible to communicate in audio and video across the two hemispheres of the world. This technology may become even more developed with time.

Healer and friend of all

On several occasions Junun cured people who were seriously ill with no hope of recovery. For example, a certain man who is still alive told me the following story: "when I was a teenage boy, my younger sister was terribly sick for one year. It was very hard time, so much so, that we prayed she would either be cured or die. In desperation we decided to take her to Junun's house. It was our last hope that he might be able to do something. So, I and my mother carried my poor sister on our shoulders to his house. We explained the situation to Junun, and appealed to him to help her. The girl was laid down in a corner of his room. After a while, we slipped quietly away, leaving the girl behind. We had not wanted to carry her back to our house. We thought that if we left her with Junun then perhaps he might do something to help.

The following day, at about noon, we heard somebody knocking on the door. We opened the door and could not believe our eyes; we were so surprised and delighted. Our sister was standing at the threshold, looking perfectly healthy. She had come home on foot!"

Junun used to go to the mountains around his hometown to spend the whole night in meditation and prayer. People would be able to hear his chanting echoing in the mountains late in the night. He had a good voice. In the mountains where he loved to stroll, leopards had been sighted several times. However, it seems Junun was not afraid of wild animals. Perhaps he was confident that they would not attack him; it may be that they, too, could feel his love and had befriended him.

Indeed Junun was full of loving kindness towards all. A few years before Junun ascended to the higher realm, his relative and voluntary house-keeper, Zahra, would write down the poems that he dictated to her. She told me, "When he was composing a poem, he would often pace to and fro in the room. While he was dictating the poem to me, his face was aglow with intense emotion. Sometimes, when I was writing down the poem I would miss a word or did not hear the line clearly. But I was not allowed to ask him to repeat the line during his dictation because he said that it might disturb his concentration. He had told me that he would edit it later on. However, when occasionally visitors would arrive while he was dictating the poem, Junun used to stop to greet them and make them feel welcome, often hugging them most lovingly. Then he would return to his dictation and finish the poem."

Years before Junun's ascent to the realms on high, he knew with certainty that he would pass away when he was seventy-four years old. He had disclosed this intuitive knowledge to some of his relatives. My mother who was Junun's daughter-in-law, the wife of his eldest son, narrated to me that when he turned seventy-four years old he started to prepare his relatives and friends for his imminent departure to the Abhá Kingdom. My mother told me that, at the time, he was still quite healthy. Yet he was saying "the time has come that I fly to the realm on high. Don't be sad. You should accept this." Some relatives and friends, who had a great love and respect for him, were in his presence at the time. They started shedding tears of sorrow; but Junun was smiling and light-heartedly trying to comfort them. Junun ascended to the Abhá Kingdom in that very same year just as he had predicted.

His passing

It was a Muslim custom in Junun's town that when somebody had passed away they would raise the *Azán*, the Muslim call for prayer, on the roof of the house of the departed. Junun's next-door neighbour was a pious Muslim clergyman who used to lead public prayer on Fridays in the mosque. When Junun passed away, the Muslim clergyman rushed into Junun's house to raise the prayer call from the roof of the house. A relative stopped the clergyman and explained to him that this was not a Bahá'í custom. The Muslim clergyman, his throat choked with tears, and his tone charged with emotion and grief said, "How can we not raise the *Aẓán*, when such a great man has ascended on high." The Muslim clergyman left the house of Junun and went instead onto the roof of his own house to raise the call to prayer. Thus, the people of the town immediately became aware that Junun had passed away.

There was a non-Bahá'í lady in Sangsar, Junun's hometown, who used to predict the future of people by intuition. The night that Junun passed away she had a strange dream. She saw in her dream that a high-ranking saint had died and some angels were carrying his coffin to heaven. When she woke up she was surprised by her dream. She interpreted it to mean that anyone who passed away that day must be of those who are nigh unto God. She related the dream to her son. In the Bahá'í eternal rose garden (cemetery) there was no grave available on that day. The son of this lady, also a non-Bahá'í, volunteered to dig the grave. He was not used to this sort of work. Nevertheless, still wearing his smart suit, he dug the grave with an amazing devotion. The fact that his suit became covered with mud did not concern him. It was a terribly cold and stormy day; a thick blanket of snow had enveloped the entire town and the surrounding mountains. There was a dreadful blizzard blowing while the coffin was being carried to the cemetery. All the mourners were covered in a sheet of snow. Notwithstanding the atrocious weather, both the Bahá'ís and non-Bahá'ís in the town attended Junun's funeral, and stood for the *"Prayer for the Departed"*. The mourning continued for several days with groups of townsfolk and government employees arriving for the wake and receiving refreshments.

A chronicler of the town, where Junun was born and lived, wrote that many of his town's people embraced the Bahá'í Faith through Junun's direct delivery of the Message; and many more came to the Faith because they were so impressed by his exemplary Bahá'í life. That was one of the reasons that his birthplace, Sangsar, became a citadel of the Bahá'í Faith in Persia.

Early one morning, when I was about six years old, I went to visit my grandfather, Junun. The door of his house was open as usual. However, an older boy blocked my way, not letting me enter the house. Junun noticed and, with a vibrating voice said: "My grandson has come to visit his grandpa. Let him come in. He is dear to my heart." He had just washed his face and was drying it with a towel; then he started combing his hair. I vividly remember that he had a partly broken comb, white in colour. At the same time he was dictating a poem, and a lady relative, who sometimes acted as his amanuensis, was writing down the verses.

His continuing influence

I would like to narrate two instances indicating that Junun's poetry irresistibly attracts even the opponents of the Bahá'í Faith. Junun did not allow his poems to be published in his life time. Whenever his relatives or the admirers of his poetry approached him begging him to allow them to publish his works, he refused to accept their request. He used to say, "The time of the publication of these poems has not come yet. In due time, they will be published. Don't worry."

A few days after Junun's departure, his relatives and friends assembled, consulted and decided that at least one piece of his poetry should be published on the occasion of his ascension. They did not know which one to choose. Over the last four years of his earthly life, his amanuensis, Zahra, used to record his poems. Later Zahra related to me how their dilemma was resolved. She said: "I had a dream, in which Junun spoke to me, saying: 'They are insisting on publishing one of my poems. I have a piece of poetry written in my own handwriting. Give it to them to be published.' He then told me where I could find it. When I woke up, I found the poem with no difficulty despite the fact that it amongst his thousands of books, exactly as he had instructed me."

A relative of Junun, who lived in the capital city, Tehran, took that piece of poetry to a publishing house to be printed. He went to a certain street where some publishing houses were located, and entered one of them not noticing that it was an Islamic publishing house. This publisher only ever printed books that were one hundred per cent Islamic. They had never published any other literature, even of the well-known Persian poets.

After the elapse of three months the relative of Junun went to the Islamic publishing house to collect the booklets. There the agent told the relative, "Don't imagine that we did not realize that the poet was a Bahá'í. His poems are about a new Revelation. But still, we had the impression that this was a great man, and his poetry expresses a deep spiritual experience. We decided to publish his poem as a sign of our respect for him." To the surprise of Junun's relative, the agent of the Islamic Publishing House asked permission to print one thousand copies of this poetry to distribute in Islamic circles. The permission was granted and the poetry was published without the slightest change and distributed amongst the Muslims. They did not even delete the expression 'O Bahá'.

I remember one day I was going to school by bus in Tehran. It was crowded and I was standing in the aisle. I saw a well-dressed man sitting down with his arms filled with several thick big books. He looked like a university lecturer. He had a full-grown beard; at that time to have a beard was the sign of being a devoted Muslim. I noticed a booklet of Junun's poetry was on the top of the other books. As soon as I saw it I asked him if I could have a look at it. The man said, "My son! It is beyond your understanding; even University professors cannot grasp the inner meanings of this booklet". He meant that it is much beyond the comprehension of a high school student like me, and he did not give it to me to look at.

Another instance, when I was a pioneer in Africa, I met a missionary of the Aḥmadíyyih movement, an active sect of Islam who believe that Aḥmad Qádíyání was the promised one of Islam, i.e. the Mahdí as well as the return of Christ. Since the missionary knew the Persian language very well, I suggested to him that we read the poetry of Junun together, which I was carrying with me on that day. I pointed out that the booklet had been printed by an Islamic Publishing House. To my amazement, after reading a few verses, he commented unreservedly and with no hesitation: "I don't know who the author of this poetry is; but he is greater than Aḥmad Qádíyání. I am returning to Pakistan. We are going to have a big conference. Could I take this poetry to read at that gathering?" I gave him the booklet but I have no information about what happened at the conference.

Junun and his poem

"*The Repository of Mysteries*" of Junun shows the direction to the Court of the inner Essence of the Beloved. It inspires in the reader an ardent passion that drives the spirit to the realm where he or she can see the Blessed Beauty face to face. The significance and the beauty of this noble book is that:

- Junun has already travelled the mystic path and reached its glorious destination;
- the door to mysteries has been opened wide before Junun's inner eyes;
- Junun has entered the presence of God and has seen the beauty of God in His Manifestation, Bahá'u'lláh;
- the worlds that Junun portrays are the fruit of his direct experience, not some theoretical view based on knowledge and belief.

The beauty and the value of "*The Repository of Mysteries*" is that it portrays:

- the rewards of spiritual development in treading the mystic path;
- the innate potentiality and the ray of divinity that exist at the core of our souls;
- how to enter a court where the Beloved resides;
- how to tap the inner reservoir of energies necessary for the evolutionary process;
- how to transcend selfishness and access the depths of perception.

"*The Repository of Mysteries*" is of great assistance to those who seek to peruse "**The Seven Valleys**" of Bahá'u'lláh, and to understand it. As Dr Esselmont says in "*Bahá'u'lláh and the New Era*", to grasp the inner meaning of "**The Seven Valleys**" is most difficult. We have to bear in mind that our understanding of "**The Seven Valleys**" depends on how pure in heart we are, not on how much information is crammed into our minds.

Rarely does it happen that the words Junun uses are exactly the words that Bahá'u'lláh has used in "**The Seven Valleys**". We have to bear in mind that Junun is not quoting Bahá'u'lláh nor explaining Bahá'u'lláh's words. Rather, Junun is expressing his direct experience and his direct vision, which occasionally coincide to some degree with what Bahá'u'lláh has stated. This demonstrates the validity of Junun's experience and vision.

I THE REPOSITORY OF MYSTERIES: INTRODUCTION

"*The Repository of Mysteries*" revolves around one central theme—how to reach a true understanding of Bahá'u'lláh as the Dayspring of a new revelation. The difference between it and many books of proofs is that the authors in those books argue, based on logical proofs, that Bahá'u'lláh is the Manifestation of God for the new era and the Promised One of all ages. But in "*The Repository of Mysteries*", the poet strives to uplift the reader to a level of spirituality whereby the dawn of the Divine Sun is witnessed by his or her own inner eyes, while becoming immersed in its dazzling lights. The love of God penetrates into the reader's being to such an extent that nothing remains save the Beloved, the Manifestation of God.

"*The Repository of Mysteries*" enkindles a passionate love of Bahá'u'lláh in the hearts and brings them closer to Him. Junun himself was a true lover of the Ancient Beauty; he was annihilated in that fiery passion. He adored his Beloved and circled around the Blessed Beauty day and night.

Junun is little known in the East; he is totally unknown in the West. Nevertheless he is, unquestionably, a great poet and mystic of the Bahá'í Era. It is perhaps too early to fully estimate and evaluate the merit of Junun's literary works. In coming decades—nay centuries—his works might be assessed by the test of time and future scholars. At this stage it can be said that he is among those who stand at the top of the mount of spiritual insight.[1] Shoghi Effendi called him a **"peerless poet"**. After the passing of Junun, the beloved Guardian, in response to the letter of a relative, wrote in Persian:

> We ask God's loving care for Jináb-i-(his excellence) Mírzá Faraju'lláh, surnamed Junun, who was skilled with arts, and in all affairs in the holy court of the compassionate Lord.

The Guardian did not use the preposition 'from' the holy court of the compassionate Lord; he used the pronoun 'in' the holy court of the compassionate Lord. To my understanding, it indicates that Junun is in the presence of his Lord. I wanted to be assured that my understanding was accurate so I wrote a letter to the Universal House of Justice to ask them for confirmation. I also requested that the words of the Guardian be translated into English, the reply I received was the translation given above and the response that my understanding was correct.

In the following poem, quoted from another book, Junun most humbly expresses his gratitude that His Lord assisted him to step on a Path that the chosen one's desire to tread:

---

[1] See Note 3 in the Appendix.

O glorious Lord! How can I voice my gratitude for Thy beneficence?
My yearning pain hath been the spur that urgeth me to seek Thy presence.
I was without a guide to lead me, yet out of Thy munificence,
Thou didst set upon the Path this soul of worthless insignificance.

This is the Path, which leads towards His sanctuary; the noble prophets
Step that way, to reach the sacred Threshold and circumambulate it.
This is the very Path the Chosen Ones desire to tread upon,
While They proclaim: "He is the Peerless One; He is the Single One".

Thou hast shown such favour unto me; that was Thy benediction.
Indeed, Thou hast immersed me in the depths of grace as in an ocean.
Whenever for Thy great bounty I have wished to show my thankfulness
I have been filled to overflowing with shame for my neglectfulness. [1]

To analyse Junun's spiritual achievements and to befittingly portray his mystical experience is beyond my capacity as he ventures to probe into the mystery of the creation and the Creator; and explores the innate reality of the cosmos. However, I remember the words of the great scholar and philosopher of the Faith, Dr Davoudi, a member of the Reviewing Committee that examined Junun's *"The Repository of Mysteries"* before its publication: "Junun wings to such heights that we cannot compete with him in flight. To comprehend his mystic poetry is beyond our intellectual concept." [2]

The beauty of the language of Junun's epic poem, the depth of its spiritual understanding, amazing mystic insight, dazzling lights of its mysteries, and the profundity of its recognition of the station of Bahá'u'lláh makes this an inspiring book through which to introduce the Coming of the Manifestation of God for this age to highly educated people, poets, men of letters and all those searching for mysticism, spirituality and the dawn of a new era.

This book of verse will attract those who thirst for spirituality, regardless of which faith they belong to. It may even lead them to investigate the Bahá'í Faith. Such true seekers will find in the Bahá'í Scriptures a treasure of divine guidance for spiritual development. And this is of particular importance in this day and age, not only for the benefit of the individual soul but for the whole of human society.

---

[1] See Note 2 in the Appendix.
[2] See Note 3 in the Appendix.

I The Repository of Mysteries: Introduction

Shoghi Effendi says:

> The need is very great, everywhere in the world, in and outside the Faith, for a true spiritual awareness to pervade and motivate people's lives.[1]

The survival of humanity depends on our spiritual transformation. When we reflect the Divine in our souls, all the virtues of godliness will inform our attitudes and our behaviour. The world's governing and administrative systems on all levels must also undergo a great change for the world polity to reflect the Divine glory in all its beauty and rectitude. When the human vices of greed, racial and religious hatred, unbridled nationalism and rampant materialism have been finally laid to rest, then will the world advance to the Golden Age of Universal Peace and Justice foretold by the prophets of old.

---

[1] Shoghi Effendi in *The Compilation of Compilations*, vol. II, p. 14.

Part II

Translated text
of

The Repository of Mysteries

by
Junun

The Repository of Mysteries

Overture

Canto 1

He is God, the Most Exalted!
O Thou, the Self-subsisting, All-possessing, Source of mysteries,
Ocean of hidden secrets! I extoll Thee; endless is my praise.
Thou art above allusion: Thou art beyond conjecture;
No intellect can grasp Thee nor can words portray Thy picture
For sanctified Thou art from Thy creation's every quality.
Bewildered is the universal mind, when contemplating Thee.
The seven seas are but a drop; while future, like the past,
Goes in a flash, when majesty Thy love makes manifest.

Impart to us Thy Wisdom, O Thou the Luminescent,
Who teacheth of beginning and of ending in an instant.
Thou dost disclose with but a hint the treasures well concealed.
Those pearls of wisdom fill the world that Thou hast thus revealed.
O Thou, the One, the Absolute! O my heart's Sovereign!
I pray Thy grace will not subside, but ever flows therein.

My soul delights whenever I, with Thee, am in communion;
With every breath I take, for Thee is yearning my companion.
Devoted ever is my heart to loving Thee assured;
To yearning, and its pain, my soul is now well-nigh inured.
My lips have quaffed from Thine own lips a cup of Love. Now plighted,
My soul is set aflame as from Thy burning blaze ignited.
My heart has sipped a draught of wine from Thy chalice opalescent;
This collyrium set mine eyes afire to shine forth incandescent.

Canto 2

The mystic speaks of God as Light in language metaphoric;
For dim souls simpler terms are used and stories allegoric.
In truth, of Light symbolic is the Essence of all Being;
A Presence sensed but inwardly, the outer eye unseeing.

Of the seven lights that mystics have oft-times specified;
A colour quite particular to each they have ascribed,

No doubt, the Light of God is neither "one" nor is it "seven";
But seven are the stages of the wayfarer to Heaven.
For each stage of his passage, the voyager should know,
Seeing red light, for example, or perhaps some darker glow.
But should the seeker's heart become attached to any hue,
Think not him liberated for he is chained anew.
He is drawn to the adornment, rather than his Sovereign Lord;
Enslaved by tint, forgetting he is the servant of his God.

Beyond the valleys fourth and fifth and, with the sixth one passed,
No effort needs the traveller make; he is as one possessed.
Love cares not which the valley—be it five or six in name;
It moves towards Almighty God; to reach Him is its aim.
Preceding all created things, God's Essence stands alone;
And His Light radiates beyond all colour, tint or tone.

A farmer cultivates his wheat to fill his store with grain;
But harvests all the stalks as well from which the seed to glean.
Thus the roving lover's wish is but to glimpse God's Beauty glorious;
Yet beholds Creation on his way, though that was not his purpose.

Open thou thine inner ear to the mystic words of Rúmí;
For that sage speaketh through his verse of every seeker's journey.
Described he thus, from insight deep, the path of spirit trod
By wayfarers sincere who seek reunion with their God:

From kingdom mineral I died, as plant to be reborn;
From kingdom vegetal I died, as animal redrawn.
From kingdom animal I died, and human now my being;
Why should I fear? I still live on despite my previous dying.
And yet again, from the human I die but to develop
An angels' wings and soar above the clouds that all-envelop.
Now, dying once again to grow, the angel state I leave;
To reach beyond what any mind can possibly conceive.
Another leap I have to make, another river crossing;
For all things perish, all except the Face of God Surpassing.
So I die! Oh yea, I die, singing as an organ with delight:
Unto God we verily return, the God of Glory and of Might.

Canto 3

Yea, yea, God's Essence undergoes no slightest alteration;
For changing, as an attribute, belongs to His creation.
Know thou! God's Essence doth not submit to any transformation—
That is the trait of bodies and of dust, prone to variation.
For the world of His creation there must ever be a turning;
Full of joy as is the bondsman to his Master when returning

Canto 4

> Myriad thanks to Thy dazzling light, blinding in its brilliance;
> O Bahá! My soul overflows, filled brim-full from Thy radiance.
> Mine eye was chosen from all eyes, thus endowed with fresh new
>   vision,
> It beheld the sun Divine in darksome night! 'Twas no illusion!
> That was Thy celebrated Grace, O Thou the Glorious One!
> Thy loving-kindness please discharge, O Thou my dearest One!

Canto 5

> O Thou, the Branch of root Divine [1] I turn to Thee, beseeching;
> That Thou should not deprive me of Thy noble wisdom's teaching.
> O Thou "Whom God hath purposed"! [2] O Thou my sovereign!
> Thy charming face enchanteth me, astoundeth me Thy mien.

Canto 6

> My heart clings tight to the hem of Thy boundless grace, and pleading
> For favour; in Thy sanctuary, Thy shelter I am seeking.
> I beseech Thee: Cast Thou a glance of favour then upon us;
> I beg Thee: Cease not from showering Thy bounteousness upon us.
> Night and day my heart seeks sanctuary in Thy dwelling place;
> With all hopes fastened on Thy kindness and Thy loving grace.
> O Thou "Whom God hath purposed", Who hath branched out from
>   God's Tree!
> For us there is no Master and no helper, save for Thee.
> Thy radiant face is shedding light upon the world entire;
> Yet, "the Servant of Bahá" was the name Thou didst desire.

Canto 7

> I acknowledge Thy loving-favour from my innermost heart's core;
> O Thou, the object of my love! Assist me, Thou Who art my Lord.
> O Mighty One! My Master; the ignitor of my zeal;
> Illumined by Thy radiance, enkindled is my soul.
> O Bahá! Thou art the light celestial, and my love's sole purpose;
> The effulgence of Thy splendour to my inner eyes gives focus.
>
> O Thou, Fashioner of the universe! Thou art our world's Protector!
> Thy beauteous Countenance is the object of my love and ardour.
> The seen and unseen worlds are intoxicated by Thy love;
> Without Thee, there is no being, not below nor yet above.

---

[1] Referring to 'Abdu'l-Bahá
[2] One of the titles of 'Abdu'l-Bahá.

Thy light hath made all particles exhibit their appearance;
Upon meadows and on deserts Thy Face doth shed its radiance.
The Daystar of Thy Countenance, having dawned in all its brilliance;
How could a shadow still exist in such sun-drenched effulgence?
Oh! By Thy alluring Beauty are Thy lovers' hearts enticed;
By Thy Splendour they are drawn towards that yearned for lovers'
    tryst.

Oh! The crux of my anticipation is with Thee reunion;
I have set my outer and inner sight on Thy Beauty's vision.
O Best-Beloved! I beg Thee shelter me in Thy protection;
Thou art the One Who doth respond to earnest supplication.
O Bahá! With all our hearts and all our souls we Thee implore
That Thy union to us Thou wouldst not at any time withdraw.
Let not the soul fall far from Thee after being in Thy Presence;
Let it not be separated after closeness to Thine Essence.
The cleaving from volcanic blast no mountain can withstand;
How can a fish pulled from the sea survive on arid land?
When once there was reunion, separation is most dire,
For heart and soul, with Thy love filled, are burning with desire.

Canto 8

On the night when love was born, my fortitude was slain;
My free will then forsook me; I was bound with yoke and chain.
When love displays its majesty in all its power splendid,
Both speaker and quiescent are left speechless and dumbfounded.
The Sovereign Lord Whom I extoll, to Whom I am alluding,
If forevermore I limned it, His image would elude me.
Reunion's path can never be completely demarcated;
Not even Resurrection's Day will find it explicated.

Canto 9

Longing for Thee is the treasure-trove gained from loving Thee;
The world of love is full of yearning grief and misery.
We are all puny mortals; Thine Essence is infinity,
Thy Countenance reflected in the mirror of eternity.
The entire world of creation is like onto a looking-glass;
In which nothing is reflected save Thine image, first and last.
Of mirrors, there are myriads, unmeasured, numberless;
But His immortal Countenance each mirror manifests.

O Omnipotent! Through Thy light was this heart set aglow,
It was by Thy help that insight into his soul did flow.
Thine assistance was the key that unlocked his very heart;
O Glorious One! The key to all our hearts is what Thou art.

So that instantly my inner eyes, becoming thus receptive,
Now see Thy shining Countenance with vision more perceptive.

Canto 10

O Thou, who art beyond all states of living and of dying;
O Thou, who art above all traits and limits qualifying.
O Thou! The whole cosmos in Thy knowledge is converged;
Both the simple and the compound in Thine Ocean are submerged.
Thine existence is Self-evident; and Thou Self-subsistent art.
O Thou, unseen by outer eye yet seen within the heart;
Nay, nay! To the people of insight, in all veracity,
Thou art not concealed to their outer eyes' perspicacity.
O Soul of all creation! How couldst Thou ever be concealed!
Save to sceptics and the negligent whose eyelids are tight sealed!
The one whose heart is not enlightened suffers ignorance;
Of God's presence his poor barren heart hath no experience.
Whoever knows Thy light, he finds Thy radiant brilliance;
Everywhere He sees Thy manifested luminance.

Hail! O Thou, our Sovereign Lord, soul-stirring and resplendent!
Thy Light that shineth on all things is clear and evident.
Who am I, a speck of nothingness, in Thy Holy Presence,
That I should say that Thou art the hidden or the manifest?

Canto 11

O my heart! It is time to elucidate the mysteries;
Expound them clearly; no longer clothed in allegories.
Detach thyself from all else save God;
With all thy heart and soul say "O Lord!"

Love is the straight path leading to thy desired end of the road;
With all thy heart, take refuge at the gate of this abode.
There the Guide that stirs the souls will take thee by the hand
And thus, detached from all save God, before Him thou wilt stand.
Once He hath liberated thee from all thy shackling chains;
Then jubilant He maketh thee, released from sorrows' pains.
That King of generosity, by the hand, He taketh thee;
And from all thy binding fetters He doth fully set thee free.
In the Friend's love thou wilt find for thee the only firm foundation,
Detached from idle fancies and every vain imagination!

O Junun! Thou must beseech the Ancient Sovereign to help thee
To expound the hidden secrets precisely and completely.

II The Repository of Mysteries: Translated text

Canto 12

Life-giving water is His love—elixir of vitality!
The Lote-tree from Whose lips pour forth pearls of His sagacity.
Rise up and from His hand receive a chalice to refresh thee
Quaff from it the potion that tastes of immortality.
Freed from earthly life and death to joyful exaltation;
Then follow Him upon the pathway straight to your salvation.

My passionate love for Him hath my heart blighted;
But He hath opened His door to His lover devoted.
O heart! Liberate thyself from every limitation;
Thou receivest from the loving Lord thine inspiration.

Canto 13

Enter this garden: gaze upon its roses delightful;
Behold how the lovers, the Ancient Beauty, encircle.
A heart-rending song each one intones, heaving fevered sighs:
"Let my life, heart and soul unto Thee be a sacrifice!"

Canto 14

O thou, the Best-Beloved of mystics and lovers!
O thou, the companion of all homeless wanderers!
O Thou, the Physician of the helpless and the sickened!
O Thou, the aim of things created—their ultimate end.
I beseech Thee to bestow on us Thine ever-loving kindness;
Grant all and every needy one a measure of thy fullness.

O Thou, Who art All-bountiful! We are knocking at Thy door
We implore Thee to relieve us from our pain and anguish sore.
Make Thy beauteous Countenance our fortune's treasury;
Remove from our hearts agitation and anxiety.
Destine for us blissful bounty that Thy Face we see;
To die of ego and live on in Thine eternity.

Canto 15

When, in the heart of Moses, God shone forth effulgent lights,
Discernment swiftly sped to Mount Sinai's sacred heights.
The Beauty of God shed its radiance; thunderstruck He fainted,
To rumbling sounds unheeding; by no tumult animated.
He swooned for a time; He returned to His senses for a time;
From eternity to infinity He flew time after time.

Moses heard the voice of God, pouring words into His heart where
God's image and the voice of God were mingled all together.

*To Moses, secrets were divulged in that court of utmost holiness;
Whilst, in His Beloved's Beauty, Moses was so utterly immersed.
Thus God secreted in His soul the mysteries of sacredness—
Such mysteries as cannot be in any utterance expressed.*

*The Celestial Guest revealed Himself within the soul of Moses,
Whose intellect and self-hood were dumbfounded in that radiance.
Now, intimate with the unseen Friend, the soul of Moses glowing
In reflection of His Best-Beloved, His grace on us bestowing;
For while His soul was orbiting the Most Desired One's throne,
Moses was man's closest link to naught but God alone.*

Canto 16

*Thus to attain the Presence of the Desired One thou must strive;
Peruse the essence of all creation His Image to derive.
He is the Physician, He Who healeth all infirmity;
And, likewise, He is the Guide for the entire humanity.*

*The inner mysteries of the divine Friend are gold of the purest;
They are the inmost kernel while the covering husk is all the rest.
Behold! Appeared a Revelation; an effulgent light was shining;
The Lord of the Day of Resurrection, now, manifest becoming.*

*The Morning dawns; the darkness of night is repealed;
Mysteries are revealed; nothing remaineth concealed.
Lo! His Beauty is manifest; the world has been rejuvenated
By His revelation all human life is newly recreated.*

*For He is the Protector, the Helper, and the All-forgiving;
He imparts reviving breath; from their graves the dead are rising.
Manifestation Universal, Promised of all Ages
Is He! Fulfilled are the prophecies; discharged are the pledges.
His revelation was foretold in all creeds and dispensations;
To Him—the hidden Truth—all Scriptures sing their salutations.*

*He hath enlightened the eye of the whole human race;
Raise thine eyes up towards His resurrection most great.
To the hearts of all men He gave illumination;
He is surely the Lord of the whole of Creation.*

Canto 17

*O my heart! Unshackle thyself from every binding fetter;
That the mysteries of the world of being thou might discover.
His lovers, inebriated by His wine, are willing to meet
Martyrdom, forgo life, to cast their severed heads at His feet.
Ecstasy and zeal have filled their senses, overflowing;
His radiance hath revived them, on them new vision bestowing.*

II THE REPOSITORY OF MYSTERIES: TRANSLATED TEXT

Canto 18

Attach thine heart to God; life earthly is a fleeting moment;
His grace is dew that moistens the heart's rose-garden fragrant.
Blessed the liberated one, full of joy, from sorrow free;
A human soul in truth he is; thy close companion he can be.

O friend! Not every man hath a heart full of tenderness;
Seize his hem when you chance on one full of kind-heartedness.
The man of God is the vital elixir for heart transformation;
Know his value; he is as a bright sun that sheds illumination!
Of the Path and its stages He has sound comprehension;
He embodies all virtues; he is a man of perfection.
He empowers us our egos rebellious to vanquish;
We receive our reward—we spiritually flourish.
If thou art a true wayfarer with virtues being blessed,
Follow thou the man of God if thou art zealous for success.

When God—exalted be His glory—guides thee on His chosen way,
Knowing of God's mysteries, how canst thou go astray?

Canto 19

The Manifestation of God is God's gift to all of mankind;
He is the Bestowal of mercy and grace, and Bounteousness divine.
Do not with ingratitude refute such a favour;
Unseal thou the eye of discernment, thou dear one!
Thou wilt recognize Him as God's Vicar on earth for this day
And distinguish Him from the ones who lead people astray.

When God's Vicar in this world was made manifest,
The effulgent light of His face from afar luminesced.
Like the sun in the sky did shine His dazzling splendour;
The whole horizon was brightened by His radiant grandeur.
He drew like a magnet all the hearts up to loftiness;
The ignoble He raised to the high ranks of nobleness.

What doth sunlight do other than to illuminate?
With its rays it doth evil's darkness eliminate.
For how can darkness resist the brightening daylight?
Behold! The whole globe is swathed with dazzling sunlight.
The oblivious are awakening from their beds of slumber;
Open thine eyes! See the sunrise on mountain peaks yonder.

With splendours immense the divine Beauty arrived;
Lifeless bodies were with spirit imbued and revived.
He appeared; again He illumined the eyes each soul;
The whole world vibrated, pulsating to His clarion-call

OVERTURE

The seven levels of heaven by His light are encompassed
Open thine eyes! See how His glorious majesty scintillates.

Canto 20

When one sets up a market for merchants to trade;
One makes sure in the shop various goods are displayed.
At day's end one must check how one's trade has progressed;
If one earned nothing one might feel ashamed and depressed.
All merchants try to make the best of their own kind of trade;
At night-time they will calculate how much they lost or gained.

Thus when souls leave their bodies and to higher realms ascend,
They will be asked to make account of all that they have earned.
O heart! Strive for something precious to carry on your journey's way,
Not to be ashamed to come empty-handed to your Judgment Day.

There is nothing more precious than love, a bounty divine,
It is the world's greatest wealth, best asset—treasure sublime.
Love's rays set the atoms of the cosmos vibrating;
Just like water from matter is life propagating. [1]
Love hath stirred up my soul as the earthquakes cause shuddering;
It was love that left my heart like a homeless one wandering.

Love aids intellect to reach its ultimate purpose;
It uncovers the meanings concealed in the Scriptures.
Love is a treasure hidden in the heart of the lovers;
Love is the ultimate purpose of our toils and labours.
When love imbues the heart with the Beloved's mystery;
The wayfarer starts his journey with heart-felt chivalry.
Out of all the attributes of the Prophets, Love is the key;
For this reason are manifest those Lords of humanity.

The lover walks on the earth with wings on his feet;
To him rose-bed and fire are equally sweet.
Without love, in this world there would be no fruition;
Probe this matter; thou wilt reach this very conclusion.
Behold! Love transformeth thine heart into a paradise;
It doth immerse thee in the ocean of celestial grace.

Lo! Love bestows upon thine eyes acuity of vision;
It parts the veils so thou canst see with new well-lit precision.
It shows the heart the way toward attaining the All-Righteous;
It doth draw all creatures to their Creator, ever upwards.
Love liberates thee, cuts the bonds that are thee ensnaring;
It bringeth thee delight and bliss, from sorrow thee sparing.

---

[1] The Prophet Muḥammad stated that all living things came from water.

Love doth release thee, sets thee free from everything save God;
It purifies thine heart until it shines like glass unflawed.
Love would become thy trusted guide whatever the conditions—
Would be a faithful friend to thee at all times and occasions.
Love is the Elias that leads thee to the fountainhead of life;
Thus it liberates thee totally from sorrow, toil and strife.

Love is the foremost treasure-trove in all the worlds of God;
Love prompts one to become a guide, show other men the road.
Love unifies the hearts of all the people of this planet;
Whether open or hidden, it is a friend most intimate.
Love is an essence sensitive—eternal, everlasting;
Towards the Most-adored One it is every heart attracting
Love is the living water, which gives life to humankind—
The pathway to salvation that God's servants must needs find.

Love motivates the martyrs to sacrifice their being;
Brave men and women are aflame with love ablaze and burning.
Like Solomon, love reigns, enshrined upon heart's throne;
With ease it solves hard problems whose solutions were unknown.
Love is the safest haven for humankind's security;
It is the unifying force cementing hearts in unity.

When the tree of human life doth reach the time of its fruition;
The fruit most valuable it bears is love, its best condition.
Of all mankind's endeavour, Love is the greatest artefact;
It is the treasured crowning glory of mind and soul and heart.

The Prophets are spiritual guides of the entire human race;
They serve the Truth infallibly; imparting hope and grace.
That ultimate Reality, the Essence of all Being
Its radiant Face to all the Prophets It hath been unveiling.

O Junun! End now the discourse; take thou pause and feel no qualms;
Nothing is manifest save God in both seen and unseen realms.
O my infatuated, fascinated, lacerated heart!
Thy love so passionate hath made thee be a wanderer apart.
Recount how treads the wayfarer along the mystic Path;
Discover and explore the inner mysteries of love.

If thou art aware of the Path and the stages of that Path,
Then thou art informed about the hidden mysteries thereof
Beseech thou, then, the Ancient Beauty to confirm thee;
He is the All-Knowing of eternal mystery.
No one, save the people of the heart, knows the veiled mysteries;
This Path is beyond the grasp of imaginings and idle fancies.
This is the straight Path that leadeth to God's Presence;
The wayfarer his end attains on this Path's pursuance.

OVERTURE

Seven are the circles within the world of being;
Seven are the scrolls the cosmos all enfolding.
There are seven layers of existence, namely, seven heavens;
To the Exalted Lord, the Prophets from Adam count as seven.
The wayfarer passes through seven stages to reach union;
He attains the aim of wayfaring—his Beloved in reunion.

If thou art in quest of God, step up onto this Path;
So that of God's mysteries some inkling thou might have.
At the start of the journey, if I speak of love and yearning,
It means that our Lord's face is hidden, not for our discerning.
Ere long He removes the veils from His hidden Countenance;
Then shines He forth brightly, haloed in dazzling radiance.

He is the Most Exalted, the Most Holy and the Most Glorious

The First Valley
THE VALLEY OF SEARCH

Before beginning to tread the mystic path of spiritual journeys,
Hearken, O my heart, to the mysteries of the spiritual Sovereigns.
Let us go to the main theme of discourse, O seekers of mysteries!
The harp of knowledge and love is tuned up to play all the melodies.

At the beginning of this path, O close companion!
Let thy heart be attuned to His love and compassion.
O dear one! Herein read of the seven vales my version;
Hallowed be the eyes that have the inner truths envisioned.

The faithful ones whose hearts reflect the radiance heaven-sent;
They have described that there are seven valleys evident.
Out of His great favour, the Sovereign Lord of bounty[1]
To these mysteries of being hath given clarity.

The mystery 'the veil would be removed' has been explained
When the fiery face of the Sovereign of Love had been unveiled—
As His Countenance resplendent was uncovered but a trace,
Myriads of veils that had masked the eyes He lifted from their place.

Since with the King of love thou art secretly in intimacy,
A priceless pearl is hidden within that holy sanctuary.
The seven states about which that King of Love doth comment;
Will become ever clearer from moment to moment.

O pen! Skim over the page like a lightning streak;
Thou must be on thy mettle this Path to bespeak.
O tongue! Talk as fast as the gale that is gushing;
Thy limbs must become as wings, through the air rushing.

Take heed! This is the book of love, O hearest thou, my dear?
Be attentive to discern the secrets that are hidden here.
Thou wilt learn how the condition of lovers and mystics
Is affected by a heart-charmer's characteristics.

Though the stages and paths that the mystics pursue
Are beyond telling, I will describe them for you.

---

[1] The poet is referring to Bahá'u'lláh, the Prophet-Founder of the Bahá'í Faith, Who wrote *The Seven Valleys* in explanation of the spiritual journey to reach the Divine Abode.

II The Repository of Mysteries: Translated text

Yet the words that I use are not coming from me!
It is He who provideth the message for thee.
He is within the mirror; I echo like a parrot what He says!
Whether He orders me to be silent or to speak, the words are His.
My heart hath turned into a reed into which doth blow the Flautist;
He stands before the glass; His voice's resonance thou hearest!

Mystic wayfarers have discarded unrealities
In portraying the concept of these seven valleys.
O thou who desirest to attain unto the Uncaused One;
Strive with every breath in unceasing search for Him, O dear one!
O thou endowed with insight! Make haste in thy quest;
To reach him, thou wouldst grow wings in thine eagerness.
When a heart in its search becomes skilled and resourceful,
Like a phoenix of love, it soars heavenwards graceful.

If to stride in the seeker's path a heart is determined,
Of all worldly defilements 'twill be doubtless unburdened.
Though the lover's heart is aflame in the throes of his passion;
Yet he must mount the steed of patience on this expedition.
If a wayfarer's effort is not by patience attended;
His wayfaring and exertion with no gain will be ended.
So my heart! Be steadfast when traveling the hard road before thee;
Be patient; for patience is, to respite and deliverance, the key.

Know ye not why love's path with sharp thorns is bestrewn?
Then learn of love's secrets from the tale of Majnún.
If thy desire is to join those who study the mysteries;
Secure the door against spurious and trivial vanities.

Say not: "A mufti or priest told me this". Such times are long by-gone.
Claim not: "Surely they know the traditions and ways of religion".
Nor say: "My father told me which way I should go;
He is older than me; has seen more than I know."
These are all idle babblings; pay to them no attention;
Discard such blind imitation without hesitation.

O informed one! Cast aside all such meaningless prattling;
This is all merely frivolous and misleading chattering.
"Those blindly imitating have the people misled;
Let blind imitation be a hundred times cursed."[1]
If thou forsake not thy forefathers' blind imitation,
I swear by God, of Faith's fragrance thou hath no perception.
O noble one! Close thy mouth and open thine inner ear
That the lessons of wisdom, point by point, thou canst hear.

---

[1] Quoting Rúmí

The Valley of Search

If thou wouldst gaze upon the mirror of thine heart;
Then detached thou wouldst be, from all creatures apart.
O friend! Distance thyself then from the people's vain gossip
So that thou wilt not be deprived of God's own fellowship.
Let neither hope nor despair affect thy composure;
And be not thou pleased by every rumoured disclosure.

The heart that is purified from mere earthly entities
And emptied of ego, is filled with mysteries.
When the heart becomes purged from all selfishness,
Naught but a mirror remains pure and stainless.
To no worldly affairs art thou henceforth attached;
Inform thine heart that the door to illusions is latched.

Bravo! O thou who wouldst tread the path of mysticism's gems!
Bravo! O thou who hast earned a crown of royal diadems!
Bravo! O thou who dost strive the ocean of light to behold!
Bravo! O thou who attainest indeed to the presence of God!
Bravo! Thy soul will become enlightened and elevated;
Thou wilt be wiped clean of egoism, and illuminated.
Bravo! Dauntlessly, the pathway of love thou wilt pace;
In thy heart such desire stirs from His loving grace.

O heart! Be thou patient in thy march on love's highway!
Thou wilt reach God's abode at the end of thy journey.
Be patient on the pathway of thy search for God's presence;
He will crown thine head with the diadem of sovereigns.
O heart! Be patient; divine confirmations be ever beseeching;
The flames of thy ardent zeal to reach God ever higher are reaching.

Be patient; be grateful to Him for the gift of such ardour;
To the friendship of the Praised One it is driving thee harder.
O heart! Be patient in the path of veiled subtlety;
As thy compassionate Friend, God will always assist thee.
Be patient. This is the road of love. There are no maps;
On this spiritual journey, Gabriel directeth thy steps.

O good-natured wayfarer! Thy guide will be Gabriel;
This is love's appeal, the response to the call celestial.
O heart! Be thou persistent on the pathway to the Glorious One;
It ends at the Primal Point—there with God thou wilt union attain.
This is the highway of love; it is a straight thoroughfare;
Blessed is the soul who is resolutely striding there.
Be patient on the path of discovery and perception;
Concealed is God's light—seen only in the heart's conception.

The heart-bestowing, Best-Beloved, comfort giver
Enchants thee and is dragging thee hither and thither.

II The Repository of Mysteries: Translated text

Nothing else remains in thy heart save the light of God;
Till thou attainest God's presence, it draws thee abroad.
Eagerly along the way, in all directions, thou dost search;
Till, in the ocean of God's radiance, thou art deep immersed.

The rolling seas, the howling gale, the planet's rocky breast
Are His tools to stir thy need of Him and urge thee in thy quest.
He makes the gentle breeze and glowing fire as the screen
On which the soft reflection of His image can be seen.
He makes water, fire and the earth only as the means
To detach thee from the world thou art entangled in.

The canvas of the Best-Beloved is nature's beauty;
The silhouette behind this screen is what attracts thee.
The reflection of the Creator appears in His creation;
It enamours the lover, overcome with intense emotion.

With but a glimpse of Him behind the veil I am astounded;
When He burns that covering veil away, I am dumbfounded.
Without the medium, melancholy is my heart;
When He is unveiled, I wrench the fetters apart.
Woodland settings attract the man of God. He is drawn to rocky
    pinnacles!
Now, just compare that with the pull of the Invisible of invisibles![1]

O Thou, the Cause of causes! Thou createst the means,
Lovingly Thou dost display Thy image on the screen.
Thou dost present Thyself as if with face and tresses;
At times Thy hair is straight; at times in curls it dresses.

Thou art the First Cause of creation of water and fire;
Thou settest the lover ablaze, overwrought with desire.
My throat pleadeth to be by Thy sharpened sword severed!
Just for Thy loving glance, my life yearns to be offered!

O Almighty! Take us by the hand out of Thy love unending;
Thou art the All-Forgiving, the All-Assisting, All-Defending.
O Thou the Lord of mankind! Fill the hearts with such ardour
In their quest for Thy presence; that they find Thy safe harbour.

Moisten our lips with a draught of Thy celestial wine;
May Thy Face light our hearts up with Thy brightness Divine.
Purge from our hearts any trace of malice or jealousy;
Make Thy love's secret known to our inner reality.

May nought remain in the heart but the most ardent love for Thee;
May all the hearts brim over with longing Thy Beauty to see.

---

[1] One of the titles of God.

Let all souls be detached both from fame and from shame;
Let Thy Countenance set hearts and minds all aflame.

Behold Junun! How besotted his yearning for Thee;
For such an effect one must find what Cause there can be.
He sees Thine imprint stamped upon each fashioned thing;
The atoms by Thine existence came into being.
The lover's eyes see in the cosmos nought else save Thee;
His mind and soul are overwhelmed in studying Thee.
Blessed are the eyes that have gazed on Thy Countenance;
This ancient world revolves through Thee—renewed its immanence.

Thy love makes the old world become recreated;
For the wayfarer it solves the hidden secret.
Thou dost energize the minds of lovers and their souls dost quicken;
Thou bestowest love upon the hearts with no recompense taken.

Thou dost assist the wayfarer from Thy love's predilection;
Thus he is able to locate his sought after direction.
Without Thy loving-kindness how can a wayfarer depend
On cherished hopes of carrying his load to the journey's end?
Thy loving-favour reaches all whether noblemen or populace;
It embraces all ethnicities in every time and every place.
Without Thy grace not a moment can anything survive;
At nothingness would all existence instantly arrive!

O Lord! Fling the door wide open to Thine all-tender mercy;
Let every heart be intimate with Thine hidden mystery.
Offer the wine of reunion for the heart's intoxication;
That love may enflame the heart in an impassioned conflagration.
With a draught of that celestial wine let the hearts grow courageous;
May the souls be intoxicated from that claret-filled chalice.

Let them shatter every fettering chain;
Let them forever impassioned remain.
Let Thy love completely shake them to the depths of their being;
Set them free from their shackles of intelligence and reasoning.
Let them be amazed and overwhelmed forevermore;
With the fire of Thy love their comprehensions can mature.
Let the hearts drink a sip of the wine from Thy goblet;
Let reason and intellect in endless raptures plummet.

Let the seekers forsake worldly shame or renown;
Every wayfarer in Thy love must let his heart drown.
Let them all earthly glamourous illusions ignore;
To Thy beauty be drawn, to the world tied no more.

II THE REPOSITORY OF MYSTERIES: TRANSLATED TEXT

When the seeker the one true God sets out to find,
He must first cast all thought except God from his mind
To God surrendering his heart in search of the Beloved,
And find the Divine Joseph by the fragrance of his garment.

The man of God befriends every created being;
In his search, he encompasses all creatures living.
At times he turns to the earth, to water, even to the wind;
He is so captivated with the Lord of all humankind.
As the wayfarer admits he cannot reach the Almighty;
He grows spiritually; slowly casts off his identity.

Hasten and be bold in thy search; beseech God that for thee
The door will be opened; God knows well what is best for thee.
Thou must search though thou art not equipped for the road—
No need for provisions when in quest of thy Lord.

The human being is sheltered under God's canvas;
And he who is searching will attain to the finish.
'If thou knock at a door', Islam's Prophet[1] *assured us,*
'Then a face will eventually appear in the entrance.'
When a well you are digging each day bit by bit,
The aquafer's depth you will finally hit.

O thou, who doth yearn to be at His beauteous Face gazing;
Search, and search, and search for Him! Thou must never stop
    searching!
Seek Him in every place, be it earth, fire or stratosphere;
Search thou for the Beloved's entrancing Face everywhere.
Associate closely with every person in thy quest for Him;
Thou might find the mystery of the Beloved in a stranger's hymn.
Be thou steadfast in thy search in spite of all calamities;
Thou might find thy Beloved in the furthest extremities.

O seeker! Where art thou? Give thou ear to His celestial tone;
He is calling thee; detach thyself from all save God alone.
In the path of ardent search make most steadfast endeavours;
Like a phoenix, on the wings of love soar in the heavens.
Make haste in thy quest; grow wings to soar through the highest
    sphere;
Leave this world behind; be amazed at what lies over there.
Release thy feet from the binding pillories of living;
Bear thou ever in mind: to meet thy Lord thou art winging.

Tell me, what does a wayfarer need who sets out on this quest?
He must mount the steed of patience for his Beloved to search.

---

[1] The Prophet Muḥammad

Look at a foetus—how it grows in the womb of its mother
With patience it passes through each stage, one after another.

Patience is required before mud transmutes into a rose;
Patience is required before the wine from a grapevine flows.
Patience is required before warmth from bitter cold grows:
As a favour from God, the pleasant springtime breeze blows.
Patience is needed while the sunlight sheds its rays
To ripen the fruit with the warm gleam of its face.
Patience is needed while the seeds grow into harvest;
And black soil transforms into beautiful rose-gardens.
Patience is needed for the sea to make rain,
In an oyster to form a pearl from a grain.
Patience is needed for the rain to transmute
The earth's soil into beautiful flowers and fruit.
Patience must wait awhile till from handfuls of earth
Human beings with pure souls in time may come forth.
Patience is wanted that from soft lumps of clay
Superb Chinese porcelain comes on display.
Patience is required: decades of pressure immense
To change copper to gold; its state must be condensed.
Patience is vital while from inanimate minerals
Plants adorn their new kingdom in myriad variables.

Behold! How great a recompense there is for patience!
Lo! His Face is shining—not hidden in abeyance.
At the outset, patience hath a bitter flavour
But, at last, rewards one with sweet fruit to savour.

Patience is needed while copper ore imbedded deeply underground
After centuries of transmutation turns itself to precious gold.
Patience is needed so that, out of the dust and grime,
The minerals transform themselves into plants sublime.
Now, every created thing is unaware of any higher realm;
It knows nothing other than the kingdom wherein it doth sojourn.
If the mineral doth not rise to the plants' domain,
And the animal doth not a human station gain,
If they remain unchanged in the kingdom of their source,
They are fruitless; ponder on it; it is obvious.

Likewise, should a human to God's knowledge not attain;
What worth is his existence and what would be his gain?
Consider! When a babe grows in its mother's uterus,
It doth develop sight and hearing for its future use.
It is preparing, stage by stage, for the world unknown outside;
When born, it sees the new-found realm where it will now abide

And if into this world the babe was never to be born,
For what purpose were its ears and eyes and feet then formed?
Eyes, ears and feet are not of any use within the womb
Meant, rather, for the world beyond the pre-birth anteroom.
The foetus in the womb needed neither ears nor eyes;
Only in this outer world would they be utilized.
When out into this wider world the babe is then delivered,
That is when its eyes and ears are for sight and hearing needed.
It is in this world the infant needs its legs and feet for walking;
And here that it will need its hands when it is time for working.
All useless if into this world the babe was never born,
Else why with eyes, ears, hands and feet should it be thus adorned?
Likewise, know another world beyond this one awaits us!
It is far beyond our earthly womb of water, air and dust.

The one, who doth discern the unseen secret and the mystery,
Speaketh not from vain imaginings, nor from some idle fancy.
He claims not any payment for the offering of guidance;
His recompenses come from God; they come in great abundance!

Peruse the book of humankind with mystic insight endowed
So that thou mayest find a trace of the traceless Beloved.
Men of deep insight are well-aware of the hidden enigmas;
They are not shallow-minded; they are beyond vain imaginings.
But one hour in the company of these Chosen Ones bestows
On thee more bounties then five hundred years of monastic vows.

Fools venerate the mosque; yet with the most cruel malice
They oppress the Ones whose hearts are God's dwelling place.
In the inner soul of the Chosen Ones is the Temple;
Here should be the place of worship; this is where God doth dwell.

O thou, the intelligent one! Open thine inner eyes wide;
The purpose of planting trees is for the fruit that they provide.
This fruit is the knowledge of God, being faithful to His Covenant;
At the threshold of the Master, thou must strive to be a servant.

From time immemorial until all eternity,
This is God's test for mankind; this is the reality.
The effulgent Orb hath shone forth; the universal cycle hath begun;
Observe thou with care to see the beauty of the Sovereign on the
    throne.

That exalted Being holdeth in His hand a chalice;
He calleth all, both nobles and commoners, to taste it
Lo! The Sovereign of love hath His Visage unveiled;
The desert of love is now by anguish assailed.

The Valley of Search

O benevolent one! Now endeth the valley of search;
Henceforward, love will be the main subject of our research.
As regards this fascinating theme there is really no end;
On the vale of love, O noble one, some time we must expend.

O Thou, who art aware of the hidden and manifest mystery;
To outline the valley of love, and limn its secrets, please assist me.
O Thou who doth enchant a myriad hearts with but one loving glance,
O Thou alluring Beauty! To me Thou art unveiled and visible perchance.

I am a smitten lover, like Majnún I am enamoured;
The lantern of my soul is with Thy dazzling light inspired.
I am neither aware of the road nor of the destination;
Neither for my life nor my heart feel I any apprehension.
Nor have I been concerned about what my future may conceal;
Nor think I of my wording when my feelings I reveal.

I am a captivated lover, a maniac besotted;
I am fleeing to the meadows and wandering through the desert.
O Thou Who art concealed amongst Thy waves of blinding brilliance,
Thy Countenance is enveloped with Thine effulgent radiance.
Untie the tresses that obscure Thy features luminous;
Unseal Thy lips to fill the world with pearls mysterious.

O Thou Who ties a myriad hearts to a single strand of hair;
With the beauty of Thy fragrant locks all hearts Thou dost ensnare.
O Thou, Who by one loving glance my heart didst captivate;
O Thou, my Loved One, look at me! Observe my grievous state.
On the very day when, by Thy love, my life was first disturbed,
My being devastated was by the slashing of Thy sword.
Unnumbered hearts are lynched upon Thine every strand of hair;
Each is like the aftermath of a mammoth massacre.

O my loved one! On which side of thy couch last night didst thou repose
That thou art so angry with me; heated, such blame on me impose?
At times thou dost bite thy lips then coil thy lariat to entrap;
Every strand of thine hair is a noose that doth lasso my heart.
O my Angel! For Thee my life I would evermore surrender;
What harm if Thou wert but to cast a glance upon Thy lover.
Thou hast captivated the hearts with the wisps of Thy hair;
Thy face sets hearts and souls ablaze like wild rue on fire.
Once again Thou hast twisted round my neck thy coiling noose;
At times Thy speech doth slay me; or else shackles me Thy voice.
Though the soul of a lover yearns to receive Thy loving-favour;
No soul is worthy even to be the object of Thy censure.

II THE REPOSITORY OF MYSTERIES: TRANSLATED TEXT

If Thou art dissatisfied, still I possess a spark of life;
Put aside Thy wrath; I offer Thee my heart in sacrifice.
I bow my neck to Thy razor-sharp sword; let it be severed!
Let Thy love's glance behead me; I beg no mercy whatever!

Myriad hearts in Thy hair strands are caught all ecstatic;
Bravo to the coil of Thy curls aromatic!
In each beauteous tress of Thine a world is enmeshed:
Both mankind and the cosmos are born from Thy breath.
By the sweet scent of Thy locks are hearts intoxicated;
Chained to the Best-Beloved's ringlets, thus captivated

Stirred by love, day and night, the cosmos is in constant motion;
It is searching for God in fervent desire to approach Him.
Let my life be sacrificed for Thy luminous Face;
Let my soul be surrendered for Thy bounteous grace.
Thy fragrant hair is the attraction that unto Thee guides us;
In our hearts Thy love's brightness shines forth and revives us.
Thy musky locks are the chains that have our necks encircled,
Drawn us to Thy beauteous Face and kept us manacled!

My all-consuming need of Thee hath robbed me of serenity;
Round the candle of Thy Countenance, like moth compelled I orbit
    Thee;
While both the worlds are fastened to a strand of Thy tresses;
Thou dost drag me hither and thither, fettered and helpless.

O Thou Who art exalted by the whole of Thy creation;
Thine Essence spurns all attributes and any limitation.
O Thou, whose attraction like a lariat doth our souls lasso;
From Thy beauteous allure, the quintessence of our passion grew
Thy flowing hair ensnared me into such thraldom unto Thee;
I desire my bond of servitude to last eternally.

The whole world hath been inebriated from Thy love's choice chalice;
The radiance of Thy Countenance to existence brought the cosmos.
Mankind, like all creation, by Thy Beauty is enraptured;
Thy locks and ringlets are like snares for hearts set to be captured.

Thy love hath lit within my heart a fire of ecstasy;
It hath robbed me of patience, forbearance and bravery.
Thy blazing love hath rendered me both anguished and languishing,
So scorched that night from day I no longer am distinguishing.
My heart is enthralled by Thy love; Thy beauty my soul doth entrance,
And their beguiling attraction robs me of my intelligence.
I know not which vessel I boarded, nor upon which ocean I sail;
Neither root nor its shoot do I know, nor tree-trunk from branch can I
    tell.

The Valley of Search

How can I care which year it is or guess what month it may be?
I am trapped in love's snare; that is my life and my destiny.
Is it midday or evening? How should I know! Neither day nor week can I date!
How ecstatic I feel! How smitten! How completely besotted my state!
I am so engaged with Thine image, I know not springtime from autumn;
I am so engrossed in Thee; neither pitfall nor path can I fathom.

"Love is a stranger to earth and heaven too;
In him are lunacies seventy-and-two."[1]
"For the infidel, infidelity; for the religious, religion;
And, for the heart of Attar, the ideal thing is an atom of Thy pain."[2]

The valley of search hath reached its finale;
Hereafter, I will speak of love in detail.
As to this dissertation there can be no end,
Tell us of the Valley of Love, O noble friend.

---

[1] Jalálu'd-Dín Rúmí (AD 1207–1273); *The Ma<u>th</u>nawí*. Jalálu'd-Dín, titled Mawláná ("our Master") is the greatest of all Persian Sufi poets, and is the founder of the Mawlawí ("whirling") dervish order.

[2] Farídu'd-Dín 'Aṭṭár (ca. AD 1150–1230), a great Persian Sufi poet.

The Second Valley
THE VALLEY OF LOVE

My patience died on the night when love was born;
My free will left me; compulsive drive doth remain.
Compulsive drive is the feathered pinion of the perfect,
While, for the slothful, it is the prison and the fetter
Compulsive drive is like the waters of the River Nile;
It is water for believers and blood for infidels. [1]
While wings carry the falcon to the king's boulevard;
Wings also bring the carrion crow to the slaughter yard.
Compulsive drive is the clarion call of love
When nothing is manifest save the Best-Beloved.

The magnet of God is like a sword with which free will is sheared;
Then only God is existent and all else hath disappeared
He is the Essence of all things, the rest are but contingencies;
The reason being that God's Oneness doth exclude all qualities.
That is the reason thou art bonded to His domination;
Whene'er He sheds His Light thou dost receive illumination.
When thine action is transformed by a single breath of Him;
Thou wilt join Him like a drop absorbed into the ocean.
This is the best achievement, if thou hast the virtuous quality,
That thy action with His action will ever be in unity.
What thou doest would be ever then with God's will in harmony;
Thine eyes would inner vision gain by God's own luminosity.

Open thou thine inner ear and hearken to what Rúmí says;
This man of the spirit hath disclosed these pearl-like mysteries: [2]

---

[1] The Egyptians entreated the Israelite, saying, "Of thine own intention fill a jug from the Nile and put it to my lips that I may drink. (I beseech thee) by the right of friendship and brotherhood; for the jug which you Israelites fill from the Nile for yourselves is pure water, while the jug which we Egyptians fill is pure blood."

[2] Junun does not quote Rúmí using his exact words. Rather, he renders Rúmí's point and meaning. Sometimes he uses different synonyms but selects more beautiful words and sounds. Sometimes he completes what Rúmí has said. We should bear in mind that the spiritual vision and world view of Rúmí and Junun are as close as if one person was saying the same thing in two different ways. Junun never borrows the views of Rúmí. It seems he confirms Rúmí's views. At the same time he wants to show his respect for Rúmí whom he recognizes as a great sage of deep spiritual insight.

II The Repository of Mysteries: Translated text

We were a simple element; we once were all one substance;
Neither head nor foot had we in our earlier existence.
When that pure light had shed its radiance, its energy took form;
Like shadows cast by crenulations, it thus grew multiform.

We were once a single substance all united like the sun;
We were pure and limpid; like a pool of water we were one.
Then, destroy ye those battlements with your trebuchet;
Let banished be those differences amidst the shadows set.

Hearken with thine inner ear not to get the wrong impression;
Beware; turn not to fatalism from hearing this discussion.
Be alert! The point is sharp—as sharp as is a diamond knife;
If thou hast no shield for thy protection, flee then with thy life.

When their souls dispense with all differentiation;
The faithful yield, like a single soul, to unification.
That is why men of insight do clearly expound:
No existence save one single One have we found.

While creation's first origin is from one source amorphous;
Plurality and quiddity are undoubtedly congruous
Then, thou must also recognize that in all created things;
He is the Essence of all attributes mirrored in their beings.
Matter's variety is to its nature inherent allied;
And to its quiddity annihilation is also ascribed.
A speck of dust is unseen, as if non-existent, alone;
It is the sun that gives it light; it has no light of its own.

O son! From the daystar no shadow falls;
Shadows are but traces of gates and walls.
The sun hath no shadows; it is all luminosity;
You can see it; it is not concealed in obscurity.

O wise man! When thou in the sunlight dost stand,
A shadow of thine doth appear on the ground.
When thou dost look in the mirror, thou seest thy face;
What thou seest is thy face's reflection—its trace.
Since in the mirror neither good nor evil is wrought,
It only returns to thee thine own features thus caught.

Though the listener should drink to the dregs from seven seas filled
With wine, just one sip of that chalice would leave him more thrilled.
This leviathan of love thirsteth for all the water of an ocean;
The more it drinks thereof the more that sea refilleth in proportion.
Love's cetacean drinketh all the water of the seven seas;
But, still athirst, that whale cries 'is there no more for me than this?'

The Valley of Love

Quenched by a draught of water, thirstiness gives way;
But this thirst makes to boil a hundred seas away.

There are unnumbered souls ensnared in His love's lariat;
The dart of His love has wounded sages a myriad.
Crimson is the symbol of His all-majestic might;
Whiteness is the sign of His authority and right.
From the invisible realm came forth the Beloved,
All in crimson, the colour of majesty, robed.

Vainglory, arrogance, earthly riches and greed
To the eyes of love seem like an onion decayed.
Mountains and meadows, orchards and streams
In love's eyes but a pile of trash it all seems.

I wish I had an intimate friend, to whom I could impart
As a confidant, the emotions that surge up in my heart.
But, with no cherished friend to confide in, I keep quiet
Though, having no intimate, the blood boils in my heart.
But sweeter than honey tastes the poison;
Preferred to life is annihilation.

Thus, with the fire of love the obscuring veils efface,
That the heart be worthy to see His unobstructed face.
The lovers enkindled a flame that now blazeth in their hearts,
It consumed their clamorous egos and any shameful lust.

Arise! In thy heart spark the tinder of love's conflagration;
Burn out all illusions of existence from thy perception.
Then stride forth; take thou the first step in love's pursuit;
In the door of the lovers' abode place thy foot.
To speak much further on this I am forbidden;
But, before the eyes of love nothing is hidden.

If thou shouldst pour all the ocean's water into a carafe,
How much would it hold? Would the portion for one day be enough?
If all the limbs of the body into a mouth were transmuted;
To encompass the Beloved and the robe it would be unsuited

Tenderly my Beloved is glancing at me, signalling to me:
O lover! Whatever of thy heart remaineth offer it to Me.
How is it thou speakest of heart if nothing doth remain?
Thy bleeding, anguished heart still recurs in thy refrain!
Wert thou not slain by Me when thou didst wager thine heart?
And yet thou still claimest what a brave champion thou art!

O bemused one! If thou hast some weapon, thou didst not yet wield;
Bring it along with thee when thou cometh to the battlefield.

II The Repository of Mysteries: Translated text

I will still slaughter thee with one stroke of My sword;
Then thy remains will be dragged off, trussed up with cord.

Hearts are mounded up on every strand of My hair;
It is the site of unnumbered souls all massacred.
Myriad hearts to one strand of My locks are belayed;
Myriad souls on one dart from My bow are impaled.

O Thou, Who by one tender glance a hundred hearts dost captivate;
Have mercy on me. Who am I? Before Thee I am inanimate
I am maddened; so fervidly in love, I am demented;
By the sword of Thy love my being is annihilated.

I have neither a heart nor a soul; my mind is astray;
From the realms of existence, all have wandered away.
Passion for Thee made me to carry my heart on my sleeve;
I gambled away my existence; of life I take leave.

I know not what is the way, nor in which house to adjourn;
Neither for my heart nor my life have I any concern.
When Thou said: 'Be', the universe came into being;
From one cask of Thy wine all the atoms were reeling.

For the Beloved, once again, hearts are enthused in their ardour;
They are immediately willing hundreds of lives to surrender.
Blessed is the soul, who, for his Loved One, such zeal hath developed,
That, in rapture, he throweth his heart at the feet of the Beloved.

How well doth proclaim that perfect master of love's litanies;[1]
He sang the song of love as an organ chants its melodies.
"Love is rebellious, murderous from the start;
"So the stranger runs from it and stays apart."

Love is discerned in men's sighs and tearful lament;
No disease is like that of the love-sick and heart-rent.
So wan a face doth bear witness to a heart in sore grief;
For the lover's wont is the shedding of tears for relief.
Such is the ailment of love and the mood of the lover;
That its state is beyond what the mind can uncover.

O young man! If thou intendest this lesson to study,
Read the book that describeth the Beloved One's beauty.
It teaches of yearning and whirling; of dancing and raptures;
It is not a book of numbers, or tedious, dull chapters.
Its theme is the Loved One's curled and musk-laden tresses;
Around the Beloved revolve all sides of their treatise.

---

[1] Referring to Rúmí.

The Valley of Love

O lacerated heart, bleeding from the depth of love's wound!
Is it again thine intention to bewilder my mind?
Hark! Whither has thy reasoning intellect wandered?
Thy passion is stirring, surging higher each moment.
O heart! I weep and wail that thou shouldst be calmed;
So why with each breath dost thou wilder become?
My tears and lamenting hath all been in vain;
For the more I wail, the more thou dost disclaim.

O mind! Do not counsel him; he is a crazed lover;
Leave him alone, aimlessly to roam the world over.
He is intoxicated with the love of his heart's desire
With no free will; to his own inner chamber let him retire.
He does not distinguish friend from adversary;
How long shouldst thou admonish a lover gone crazy?
He is inebriated with love; he pays neither attention
To man-made conventions, nor listens to misleading direction.
To one who is love-sick and whose heart is perturbed,
The whole world and its dealings are but a canard

The heart felt the flame of love in its conflagration;
The wise man saw love's charm in his infatuation.

O Thou, the Absolute, the Ancient, the Ever-Living!
The faithful companion of lovers is yearning for Thee.
O Sovereign of bounty and kindliness, O Forgiving One!
Nourish our souls with the food and drink that cometh from Heaven.
O Thou! Both the worlds are humble before Thy boundless grace;
The ultimate goal and desire of all hearts is Thy face.

The fire of Thy love in my heart hath flamed up in a blaze
My mind and soul hath strayed away from the world in a daze.
Lo! In my heart Thy fire is flashing and flaring;
Leaping flames, with each moment, are dancing and swirling.
Burn! O my heart, burn! How that burning has spread!
For lovers such burning is their daily bread.
Let thine ego—that hindering veil—be consumed in the flames;
As thy self is annihilated; His existence remains.

O my heart, burn! Then sweep out the ashes from the fire;
Place them in thy palm; inhale to feel how fragrant they are!
They are redolent of the Divine Beloved's presence.
Though only dust, yet they carry the Loved One's fragrance.
Use this dust as a collyrium applied to thine eye;
New vision thou wilt gain; the celestial King thou wilt espy.

Once again, before the inner eye, doth emerge the Sovereign;
O lacerated heart! Beware; His glory doth all overwhelm!

II THE REPOSITORY OF MYSTERIES: TRANSLATED TEXT

Oh! What a wondrous countenance, shining with dazzling radiance!
Oh! What penetrating light! Mount Sinai burns with its luminance.
Both humans and angels His footsteps trace;
Like shadows, they follow His beauteous face.

A ray emanating from His face became reflected;
And on its pattern all creation was perfected.
The reflection of His face in all creation has its image;
All created things circle His abode, day and night, in homage.

O Thou, the Absolute One! O Thou, the most loving Lord!
Thy beauty brought into being the seen and unseen world.
All created things, as a whole and in parts, towards Thee are reaching;
*They are on their journey of return to Thee; for Thee they are
    searching.*
All are striving to attain to their Origin,
Both atom by atom and mountain by mountain.
They will not stop for rest until they have reached their Source;
The whole cosmos is orbiting around Thee in force.

Thine energizing love inebriates both mind and soul;
In Thine Ocean the soul of the whole cosmos is a pearl.
Thou art the origin and the ultimate end of my existence;
Thou art my soul and my heart and my life—my very essence.

The ego's 'I' and 'we' are veils that obscure our vision of Thee;
Thy cup inebriates my heart; when the veil is gone then I see.
Whosoever effaces his selfness becomes spellbound by Thee;
He is filled to overflowing with his ardour and ecstasy.
He hath died to the body to be quickened in spirit;
From ties worldly released a saintly life to exhibit.

His life is submerged in the world of eternity;
Nothing remains in his heart except for divinity.
His heart fills to the brim with the radiance of devotion;
All his mind doth discern is the passion of adoration.
The wine of divine love hath robbed him of all other thought;
He is in Thee, The Glory of God, entirely engrossed.
That self-effaced soul hath no desire now except Thee;
His heart and his lips sing no song save Thy melody.

Thou dost guide humankind chanting Thy celestial refrain;
Representing God on earth, His Cause Thou wouldst proclaim.
Spiritually and temporally mankind Thou leadest;
Thou art a Servant, yet what only God doeth Thou doest.
Thus His wrath is also Thy wrath, O Thou, the Most Beneficent!
And His favour Thy favour; on high and low Thou bestowest it.

*Whoever in his heart entertains hatred towards Him,
In fact, is battling against God manifested in Him.
O God! Against such severe testing safeguard Thy servants;
Take them by hand; to the right path grant them Thy guidance.
"The people's perceptions are like riding a lame donkey,
While God flies on the winds like an arrow's trajectory."
I can say no more than what I have said; I extol Thee
Yet not content am I with how much I exalt Thee.*

*In His proximity, my breath I held;
He signalled; to silence me compelled.
With His sugar-shedding lips, He sweetens His reproach;
He explains to this poor lover, where he doth encroach.
Thou speakest again of pitfall and pathway;
O thou! Besotted art thou by My beauty.
O thou, who hast been enraptured by love's passion!
Like a droplet, thou art absorbed into love's ocean.
Oh thy life is in turmoil because of thy love for Me;
Oh thou art a wanderer because of longing for Me.
O thou, who hath gambled thy being away in only one game;
Thou art galloping thy steed in the field of reunion's domain.
Oh! Thou art alone; there is no one to share thy ardency;
Oh! In thy defeat thou hast beaten the drum of bankruptcy.*

*O thou, who for Me hast offered up thy very existence;
Nothing—not thine heart nor thy mind, nor thy body—remaineth.
Thou hast gambled away thine existence and art lying slain;
O thou, who art confounded, ever longing Me to attain.
If the slightest trace of thy being doth in thee remain,
Then offer it to Me, O wanderer in My domain!
I will stain My sword red with the colour of thy blood;
I will rope thy corpse with my lariat and drag it out.*

*O friends! Once again rebuketh me my Beloved;
It befuddles my senses, makes me empty-headed.
O comrades! Once again Love draws the bow to let fly the arrow,
Raging in battle against the heart of this bewildered fellow.
O friends! Once again I scented from Love's angry libretto
The smell of blood; it immersed me in an ocean of sorrow.
Once again Love's passionate glance my heart penetrated;
Dart-like, Her alluring eyelashes knocked me prostrated.*

*Last night, Love sent a message of furious reproach;
I know not on which side She hath slept on her couch.
I feel in Her heart She fosters a hatred of me;
Though barely wakened, Her outrage is easy to see.*

My Love is twirling and twining Her locks in my presence;
She casts a spell that refastens my neck in Her tresses.

Pray! Do not be angry! Raise the stakes of Thy ruthless reprisal;
For more of Thine onslaughts, my heart is at Thy disposal.
My heart never complains of Thy cruelty;
Enchained in Thy love, it bears all patiently.

I leave aside details of Love's behaviour;
Rather, I will try to explain it further.
To a strand of Her hair myriad hearts Love hath bound;
Lo! With Her arrow myriad souls doth Love wound.
But it is as sweet as honey to the lips of the lover;
Yet so much more honey-sweet is Her rebuke and Her anger.

Annihilating of self is more exalted than a life of selfish strife;
Without self-annihilation how could anyone achieve eternal life?
In the presence of the King of Love one must be self-effacing;
One must traverse through the wilderness of self-annihilation.
No doubt, one must break the fetters in order to move onward;
When freed of fears for life and limb, then one can journey forward.

For such a one is not allured by worldly matters or life mortal;
What to him doth taste as pleasing sweet is a draught of poison lethal.
No more concerned if he be a believer or disbeliever;
His heart doth bleed; he hath been brought down with the blade of
  love's cleaver.
Between guidance and misguidance he no longer doth distinguish;
No imaginings he entertains—all thought he hath extinguished.
Of belief and disbelief love's zeal him hath deprived;
It is as if he hath not into this world arrived.

No other rule doth Love allow except its own command;
Love's mystery no intellect is fit to understand.
Both the mind and soul astounded are at Love's majesty;
No place for fame or shame is in its realm of dignity.
Love is beyond the mortal world's renown or infamy;
When, through a reed it blows, both worlds, like breath, before it flee.

O my dear! Blow with the bellows of love for an instant,
That the human mystery to thee becomes evident.
Blow with the bellows of love to see life as a moment fleeting;
Whoever becomes intimate with love's melody is a true human being.
Blow with the bellows of that love that maketh thee restless;
That thou become aware of the mysteries of the Peerless.
That one who is not intimate with this melody is a scorpion;
Nay, he is a bloodthirsty wolf that amongst humankind doth sojourn.

The Valley of Love

Pain forces men to search for a cure;
Pain drives men to find the healer's door.
Pain makes man restless; it compels him to cry out;
Like Jacob he doth wail from the depths of his heart.
Pain robs man of patience and fortitude;
Pain drives man to the path of rectitude.
Pain robs man of calmness and slumber;
'Til his prayers bring forth an answer.
Lo! If bodily pain such an effect doth induce;
What effect would the pain of the spirit produce!

How discerneth the lover the trap from the lure?
How should he then distinguish unripe from mature?
That poor one hath left the world of being far behind;
Love hath severed him entirely from all else save God.
He is now placeless and alone, completely selfless;
Released from all fettering bonds, he is a dervish.
When the love of Laylí[1] left him demented;
He turned to his broken heart and lamented.
Love of Laylí lacerated his heart, leaving it bleeding;
Love of Laylí carried him away from this world of being.
Love of Laylí robbed him of sleep and quietude;
Love of Laylí robbed his heart of all fortitude.
Love of Laylí turned him to a homeless peripatetic;
Love of Laylí rendered him wounded, tear-shedding, pathetic.
Love of Laylí devastated his earthly reality;
Love of Laylí hath led him to homeless itineracy.
Love of Laylí hath left him in a world of isolation;
It hath robbed him of all life and all earthly consolation.
Love of Laylí from this whole world had so set him apart;
From when the call of love was raised from the depths of his heart.
Love of Laylí had left him disturbed and sore troubled;
His longing for her was, every moment, redoubled.

The daystar of the lover's yearning for God hath now dawned;
To the yoke of the Beloved the lover's neck hath been bound.
When his neck was ensnared in the tightened noose,
From all other binding ties he was cut loose.
The Beloved's ringlet is coiled round his neck like a tether;
Enraptured, he is being dragged around hither and thither.

He runs in all directions in search of his Loved One;
He tries streams and then rivers, then even the ocean.

---

[1] Laylí is the sweetheart of Majnún in a legendary story. In Persian literature, Laylí is a symbol for the Beloved. The term is even used for God as the Beloved of hearts.

Sometimes this lonely one, from the world disconnected,
Leans with face to the wall, and sheds tears undetected.
Drunken with love, he tells of his longing, his open heart throbbing;
He cries: "Of quietude and rest the pain of love is me robbing!"

Pain compels the wayfarer to the end of the journey;
As pain drives the ailing to find a healing remedy.
Why should the Physician come when there is no pain?
He Who is the celestial Friend is the Healer of every blain.
We are ailing and helpless, anguished in our aching;
He is the Healer of all, the Balm, the All-loving.
From head to foot we are sinful and full of transgression;
He is full of tender mercy and loving compassion.

O God! Shut Thine eyes to our flaws and our failures;
Oh! Thou art Love, the All-Bestowing of favours.
We are full of sin and shortcomings in every inch of our being;
He is all Favour, the All-bountiful, and the Ever-forgiving.
O God! We beg Thee to overlook our shortcomings;
Oh! Thou art Loving Bounty in all of Thy Being.
We are but puny mortals; insubstantial and ailing;
Cast a glance at these souls of Thine, enfeebled and failing.
All our hearts are melting away in the blaze of our love for Thee;
O Thou All-Possessing! Cast Thou a glance on us of sympathy.
Like fish, we thirst; where is the river and sea that we search for?
Oh! Thou art our Succorer, our Draught of life-giving water.

Let our abasement turn into glory and loftiness;
Let our poverty be changed into honour and richness.
Let our minds be worthy of the blissful joy of Thy bounty;
Let our intellects be immersed in delight to have found Thee.
Make us dauntless; free us from the fear of anything save Thee;
Grant us a portion of Thy love, and Thy hidden mystery.
Let Thy love shield us against any harm or ill-will;
Let Thy love lift us above earthly good and evil.

Let the burning fire be transmuted to a rose-garden green;
As Abraham hath done, we say: O fire! Be cool and benign. [1]
Let us follow the example of all Thy lovers;
Assist us to tread in the footsteps of Thy prophets.
Part Thou the sea to make passage for our safe crossing;
Change the fire to a garden of roses refreshing.
Help us to recognize those who know Thee and love Thee;
Help us to identify those who have faith in Thee.

---

[1] Referring to Qur'án 21:69: "We said, 'O fire! Be thou cold, and to Abraham a safety.'"

The Valley of Love

We do not turn away from those who are Thy Chosen Ones;
We prostrate at Thy threshold and become Thy custodians.
Let our necks be worthy to be noosed in Thy lariat;
Let our necks be fastened to Thy fragrant hair's ringlet.
So that to this mortal life we attach no importance;
We grow wings to be soaring to the heights of love's heavens.
That in dying to self we attain existence eternal;
Release us from living this life, debased and delusional.

Elevate us unto the highest level of servitude;
We attain everlasting life in shedding our selfhood.
By the crown of loving Thee let our foreheads be blessed;
By our servitude to Thee let our necks become noosed.
Let us scorn ego degrading and selfishness shaming;
Let us be smitten by love for Thy Beauty disarming.
Let us ignore all other learning save that knowledge of Thine;
Well is with him who bows down before Thy knowledge divine.

We prostrate ourselves before the wealth of Thy Divine knowledge;
Nothing other than our love of Thee do we prize and acknowledge.
Bring to our lips a draught of Thy chalice our hearts to revive;
Arouse in us the desire our beloved Master to serve.
Overlook our shortcomings, O Thou, the Righteous One!
For our sins and trespasses we beseech Thy pardon.

Let us turn ourselves to Thee entirely, seeking only Thy grace,
To be purged of perversity and disposition to transgress.
From the fetters of all earthly matters let us all be free;
Swift and nimble make our footsteps on the path of love for Thee.
We must be non-existent, the real existence to discern;
Illusive worldly matters we must pass beyond and spurn.

O Lord! Burn up our avarice, hatred and arrogance;
To be Thy love's abode, make our hearts pure with innocence.
O God! Cleanse the hearts from debasing jealousy;
Enlighten the souls with the radiance of love for Thee.
O Bahá! Purge us from deceit, corruption and hypocrisy;
Cleanse our hearts from every mortifying and sinful tendency.
That the hearts become cognizant of Thy hidden mystery;
And breathe from the rose-garden of reunion its fragrancy.

O thou, who art unaware of how I love my Beloved!
How wouldst thou comprehend the state of a heart by love maddened?
The true man of faith is the one who suffers the pain of yearning;
Unlike those who are filled to the brim with arrogance and loathing.
Purify thy heart from the defilement of hatred and enmity;
Thus, thy heart is the abode of the love of God and its treasury.

II THE REPOSITORY OF MYSTERIES: TRANSLATED TEXT

Let love instigate thee to cherish high aspirations;
A carnal self is not worthy to be caught in love's chains.
Uproot from thy heart all trace of haughtiness and hostility;
Eliminate thy self so that the world might be quickened by thee.
Purge from thy heart all jealousy and resentment;
Do not hurt the hearts of those who are innocent.

Why would the royal falcon hunt a dead mouse to devour?
O man! While his ego lives, a man is but a cadaver.
Light a fire of love in the inmost core of thy soul's recesses;
Burn away all idle words and useless thoughts and excesses.
To uproot the shameful ego, exert the utmost efforts;
Then take but one step, set thy foot in the land of the lovers.
O young man! That is the meaning of dying before thy demise;
It is through self-annihilation that thou attainest eternal life.
When, in union with God, the soul and the heart are annihilated;
Then before our inner eyes the mysteries become unveiled.

O noble reader! The Valley of Love hath come to its ending;
Now, on the Valley of Knowledge[1] hear the treatise impending.
O my heart! Thou art lacerated with a burning passion;
Why, with every breath you take, do you heave sighs of emotion?

O Junun! Blest are thine eyes with their tears of love shedding;
Thou art constantly immersed in the ocean of yearning.
O dear one! Stop composing dirges for a while; this Valley endeth;
Now, like a brightly blooming flower, smile in front of thy Beloved.
O thou, bewildered one! Thou didst define the second Valley;
Thou didst some verses compose, this Vale to illustrate truly.

Now is the third Valley's turn to be drawn;
The sun of knowledge doth in the soul dawn.
O gentle composer! Record in ink these profound commentaries;
Thus expound the subtleties of knowledge of these divine mysteries.

With the assistance of God, the Valley of Love was portrayed;
Now must be an image of the Valley of Knowledge conveyed.

---

[1] Ma'rifat in Persian has no single word equivalent in English. It is a combination of three meanings: knowledge, wisdom and insight. The third Valley is the Valley of Knowledge. But the reader has to bear in mind that by the word "knowledge" is meant "knowledge with wisdom and insight".

The Third Valley
THE VALLEY OF KNOWLEDGE

O nightingale of the soul! Warble the melody of knowledge;
Spread out the pinion wings of love to soar in the realm of knowledge.
The heart was born in the higher sphere of all things spiritual;
In the inner chamber of the soul, hath opened the sacred portal.
Open thou thine inner eye to the veiled and hidden kingdom;
The sun of knowledge hath now dawned from deep within thy bosom.

The mystic hath seen the signs of God in creation's entirety;
Like the radiance from the Beloved's face in blazing intensity.
Both physical and spiritual worlds are His evidence;
The mystery of each realm is testimony to His presence.

When an infant is born into this earthly realm,
Things he sees; if foul or fair, he cannot judge them.
Later he travels the world; on diverse places his eye falls;
There a synagogue, then the Ka'ba; and, here, monastery walls!
He paces the terrain with his firmly treading feet;
Inspecting all created things that his eye doth meet.
Of the world around with his outer eyes he becometh aware;
He wants to distinguish the good from the bad, the seed from the snare.

Likewise, he traverses the realm of spirit with his inner vision;
With every experience, a door opens to his inner perception.
He traverses the spiritual sphere and observes with a sharper sight;
As he gaineth new vision, he starts to see with the eye of the heart.
Lo! He hath been reborn with new inner powers of observation;
Born into the spiritual realm, new visions come to his perception.

He hath emerged from the darkness into a sphere of light;
Like Moses, he hath stepped onto Mount Sinai's sacred site.
When his inner vision was opened and new insights he had gained
Entry to the realm of mysteries, in God's Presence, he attained.
In a state of deep supplication, unto God he is humbly turning;
He slams shut and bolts the door to idle fancy and vain imagining.

From perdition unto guidance he now hath turned his face;
An epitome of virtues his whole being doth embrace.
To whatever holds his destiny, he is fully acquiescent;
He maintaineth that in every war only peace is the requirement.
In dying to selfish ego, he attains to life eternal;
Every bough or leaf for him becomes a bed of roses vernal.

II The Repository of Mysteries: Translated text

With spiritual heart, he traverses through the realm of the Beloved;
In that spiritual sphere he doth observe those mysteries unnumbered.

Although the soul of a true listener is able an ocean to drink,
The more that he drinketh, the more the waters will rise again to the brink.
This book of rhyming couplets is alike of love a fount;
The more one quaffs its waters, the more that gushes out.
Along every stage of thy exploration may God assist thee;
Hopefully, thou seest not as a pond this billowing sea.

God hath opened to us the door of inner mystery;
Who could stop the flow of this stream because of jealousy?
Although by language a topic is explained and the theme conveyed;
Yet, by speechless love, the feeling much more deeply is displayed

To fall in love with some beauty, and between this one or that one decide,
Eventually leads to the sanctuary at the majestic Sovereign's side.
Hearken again a story that enshrines a mystery;
That of its hidden secret thou wilt not divested be.

A mystic was recounting a tale to a companion
Of an intimate nature, he had kept close to his bosom.
He said: There was a time when I was in love with a sweetheart;
I was restless; I would run here and there hoping to meet her.
I was searching for her, hopelessly weeping and groaning;
I was enamoured and bewildered, heart-sore, bemoaning.
At times, in my search for her, I even approached her abode;
Sometimes, in rapture, I sought the seas, or up mountains I strode.
At times, as if riding on the wind, I journeyed everywhere;
Sometimes, I stayed static, enchanted by the beauty of her.
There were times when to Mecca and Madínah I trekked;
In all lands and locations for her presence I checked.
I sought her in the wine taverns, and then within a nunnery;
Whether Ka'ba or pagoda, all endured my scrutiny.

At times I strode through valleys deep; at times I climbed the steepest hill;
At times I would sit shedding tears, and plead with my whole heart and soul;
Many streets of Rome I trod, or strolled through Paris boulevards;
It was as if I sought her beyond this world of dust and shards.

At times in the bonds of being, it seemed that I was fettered;
Yet there were times that I felt free; all binding chains were shattered.

THE VALLEY OF KNOWLEDGE

One night, while I was in a state of contemplation in my quest;
By the sight of her wondrous face unveiled, I suddenly, was blest.
For visions of sheer beauteousness and such attractive stature
To leave both men and women spellbound it is their true nature.
When comeliness reveals itself, a tumult can ensue,
Hundreds of hearts, each one like mine, can then be broken too.

She entered my room. No hijab did she wear to my amazed delight;
Uncovered was her lovely face; her lower lip I saw her bite.
Her long musk-laden hair was cascading down her arms;
The whole world would have been smitten by that glimpse of her charms.

She whispered: "O thou, my crazed and infatuated one!
O thou, my enraptured lover! What love's anguish is thine!
In the fire of separation from me, how fares thine heart?"
"I swear by God," I replied, "I can no longer bear it."

She sat down on my bedside chair for a moment brief;
She carried away my heart and my mind as she left.
I asked, "O thou who art so gracefully withdrawing! When will I see thee again?"
She responded, "Only in the middle of the night, and only deep in thy dream."

No knowledge save the knowledge of love is genuine;
The rest is but the conflicting theories of Satan.
Begone! Uncover the secrets of love and learn them;
Find a sweetheart; and for her be ready to die then.

Gradually the Beloved's hidden secrets become manifest;
O lover! Gaze at that supernal Beauty with thine inner eyes.
The knowledge of God is ever a direct vision;
It cannot be acquired from any theologian.

Remembrance of God is not a number of prayers to chant;
The true remembrance is but the one that assisteth the heart.
The right thought is the one that revealeth the right road;
The right road is what leads to the Sovereign's abode.

The true King is He, Who is born to His sovereignty;
Not the one that depends on an army and treasury.
Observing that Face, thou wilt discover mysteries divine;
His image reflected in all creation thou wilt find.

All the atoms are restless and magnetized by that Countenance,
Their particles quivering like the pointers of compasses.
Jacob-like they are searching for the celestial Joseph;
Unconsciously they are striving to attain their Beloved.

II THE REPOSITORY OF MYSTERIES: TRANSLATED TEXT

O thou, searching for the Beloved! Where art thou?
Gird up thy loins and hasten to reach Him now.
Come hither! For love's courtship the time has arrived;
Hurry! The door to the tavern is now open wide.

Once again the barrel of wine is fermenting;
The Wine-seller stands at the door calling, "Welcome!"
Drink a glass from the hand of the Cupbearer celestial;
Thou wilt be overflowing with words inspirational.

The head without one eager thought would make a better tail;
While lost in its own negligence, it leads to no avail.
When a jug contains no water, it might as well be broken;
When lips no wisdom utter, it is best they had not spoken.

A heart with no yearning pain might as well not be throbbing;
A rose with no fragrant scent might as well not be blooming.
An eye with no vision might as well be sightless;
Leave it closed. Surely to open it is pointless.

Take up a white cane and feel thy way to the bazaar;
While thou art passing, raise this petition everywhere:
Say! O my God! I am blind. I beseech Thee, light on me confer;
Instead of a life without insight, lay me in a sepulchre.
I desire not a life with no yearning for Thee;
Without a longing for Thee, death better would be.

O Thou Radiance of God! Thou Lord of religion and heart;
O Thou, at Whose feet both the heart and the soul must submit.
Out of jealousy, they are attempting to overlay
And obscure the lights of Thy Sun, these common clods of clay!

I beseech Thee that at them Thy wrath's dart Thou let fly;
Surely better they are blinded than gaze with squint-eye.
Let the Royal Falcon be released from their talons;
Let the hearts be relieved from such shameful actions.
Those horned owls treat the innocent Falcon unjustly;
Its feathers and plumes they tear out with sheer tyranny.
They ask 'Why dost Thou of that yonder land reminisce,
With its palace, where Thy perch was the Emperor's wrist?'
It hath committed no crime except being the Royal Falcon.
What was the crime of Joseph except being honest and handsome?

To suffer from adversities attracts Divine mercy,
Whereas folly is an illness that brings down God's fury.
There is no remedy that will cure the illness of folly;
'It is the sign of the wrath of God', so sayeth Rúmí.

The Valley of Knowledge

Fools turn away from a treasure of wisdom, an erudite Elder;
Instead, they set up any monkey as their spiritual leader.
For them an eloquent man of wisdom is an outcast apostate;
While an arrogant and ignorant churl as their guide they will instate.

They rebel against the wise Sovereign of luminance;
But they are well-pleased with the father of ignorance. [1]
Out of folly, they worship a calf [2] *as their god,*
But they will not adhere to the Prophet of God.
They cherish idle fancies; God's Vicar they wish not to see
Because the blood is boiling in their veins out of jealousy.

O God! Heal their souls from their skew-eyed disease;
Thou art the sole One with the cure for their eyes
They are enveloped in darkness and bereft of cognizance;
As stupid as Abú-Jahl, [3] *they are steeped in their ignorance.*

O God! Either scour the tarnish from the mirrors of their hearts;
Or release us from the degradation of their shameful acts.
The dust blessed by the touch of God's Vicar is the remedy
To heal the eyes and hearts, which are of such a blessing worthy.
This refers to the hearts, which are free from the ailment of
*   foolishness;*
Not the heart of a fool who hath been born inwardly blind and
*   mindless.*

O God! Heal the eye that is blind; we refer to the blindness
Of folly, not loss of sight due to injury or sickness.
Thus, there is still a chance to heal that inner blindness;
For treatment, one has to search for Celestial Guidance.
As thou art a human, let a source of healing be thy quest;
O dear one! A human soul should not be lower than a beast.

O my dear! With love, a person's true humanness doth prevail;
The head that cherishes not love doth not differ from a tail
For spiritual blindness, one must find the remedy;
The therapy for those who bear the cross-eyed malady;

---

[1] This refers to the tribes in Arabia rejecting the Prophet Muḥammad, having been swayed by the Prophet's uncle who was against Him. Muḥammad called him 'the father of ignorance'.

[2] Referring to the followers of Moses who made a calf of gold and started to worship it as a god.

[3] Abú-Jahl, the 'Father of Ignorance', is a title given to the uncle of the Prophet Muḥammad when he rejected the Revelation of the Prophet Muḥammad. He was originally called Abu'l-Ḥakím, the 'Father of Wisdom'.

II THE REPOSITORY OF MYSTERIES: TRANSLATED TEXT

Knowest thou the treatment for blindness of the spirit?
Find the dust where the Envoy of God on earth hath trodden it.
To search everywhere for this remedy, exert thy utmost effort;
Thou may find the collyrium, which to the eye gives insight.
If thou couldst be relieved from this, thy squint-eyed degradation;
Thine head would be crowned with the diadem of inner vision.

When Almighty God was moulding the clay of thy creation,
In His wisdom, He balanced lust with reasoning perception.
For reason grasps the import of divine decrees and pays them heed;
Thus, God enjoined thee to obey His Word in every goodly deed.
So whosoever puts aside his reasoning, and disobeys,
He deprives himself of sound obedience and its virtuous ways.
Ego tempts man to rebel; and break God's Law till, blighted,
He falls far from God. He has been squint-eyed and short-sighted.

The basis of worship is submission to the Messenger of God;
To disobey God's Messenger is the action of a cross-eyed clod.
This hath been from immemorial time unto eternity
And will ever be the test of God for all humanity.

To ensure you always take the right path consciously,
Harken! Be awake; do not walk round so drowsily.
God, the exalted One, hath acquainted thee of the rightful way;
Open thy eyes! Do not grope blindly on a road that leads astray.

In this world, one must ever avoid being
Haughty, jealous, greedy and patronizing.
If to judge in a rich man's favour a magistrate accepts a bribe,
How can he defend the rights of the oppressed, and justice true
    prescribe?
One should avoid being proud of one's prestige and prosperity;
One must take refuge with God from such pride to have immunity.
Seek God's assistance to overcome this evil-minded part;
Let the light of the All-Glorious shine forth within thine heart.

O ignorant one! Avoid being jealous of the mystic;
Such envy becomes a cord of palm-fibres tied round thy neck.
Sweep the threshold of this tavern with thine eyelashes;
Seek assistance from the Knower of unseen matters.
The Knower useth every means in order to help thee;
He flings open the portals of inner knowledge for thee.
Deprived of the favours of God and His Chosen Ones,
Even wert thou an angel, thy name thou wouldst blacken.

Turn to God for His help and have trust in His favour;
Follow the path of God in thine acts and behaviour.

THE VALLEY OF KNOWLEDGE

Know thou that there is a light concealed deep within thee;
Know thou, too, of the egoistic conceit in thee.

Restrain thy hands from harming thy innermost self;
Beware that thou art not made proud by thy triumph.
Do not treat thy meek and hidden self cruelly;
Be not like a scorpion that stings its own belly.

Take thou a lesson from what befell Satan;
An angel he was until doomed by his action.
Through pride and defiance his good name he destroyed,
When he would not bow down, and was cast out by God.
Each new era begins with the same test severe;
In each age a new Adam and Satan appear.

To worship God without loving His Manifestation;
Hath no spiritual root so leadeth not to fruition.
Although many acts one performs of worship external;
Outward worship hath no credit—like husks with no kernel.
Satan loved not Adam and would not pay homage before Him;
Instead he bowed to his own ego, to his eternal shame.

Can to the hypocrites the door of divine mercy be opened?
The whole harvest of their knowledge hath gone with the wind.
Like when, heedless of the flooding rain, a miller soundly slept
While the whole mill of his worship down the raging stream was
*   swept.*

Now follows a commentary on people of vision;
About the works of Ba-Yazíd I give this depiction.
Thus spoke forth that most masterful of all story-tellers;
As he narrated a parable for besotted lovers.
Most pleasingly hath taught us that king of love's secrets
In his concise account of love's gambits and tenets.
How graciously that master of love's portrayal would talk;
Here is his limning of the path of perfection we walk.

"For twelve years I was living the life of a hermit,
Like a blacksmith, I hammered my ego to mould it.
As a pious practice, I threw it in the furnace of punishment;
Using the crucible of hardship for self-discipline's management.
With the sledgehammer of reproach I would admonish it;
Until it became like a mirror when I polished it.

"For one year I admired it with pride and fulfilment;
I regarded it with joy as a great achievement.
Till, having looked at my triumph for a while in conceit,
I spotted round my waist a girdling sash of self-deceit.

"For another five years, then, I struggled and strived;
And I cast off the girdle of deceitful pride.
Five years later, I had become the mirror of my own self-scrutiny;
So I could grind away from my actions any rust of hypocrisy.

"It was then I renewed my faith only in God,
Having found folks around me were spiritually dead.
From then on their company I completely eschewed;
I said a prayer for the dead and was greatly relieved.
I left those corpses disporting themselves in their cemeteries;
Now with no one save God do I share any intimacies.
The profane being purged from my tablet of existence,
To union with God I arrived through God's own assistance.

"When I emptied my heart of all ego and selfishness,
My whole being was aglow with my inmost core's essence.
Then I opened my inner eye in the realm of unobstructed vision;
And saw the lights of divine Reality shining from six directions.

"How could I see the creatures; I saw only the Creator!
I saw Him radiating from all sides with no barrier.
The lights of the Creator were displayed everywhere arisen;
I opened my inner eye; His lights shone around the horizon.
Having reached the summit where there are no limits visual;
All I saw before me were hailing that Light perpetual.
A trace of God I could in every single atom discern;
His blessed Countenance I perused in each and every sign.

"All created things were the signs of the Lord All-illustrious;
All atoms became visible in the light of His Countenance
The radiance of His Essence was manifested from all around;
Since points of location are excluded in the Oneness of God.
The Sun of His Countenance was blindingly bright;
How can shadows exist in that Sun's dazzling light?
The light of His Face on every side was evident;
All creatures disappeared; only God was apparent.
Only God was manifest in the entire world of being;
In that light all-effulgent, darkness paled, disappearing."

O seeker! Open thine inner ear! Do not infer from what I tell
That the contingent world is the embodiment of God. Not at all!
The light of God is shedding its radiance on the entire cosmos;
The whole creation is harmonized by the brightness of His face.
The radiance of His Countenance unifies the souls;
Hearts are illumined when the Unborn's light on them falls.
The Supreme Being manifests from every side His luminescence;
Both invisible and visible are made apparent through His Essence.

To see the Beloved's full lustre in all six directions gleaming;
Attests that the fire of inner knowledge is vigorously flaming
In the same way that sunlight in this outer world is obvious;
I saw nothing save the Beloved in all of the cosmos.

O intelligent and quick-witted reader!
If you put a piece of iron in the fire,
It is purified, turns red and, like the fire, glows;
It acquires the same effects as what the fire shows.
If you touch the fire, it will feel identical
To touching that fragment of fiery metal,

You will find that the action and the effect for both is the same;
Like a ray of sunshine when reflected in a faceted gem.
Likewise copper its own traits loses to be transmuted
Into gold by the elixir of forces imputed.
After this process, one can call it copper no more;
Transmuted to gold; it no longer is as before.

The heart can discard its base copper quality;
When transformed by the divine elixir's bounty.
The elixir of love will transmute a heart of base copper;
It is God's mystery that love is that transmuting elixir.

The bounteous elixir bestows on all its gift of transmutation;
Through the agency of love, every heart secures such transformation.
The elixir's role is to help each one to attain his goal;
With its aid can be fulfilled the heart's desire of every soul
Whenever to this transmuting elixir thou shouldst gain access;
The warmth of thy love will throughout the whole world spread
      happiness.

One's desire is fulfilled when one attains to one's goal;
One extols one's Sovereign Lord with words like unto pearl.
To what is enshrined in the heart doth bear witness the tongue
That, as a gift from that rose-garden, this blossom hath sprung

Thou wilt know every tree by the fruit it produces;
With all thine heart and soul study its leaves and blossoms.
A heart that from its fetters is detached and now free,
Is attached to the rose-garden of reality.
Day and night, in their searching such hearts are determined and
      most ardent;
They yearn unceasingly to see the Beauty of the best-Beloved.

Day and night their minds are turned towards their Hearts' Desire;
Their hearts are bound in a lock of their Beloved's hair.
This is the feeling and the mood of the wayfarer as well;

II The Repository of Mysteries: Translated text

I said it briefly; I do not wish to say more. So, farewell!
This is how the men of God every moment expend;
They are communing with Bahá their love to extend.

O Bahá, Glory of Love! O Thou, elixir of the soul!
Thou dost infuse love into the hearts; Thou dost grant it to all.
We implore Thee to touch our hearts with Thine elixir of
*   transformation;*
That Thou wouldst spread once more the light of reunion is our
*   supplication.*

Let Thy sacred books give illumination in all the six directions,
So that those who were before withheld, round it make
*   circumambulations.*
Thy light it doth generate radiance, power and Glory;
Many a Moses doth kneel down on Thy sacred Mount Sinai.

O Thou, the most Beauteous One! Myriad Adams, Noahs
And Abrahams are stunned and rapt by Thy Countenance.
Many a Jesus Who is seated by the highest throne;
Is bewildered and astounded by this Beloved One.
Many a Joseph to Thy beauty is attracted;
In myriad hearts such great turmoil Thou hast created.

Myriad pure souled Muḥammads are left all in confusion
Bewildered at what they see with their limitless vision.
Many a Moses in the inner Mount Sinai doth kneel before Thee;
Each ardently supplicates: O Lord! Show me Thy face, I beseech Thee.
Many a Friend of God[1] blest with a heart sanctified
Is, by Thy hidden mysteries, stunned and mystified.
Many a charming Joseph, of all hearts the enchantment,
Standeth wide-eyed and open-mouthed in total amazement.
While many an Aḥmad[2] possessed of every good quality,
Is astonished and astounded by Thy most peerless Beauty.

The veiled Beloved One hath been unveiled in my heart;
The compassionate Lord with His fiery face hath appeared.
The Sovereign hath removed the veil and doth Himself reveal;
Then, how could a lover be patient and at ease prevail?

His Face shining with God's Beauty, He hath manifested;
How delightful! He hath returned in all His glory vested!
Hurrah! The hearts and eyes of the lovers are illumined;
Their souls are refreshed and, like a rose-garden, are blooming.

---

[1] Abraham
[2] Muḥammad

How much sacred blood hath been in His pathway shed!
How many lovers to the gallows swiftly sped!
Many people there have been who for His Cause their lives did offer;
Round the Beloved they circled like moths round a candle gather.

O thou, the incomparable Sovereign, the Matchless, the Peerless!
We beseech Thee to take us by the hand out of Thy loving kindness.
Out of Thy favour, pour into our chalice a draught of Thy wine
That our hearts be illuminated by Thine Ancient light divine.
Thy radiance rends asunder the veils of idle fancy;
Thus, the Beloved through the Beloved's own eye we can see.

When the lover discovered that the fire was his remedy,
He saw his heart, like a piece of iron, in the furnace fiery.
He cried: "O Lord! Fuel up the fire to refine and purify
So that, like a candle, I become consumed, and melt my life away."

The fire of Thy Beauty deprives the lover of all ease;
The pain of yearning makes him writhe, his aching to appease.
He crieth out when the fire of longing blazes:
"O Lord! 'Verily we have done wrong to ourselves'." [1]
The misdeeds he hath committed revisit his mind's eye;
He pleadeth that this flame may him of his sins purify.
He crieth out: "O Thou, my compassionate Lord!
We have offered our lives and prestige in Thy path.
O Thou the Righteous One! Please, accept our supplication;
With Thy glance of loving-favour grant us absolution."

We will be saved from the dangers of temptations degrading;
Aid us, to reunion with Thee, to ensure our attaining.
Let the hearts and the souls attain to Thy presence;
Our souls are astounded by Thee like Moses was.

Detached from any fancy or perception excepting Thee;
Our minds and souls are intoxicated in observing Thee.
Monastery or Ka'ba is all one in the light of Thy countenance;
We are astounded at beholding Thy most bedazzling radiance.

O Thou, the Knower of all mysteries! Who, then, are we?
We are a mere handful of dust; upon us have mercy.
Thy loving mercy surpasses the entire world of being;
Whoso effaceth his selfishness is truly wayfaring.
Whoever seeth himself as unknowing, is a knower;

---

[1] This refers to Qur'án 7:21. When Adam was thrown out of the Paradise he prayed, begging for forgiveness: "*O our Lord! With ourselves have we dealt unjustly: if thou forgive us not and have pity on us, we shall surely be of those who perish.*"

Whoever hath reached self-effacement, he is all the wiser.
Whoever sincerely doth express his humility,
He putteth aside all disturbance and anxiety.

The more he approaches perfection and maturity;
The closer he is to selflessness and humility.
The higher he ascends the ladder of spiritual perfection;
The greater is his enchantment, self-effacement and devotion
He doth dispense with every degrading temptation;
And enrols in the school of spiritualization.

In this school there are no hollow words or empty noises;
The lessons taught here are of delight in the mysteries.
People of fidelity and faith are tutors of this college;
There, of purity, honesty and truthfulness one gains knowledge.
It is a celestial school beyond the world material;
There one learns fellowship, faith and all values spiritual.
At this school, one can gain in love and friendship a high degree;
Its curriculum includes world peace and global unity.
Harmony and loving unity are the lessons of this institute;
All the principles of rapture, bliss, and celestial melodies are taught.
This college runs courses in enthusiasm and eagerness;
At this seminary, saints and angels serve as janitors.

O seeker of God! Where art thou? Hasten!
Gird up thy loins! Come on! Hurry up then!
Open up thine inward eye and see with clear vision;
The lights of God are shining from every direction.
The divine Countenance hath spread its wondrous radiance;
Open thy inner eyes to the Beloved's effulgence.

Now everything thou canst see is light everlasting,
As with limitless vision thine eye thou art casting.
All atoms are immersed in His dazzling illuminations;
Thou canst read His signs in creation, His Face's reflections.
The light of His Essence is on all sides being shed;
It transmutes death to life where're it doth spread.

When one's vision is neither distorted nor blurred, one can find
That in every human being there is a mystery enshrined.
In every mind a secret of His enigma is hidden;
And every soul is but a sign that doth reflect His image.

God hath opened the door of the spiritual tavern;
The wine hath been clarified, of sediment siphoned
The Lord of souls hath raised up in His hand the chalice of wine;
He hath called out to all humans and angels a draught to imbibe.

Those whose spirits are quickened have been moved by His clarion call;
Prostrating at His threshold to serve Him with full heart and soul.

God hath breathed the Holy Spirit into the whole human race;
It hath been wafted over all like springtime's reviving breeze.
The vitalizing breath hath quickened, in the hearts, the sterile loam;
Every tree is now festooned with fruit and adorned in blossoms' bloom.
Through the reviving spring breezes the world is rendered pregnant;
All the atoms have raised their voices joyfully exultant.

But where there was a withered twig that had hung from lifeless bough,
It hath, with the breezes of spring, become still more withered now.
Watch how the spring breezes blow around everywhere,
Wafting over all the plants whether fresh or withered.
All bring forth what belongs to their innate potentialities;
They reveal clearly what lies in their hidden capacities.

How could the cruel cold of winter snow;
Withstand the burning summer winds that blow?
While everything else melteth like ice in hot water,
How would snow and ice survive in the sunlit summer?
When the spring breezes waft with their soul-stirring forces,
How could a trace of cruel winter remain in us?
Likewise, the hardship and cruelty that the faithful have faced
Surely, from their minds and their memories, all will be effaced!

Take the story of the lover who, pursued by a watchman,
Fled distressed in the darkness and, thus, found his beloved one.
He saw immense favour in the harshness of the sentry;
When, through that cruel disgrace, he became honoured greatly.
Likewise, be sure that, with any hardship one might feel,
That suffering a blessing in disguise doth conceal.

When in winter, the snow and ice are hard to withstand,
The cold penetrates to the very bones of the land.
No tree can bring forth fruit in that bitter chilled air;
The leaves have fallen, leaving the branches all bare.
Then, when the quickening spring breezes blow,
In all trees and bushes, new life doth flow.
The flowers beam, the leaves applaud, everywhere is verdant;
The fields are clothed in green; the whole world is a rose-garden.

In reality, the leaves and blossoms of the rose-garden
Are the rewards of having borne a cruel winter's burden.
So it is with the hardships imposed on all the believers;

II The Repository of Mysteries: Translated text

O man of intelligence, in this vile world each one suffers.

After this world, they will enjoy the blissful spring of eternity;
In the world to come, they will be established on the throne of glory.
They are forever seated on the throne of honour and splendour;
They are eternal and immortal with no limit or border.
The gate of celestial mercy is opened to them wide;
Grandeur and glory encircle the spot where they abide.

The more misfortunes the believers bear for the sake of God,
When they stand before the righteous God, the greater their reward.
The faithful bear so much adversity in this world;
'Calamity is the sign of My love', God hath said.
Because to God's loved ones is allocated calamity,
Welcome it! Turn thee not away from God's Divine decree.

The prophets are ever besieged by trouble and affliction;
Their lives are well familiarized with pain and persecution.
Joseph was afflicted by the malice of his brothers;
In his grief he turned to God and uttered mournful prayers
"At the hands of my family, so many sufferings I did tolerate
That, to the end of the world, I could not all of them enumerate.
What am I saying? Surely Thou dost know of them already;
Thou art the All-knowing, All-informed, All-seeing Almighty."

God responded to his lamentation and said:
"O prophet! Do not by such thinking be made sad.
Thou art the light of the eyes, an example to humanity!
Be thou steadfast and firm; turn thee not away from calamity.
All thy suffering doth draw thee toward My Divinity;
Every prophet must taste of this sort of adversity.
This calamity hath caused thee to come nigh to Me;
Yet it, constantly, hath been making thy heart to bleed.
O enlightened one! This calamity hath made of thee
The most distinguished of all servants of God Almighty."

In this world, the more intimate to God is a lover,
The more hardship he bears when compared to another.
No religion hath ever appeared without raising opposition;
No heart hath ever been purified without passing through affliction.

When the diamond hath been faceted and shined;
It dazzles the eyes as its radiance is refined.
The more grinding and buffing goes into its processing,
The more it takes on lustre, with its value increasing.
It is like the difference between porcelain and clay pitchers,
Thus the glory of the soul doth depend on bearing hardships.

Look around and observe everything carefully;
Inspect whatever exists in this world closely.
Its value depends on the measure of hardship involved;
Without bearing hardship, not often does one reach one's goal.
A believer's torment is a testament to his spiritual degree;
For the people of God must be always accompanied by misery.

God said: "O Joseph! Do not shed those tears of lament;
Do not thou be aggrieved and gloomy, by such anguish rent.
The chosen ones must needs tread the path of affliction;
They must traverse the field of self-annihilation.
Thou art a chosen one, my prophet to the people;
From amongst these shells thou art the bright pearl, the jewel.
Thine affliction doth testify to the mystery hidden in thee;
From the beginning to the end it will always thee accompany.
Of thy spiritual value all thy hardships are evidences;
Suffering refines thy heart and makes it a garden of roses.

"O Joseph, My moon of Canaan! I will this tale cut short;
In Me thou art annihilated with all thy soul and heart.
I send thee My praise, benediction and loving salutation;
At dawn and dusk, let thy companion be My celebration.
Thy love for Me will ever be a Gabriel for thee;
While being thine own spirit's guide, it leadeth thee to Me.
My love is a mercy that doth the whole world encompass;
For all the prophets, love hath ever been the driving force."

For love of God every prophet calamities bore;
Each one of them suffered countless adversities sore.
Evil-natured people worked to cause them harm and tribulation;
All the prophets suffered every type of mischief and affliction.
Noah, cried out from the depths of his heart, imploring: 'O God!
Leave no unbeliever on the land!'[1] *And all perished indeed.*
Húd and Ṣáliḥ suffered greatly, by wicked people victimized,
Burdened with many afflictions; their hearts bleeding and agonized.

All the prophets had to flee from their hometowns as outcasts;
Severed from their kinsfolk by the populace's malice
Behold! The Friend of God, the exalted being, Abraham!
All the malicious people of his town amassed to stone him.
Moses suffered hardships when from Egypt he was forced to fly;
He trudged through meadows and mountains and even through
    deserts dry.

---

[1] This is a reference to Qur'án 71:26: "*Lord! Leave not upon the land a single dweller from among the unbelievers.*"

II The Repository of Mysteries: Translated Text

Isaiah was, with a wood-saw, in two pieces rendered; [1]
John the Baptist's severed head was on a platter tendered.
Likewise, when the life of Jesus with groans of pain was ended,
He heaved a sigh as to the heights of heaven He ascended.
The Prophet Muḥammad's teeth were splintered with stones;
Tribulation forced him to flee far from his home.

When, for the Primal Point Himself, [2] *the path of love came to an end,*
That Sovereign of love called: 'Is there one who would My Cause befriend?'
His lovers responded: "yea", and arose His Cause to aid;
Thereby, the secret 'if the veil is removed' was portrayed.
His lovers, to fulfil the Covenant, raised His standard high,
Each one crying out from his heart's depths: "Here am I! Here am I!"
Those noble followers rushed towards that Sovereign of love,
All chanting: "O Thou most Holy One! O Thou most praised One!"

Myriad lovers stood steadfastly, all faithful to their Lord;
For His sake their heads they gave; martyrdom their lives adorned.
Myriad people of deep insight sacrificed all they had;
Burning with passion, they circled round that candle of love.

O Junun! Bring to an end this chronicle; tell it no more!
From this field wafts the odour of the martyrs' blood and gore!
The one true God is shedding on the whole cosmos His radiance;
All created things are in harmony through His incandescence.

Sunlight transmuteth a pebble to appear as a precious stone,
Sparkling from every surface just like a priceless paragon.
All the souls are unified by the light of His Countenance;
The hearts are enlightened by the Unborn One's magnificence.
From every side is manifest the inner light of Being;
Both the seen and the unseen worlds, that light is now revealing.

Every face is unique because of His Beauty unique;
The lights of the All-Glorious Sovereign, all souls bespeak.
Truth-seeing eyes can penetrate through all of creation;
To truth-seeing eyes a pebble becomes as a gemstone.

Where is the immortal eye that can perceive the Being immortal;
For whom a glimpse of the Cup-bearer and the cup is ambrosial?

---

[1] According to *Babylonian Talmud* (*Tractate Yebamoth*, folio 49b): "Manasseh slew Isaiah; for he commanded that he should be slain with a wooden saw. They then brought the saw, and cut him in two; and when the saw reached his mouth, his soul fled forth." From commentary and critical notes by Adam Clarke, *The Holy Bible*, vol. II, p. 1793.

[2] The Báb

The Valley of Knowledge

God's Beauty can only be seen by an eye that from God hath been borrowed;
A ray that from God hath been emanated, back to God will be mirrored.

To fly to Sheba with rapture is required a hoopoe bird
That, entranced, it might in circles swoop around Sheba's abode.
The zeal of a phoenix is needed, the summits of Mount Qáf[1] to seek
A peregrine is needed to circle around that celestial peak.

The rose-garden deserves that a nightingale in it should warble;
High aspiration is wanted to reach the Beloved's arbour.
Only another sincere and honest Joseph has the nature
To attain in Egypt such an honoured and prestigious stature.

O thou noble one! The heartfelt lamenting and prayers
Of Noah are needed, before one can hear God's answers.
It was required that Adam by the divine breath be quickened
So that he could traverse both worlds in the space of a second.

Jacob's lamentation for his son was sorely needed
So that, by the righteous God, his eyes would be illumined.
An enlightened one like Buddha is essential to attain
To Reality's quintessential light of the Peerless One.

Seek a friendship like that of the sore-hearted Abraham
That the burning fire may transmute into a rose-garden.
An ardent Abraham was called for idolatry to break;
From his homeland he was ready to be banished for God's sake.
The ensign of the Unity of the one true God He hoisted;
All the fettering chains and binding superstitions He shattered.
To rebuild the Ka'ba and, out of it, the house of God to fashion;
For God's sake, He was ready His son to sacrifice as ransom.
For his Beloved's love, a homeless exile's path he trod,
Eager to submit his life and heart in the Cause of God.

An alluring and ardent Ishmael must needs be, for God's sake,
Willing to be sacrificed—of his life an offering to make.
The Son of Imran, Moses, on Mount Sinai must emerge
That, in those dazzling lights, He might be totally submerged.
O trusted one! There is need of a David's melodious tone
That his enchanting voice be echoed in the highest heaven's dome.

Those with enthusiasm are needed for this path to tread;
To uncover, point by point, mysteries a myriad.

---

[1] Mount Qáf (Jabal Qáf)—a mysterious mountain of ancient Muslim tradition known as the "farthest point of the earth".

II THE REPOSITORY OF MYSTERIES: TRANSLATED TEXT

Where is the Solomon who every secret unravels
And, from beginning to end, can explain all the marvels?
Every species of wild creature doth conform to His commands;
Submitting with their hearts and souls, they all bow to His demands.
The birds, the fish, the mountains, the rivers, gusting winds and fire—
To come under His dominion, all creation doth aspire.
He embodies all the attributes, knows the language of all things;
Divine knowledge He doth manifest, and new life to all He brings.

When once He hath unveiled His face in the heart's most hidden sanctum,
His love doth humankind unite in the chanting of love's anthem.
His love elevated all the souls, and all the hearts enflamed;
All prostrated at his threshold, and his devotees became.

A Mary is needed to bring forth Jesus to this world
That He might bestow spiritual life to all humankind.
A Christ is needed to ascend to heaven's heights celestial;
Detached from the conditioned, to attain the Unconditional.
A Mary Magdalene was needed with her burning faith,
For the sake of her beloved Christ, her total life she gave.
A Peter is needed to risk his life in servitude to Christ;
Into the path of his love for Christ, his whole being he did thrust.
An Aḥmad, Muḥammad,[1] is needed, motivated
By the love of God, His cause will be spread far and wide.
Where is Khadíjah,[2] of those times the best woman becoming?
Where is Fáṭima,[3] the solace of the eye of Muḥammad?[4]
For the martyrdom of a Hussein there was a need,
With his kinfolk and companions in the path of God.

Then, the Lord of the new Age, the Báb, made His appearance,
Being the spiritual Guide for both angels and humans.
He was the promised Qá'im and is the Exalted Lord
Who laid the first foundations of new Faith for the whole world.
In the Holy Qur'án, God hath called Him the Lord of mankind;
God hath elected Him, for all paths, as the celestial Guide.

When what is true and what is false for thee is clarified,
A rose-garden thine heart becomes, of ill will purified.
Quddús, that unique personage, gave his life and sacrificed,
In the path of the Exalted Lord, whatever he possessed.

---

[1] Prophet Muḥammad
[2] The wife of Muḥammad
[3] The daughter of Muḥammad
[4] The Prophet Muḥammad

For the love of the Báb, Bábu'l-Báb his life surrendered;
He forsook everything for the sake of his Beloved.

Myriad enraptured lovers towards their Best-Beloved hastened;
Drawn to the celestial Friend, they found at His side a safe haven.
Ṭáhirih, 'the Pure One', her heart purified from all else save Him—
That woman shed radiance over creation like a brilliant gem.
When Bahá's Beauty removed the veil from His Countenance,
His wondrous Face shone forth with a sun's dazzling radiance.
That Self-Subsisting, the Glory of God, in Tehran first raised His clarion
   call;
Then in Baghdad, Constantinople, Adrianople, and 'Akká's prison cell.
He endured divers calamities; was banished, held in prison;
For forty years He was raising His call between earth and heaven.

With His divine wisdom, He freely admonished humanity,
Showing the way to universal peace and global unity.
The Book of the Covenant of His Faith He revealed
In which the Centre of the Covenant He bequeathed.
He defined it as the secure cord to which we should cling
So that we could serve His Cause faithfully in everything.

O dear one! Cleanse thine heart of everything except His love;
All created things would perish but for the Face of God.
At this time, there is no one in the world except the Best-Beloved;
No one resides in the house save the Loved One, the Most Exalted.
At this threshold, we are privileged to be chosen as servants;
Before the porch of this King of kings we bow in subservience.

We have emptied our hearts of all save the love of the Beloved;
From the mirror of our hearts all trace of tarnish is removed.
What is that tarnish, if not arrogance, hatred and hypocrisy?
It is all malice and deceit, and the unbeliever's treachery.
When our hearts are freed from hatred and iniquity,
We are treading the right path in all sincerity.

The people of God discern their King because their hearts are pure;
They recognize the Sovereign despite the robe that He might wear.
If the mysteries of the people of rapture, I were to expound,
I would not have concluded even unto the end of the world.

Once I had a heart that pulsed with sanguine love. It bled
Out unstaunched from my eyes in the countless tears I shed.
I asked my heart: "How do you feel?" In anger it forsook me
And, running from my tear-filled eyes, it departed hurriedly.
It became a vagabond; any refuge it forswore;
Now, as regards its whereabouts, I ask around no more.
No one knows its hiding place, so asking is of no avail;

II The Repository of Mysteries: Translated text

For I might as well an oil lamp carry in a howling gale.
You might, now, have some concept about the situation;
This is, for besotted lovers, a typical condition.
I, too, have neither heart or soul or my own mind today;
From the land of existence they have wandered far away.

O thou master of the dice! In love's gamble, with besotted
Passion, I played and lost all my belongings and my assets.
I have no attachment to property or to riches;
Nor is there any worldly thing that my heart cherishes.
With that frenzied love, my mind is preoccupied
In my heart, all other thoughts have been swept aside.
There is nothing in my heart remaining, save for Him my love;
It ignites a fire in my soul with every inward breath.

There is one notion only that captivates the chosen ones;
It is the charming image of the maidens of paradise.
The fleeting world matters not a whit to me;
Only in one's love impassioned one must be.
I found, for me, all else save God is non-existent;
I therefore have renounced the false and evanescent.
What is the worth of this world that one should be so attached to it?
If its profit hath no value, then, what about its deficit?

My answer, if thou shouldst ask me how I earn my livelihood,
Is: "No worries! The Provider of our daily bread is God."
Thine eyes are bedazzled by mere worldly tenure;
Thine heart is not enlightened; thou art not aware.
What I am saying is not for those of heedless ignorance;
Rather, I speak to the mystics whose hearts are vast as oceans.
People of enthusiasm are needed to come with me
Because, I do not deal with people of banality.
O thou who hast not ever learnt the lessons of love!
Thou art as a pebble left behind one on the path.

This world with all its layers of mystery on mystery,
Except for the appearance of the Chosen Ones, would cease to be.
Therefore, in every era, a Vicegerent of God doth appear;
It is a test for the people of the time they have to endure.
In the world of existence are courageous men of God;
Who every evil act will weigh against each action good.
These are men who can judge, with deep insight and sharp vision,
Which deeds should be condemned and which merit approbation.
Thou canst be sure that the world is at all times sustained
By people of God who have mystic vision attained.
Thou shouldst know that the world is never left destitute
Of chosen ones with mystic sight and vision acute.

The Valley of Knowledge

Try to understand! For the world there is no likelihood,
In any era, to be left without the men of God.
If thou ever shouldst imagine such a possibility,
Know thou! No heart is denied the light of Divinity!
It would mean that Divine Grace could stop flowing! That is
   preposterous;
The world's existence is contingent on the lights of the All-Gracious.

God hath said: "The earth cannot contain Me, nor can heaven;
I am only to be found in the hearts that have been broken.
Wherever there is a broken heart, thou wilt find Me residing;
Only the eyes of love can perceive Me within that heart shining."

O heart! Be freed from every fetter of the material world;
Be the collyrium to cure the eyes of every ailing soul.
Because the broken heart doth accommodate the divine Friend,
Therefore, a bewildered and broken heart is a dividend.
This doth not refer to a pampered heart that simply is upset,
When vain opinion, like some noxious spell, doth trap it in its net.

Until thou dost see in the world nought save the Beloved;
Look where thou mayest, save His Face thou wilt see no other.
Traversing throughout His creation with thine inner eyes,
Thou wilt see naught save Him whatever thou dost scrutinize.
He is the familiar Face seen everywhere, but He is nowhere;
He doth associate with all and yet is far beyond elsewhere.
He is sanctified from the entire world of His creation
While manifesting attributes that cause inebriation.

Myriad paths merge into one when they reach Thee;
Into fragments Thy blast doth shatter Mount Sinai.
O Lord! Enable me to see, of all things, the realities;
Out of Thy grace, offer me, of Thy divine knowledge, a chalice.

O Loving God! Show me the path leading straight to Thy Mansion—
The same path to which Thou hast kindly guided each Chosen One.
Thou art an ocean, and the world of being a droplet of dew;
Thou hast created both the worlds in the mere twinkling of an eye.
At Thine order: "Be", the whole cosmos came into existence;
Intoxicated by Thy wine were the deserts and mountains.

The inner realm of all prophets is in essence identical;
To the citadel of Thy knowledge, each of them is the portal.
Spiritual paths a myriad are but one path;
All the religions are indeed the same Faith.
There is neither old neither new in Thy bazaar;
The old becomes new with each Divine Avatar.

To unfold inner mysteries, Love takes on substance diverse:
Once in Adam then, later, It was in Noah manifest.
Once in Abraham revealing Its garden-bed of roses;
Once with physical beauty, It came in the form of Joseph.
Once, manifest in Moses, Its radiance hath Sinai bedazzled;
Once in Jesus manifest; one time It sparkled in Muḥammad.
Once being the Mahdi who had emerged in Shiraz;
Once it was through Quddús that we heard the song of love.
God unveiled His Face in the Shiraz of the inner soul;
Myriad infatuated lovers were thrilled and enthralled.
A multitude of rapt lovers, including Ṭáhirih,
Became attracted to the light of that Divine Beauty.
Once manifest in Bahá with majesty and glory most absolute;
Once again in the Mystery of God, the Branch out of that Ancient Root.

Yet, He is also separate from the whole of His creation;
His Essence from all attributes is in impervious isolation.
Love functions in a way that is verily remarkable!
One cannot but repeat the words: How splendid! How wonderful!

In Arabia sometimes He appears; next in Persia is discovered;
"He-God" we sometimes label Him, sometimes we speak of "She-Beloved".
No matter where a rose buds forth, it is nonetheless a rose bloom;
In whatever cask the wine ferments, it is wine that we consume.
If the sun rose from a point upon the western sky's horizon,
It would be still the self-same sun we ever cast our eyes on.

If the apples that you counted add up to some two hundred;
They would only count as one when they are crushed and blended.
Though the sun doth shine through various and unnumbered window-panes;
The rays are from one sun through whichever window it attains.
Such diverse entities have come from just one Source divine;
No soul exists that was not stirred by that vitalizing Wine.

For that very reason, the Lord of all worlds hath said:
'There is no difference amongst the apostles of God.' [1]
Though all forms of existence are from but one Existence;
They have multiplied to hundreds of thousands of species.

The believers are united by a spiritual chain;
Of any difference amongst them there is not a grain.
How beautifully Rúmí hath this theme illustrated;
Such secret treasures for us he hath elucidated:

---

[1] From the Qur'án

The Valley of Knowledge

"While the souls of wolves and dogs are separated,
The souls of the lions of God are united." [1]
All existence exists because of that one Existence;
All are intoxicated by the same wine's indulgence
When He removed the veil from His shining Countenance,
All the atoms were lit up by His Face's radiance.
O thou intelligent one! This is the meaning of the word 'Be';
By the brightness of His face came to exist every entity.
The entire cosmos is the manifest sign of His Beauty;
To His Face and His Eyebrow all things are testimony.

Observe thou all the atoms with thine inner vision;
Of His Beauty both the worlds are but the reflection.
Of His Countenance the universe is the indication;
The world entire revolves around His lofty habitation.

No sooner did He remove the veil from His shining Face,
Then it shone forth, generating the entire universe.
The inmost Essence manifested in His unveiled Features;
By virtue of His Grace appeared all His living creatures.
Were it not for the effulgence and glory of that Beauty,
How could creation's kingdom include a single entity!

The entire world of existence is the emblem of His Beauty;
Both the inner and the outer realms echo His reality.
A dazzling light was shed by but one ray of His Countenance;
Thus, the sun came into being by that very radiance.
O man of insight! Know of 'Be' this is the meaning:
'Twas His Being that brought forth all atoms into being.

Absolute Unity is His Face; diversity is but Its reflection;
Ponder upon it with thine heart and soul; thus attain to
    comprehension.
There is no doubt the Countenance of God is Unity,
Though Its effect doth bring forth forms of great diversity.

After separation, those souls that attain unto reunion
In the light of His Countenance, become submerged in His Ocean.
There is no doubt that all emerge forth from the one Existence,
Yet they seem as myriad forms on superficial evidence.
Undoubtedly, one can assert with certitude, maintaining
The existence of all created things cometh from One Being.

What an inexperienced youth within a mirror can perceive,
An older, wiser man from an undried mud brick can conceive.
In the light was Satan tempted, then was outcast and accursed;

---

[1] Rúmí, *The Mathnawí*, Book IV:414

While from darkness Adam was redeemed and with all honours blessed.
A person with a pure heart, when he looks at anything,
Sees nothing save the light of Bahá within everything.

My wonderment increases when my inner self I see;
I am dazed by the effect my Beloved hath on me.
In what a wonderful, delightful mood of marvelling am I!
Since, from the bondage of this world hath now been freed my inner eye.
Wherever I search, nothing but God do I find!
By the lights of Bahá my eyes are illumined.
Lo! What an amazing state I have reached! It is delightful!
One cannot but repeat it: How marvellous! How wonderful!

O Bahá'u'lláh! O Thou, the Sovereign of bounty!
All the mysteries of being were revealed by Thee.
The two worlds are illumined by the light of Thy Countenance;
No eye would have light by which to see without Thy radiance.

O Thou Who, on mankind, doth ever cast Thy light gratis!
O Thou Who bestoweth love upon the hearts of lovers!
O Thou whose lights have filled up the souls with radiance!
The eyes of the world are enlightened by Thy brilliance.
Thou conferrest on the hearts the high lustre of Thy kindness
Thy light of unity createth vision out of blindness;

Oh! Thy Face is unsurpassed in Its shedding of splendour!
Thy light illumines the mind of every human creature.
It was Thy light that filled all the hearts with brightness intense;
It was Thy light that to the world's eye gave its radiance.

Eyes receive vision from Thee to discern reality;
The hearts are illumined by the light of Thy Unity.
Thy love doth bind together the scattered leaves of humanity;
Thy glorious Face fills earth and heaven with luminosity.
O Bahá! Unmeasured is our gratitude for Thy dazzling lights;
Thy effulgent splendour bringeth illumination to our hearts.

O Thou Faithful One! I must request a shaft of light from Thee;
By Thy light the hidden mysteries are visible to me.
O Thou, the Almighty! Baring the inner reality
With insight acquired from Thee, one seeth all with clarity.

The outer eyes see nothing other than the outer entity;
I beseech Thee; bestow on me the inner eye's acuity.
An insightful eye is needed to penetrate into creation;
It removes the obscuring cover from the roots of its foundation.

The Valley of Knowledge

What the mortal eye can see is only what is mortal;
Whatever it discovers is of the world corporeal.
Yea, yea, the intellect is a mortal tool in this arena; leave it be;
For the intellect hath not the means to grasp that innermost Reality.
Yea, yea intellect is but a tiny bristle in this province;
A small prickle cannot comprehend the fathoms of the oceans.

The eye of a mystic extends its view far beyond this finite world;
This world is a glow-worm; that inmost Reality a shining orb.
How could the outer eye be able to see God's Countenance
Unless, by the loving-favour of God, it should receive assistance!
The full workings of the outer world no outer eye can see
Without a new God-given glimpse of inner reality.
The inner eye sees nothing but the inner life forsooth;
The inner ear it heareth naught except the inner truth.
How would the mortal eye see aught but transient entities?
To what could hearken mortal ear if not to idle fancies?
How could the worldly eye see more than merely worldly matter!
How could the worldly ear hear more than crude and worldly clatter!

While the outer eye sees nothing but created things material;
The inner eye is channelled to see the yonder world ethereal.
What is immortal can be seen by an immortal eye
While what the inner ear doth hear comes from our God on High

This world can with the outer eye be viewed;
That world can be seen with vision renewed.
This world is all that can be seen by the eyes of flesh and blood;
That world becomes visible but through the eyes of the Beloved.
This world is as a shadow; the next world is as the sun's radiance;
How could a shadow be aglow as against the sunshine's brilliance?
This world is like a fancy, just an optical illusion;
That world is like a shining sun's everlasting effusion.
This world is like a photograph, an image of that world;
That world has a compelling power that enlivens this world.
This world is like a gloomy winter while the next is like a vibrant
    spring;
This is a dull autumn; the next a tulip garden, ever flowering.

That world is like an ocean while this is like a drop of dew;
That world is full of gladness while this hath always sorrows new.
That world is like a sun and this world is like a lantern;
This world is a leaf; the other world a hundred gardens.
This world is like a seed; that world is like a forest;
This world is like a bough; the next, of fruit, the choicest.
That world is like the soul and this world is like the flesh and bone;
That world is like the candle light; this world's lamp hath never shone.

II The Repository of Mysteries: Translated text

Neither is the body hidden nor is the soul concealed;
But life's reality is not to every eye revealed.
Whatever mortal eyes see of this world are the limits;
What the eyes of the heart see is the light of the Essence.
Mortal eyes must deal with constraints, limitation and boundary;
While naught but the One God is seen by eyes of immortality.

Whatever the immortal ear hearkens to is the eternal Voice;
It is beguiled by the melody of Its heart-ravishing chorus.
Whatever emanates from the people of God is good;
Whatever is imparted from them are the lights of God.
The outer eyes see only what the outer world doth flaunt;
The inner eyes can see the splendour of His Covenant.

If thou wouldst once behold the world through the Eye of the Beloved,
Thou couldst the Centre of the Covenant's glory soon discover.
Then with breakers of the covenant no coalition thou wouldst make
Nor fall thou for illusions—the mirage as water to mistake.
A human's constraint is the duty to serve God and to obey;
The lover's constraint is love's rapture and a life of ecstasy.

What, save God's artefacts, can the outer eye distinguish?
If you gaze through the heart's eye, those artefacts will vanish.
Beseech God to grant to thee the gift of the immortal eye
To see naught in creation save the Creator's mystery.

O my dear! Beseech God to endow thee with God-seeing vision;
Then, thou wilt clearly see the Creator's signs in all creation.
While thou lackest insight to see God's image in His emanation,
Thou hast not yet attained a state of rightful comprehension.
Those endowed with knowledge have described creation thus:
A gem-like point; all effects are but contingencies.

It is vital to obtain the knowledge of eternal verity;
As thou knowest, contingencies will fade away eventually.
That is why the men of mystical vision have been stating:
That, for the mystic, the Source is naught else but the Being.

The origin of all creation is nothing but one substance
While artefacts are subject to diversity and variance.
Thus, what doth originate from One God must be oneness;
Only an atheist will believe it to be otherwise.
Since we believe that the Essence of God is Singularity,
We maintain that from one source issues one eventuality.

Much have we been expounding so that thou shouldst be cognisant
Essential, thus, is naught save God; all else is non-existent.
Hear with an attentive ear, to avoid misunderstanding;

*Do not become a fatalist through what we are propounding.
Do not think that the wayfarers of the Path would imagine
That different people are predestined to good or bad action.*

*O man of wisdom! If thou in sunlight shouldst stand,
It is thine own shadow thou wilt see on the ground.
When thou dost gaze in the mirror thou wilt see thine own image;
Thy character reflects thine own self and no other visage.
In the mirror's image there is neither goodness nor badness;
It reflects only the goodness or badness thou possessest.*

*If thou shouldst question from whence the good or bad cometh:
Good or bad is our shadow, we carry it with us.
'Me' and 'we' is our veil between us and His Beauty resplendent;
Sunder the veil to see the Beloved's Face clearly evident.*

*As long as thou art wrapped up in the shroud of existence,
How wouldst thou see through a peephole into yonder distance?
Renounce the hindering selfhood; the obstructing veil of ego rend;
Only then, wilt thou find thyself at one with that Celestial Friend.
Enter the field of battle against thy sensual desires
So that to thee may be revealed the ancient mysteries.*

*When all obstructing attachment to this world is removed,
Naught will be seen in thee but the ray of the one true God.
When thy thou-ness melteth away, thou art a mirror of Him;
Simultaneously, thou art the creek, the river and the sea.
When neither the ego of 'me' nor 'we' remains within thee,
This self-effacement gives thee glorious immortality.*

*The ocean surged; the creek and river had become merged;
Wonderment arrived; way and by-way as one emerged.
Union hath come; duality hath gone its way;
Love is here; of free will there is no more to say.*

*O dear one! Thou hast observed it every day
That, when the sun rises, the stars fade away.
How should love, with all its overwhelming dominance,
Let lovers of God do other than its ordinance?*

*Love battered my brain; my mind was fleeing;
Love hammered my head and sent it reeling.
The sun was rising; my lantern held no sway;
All my thoughts and fancies now melted away.*

*Sacrifice whatever thou possessest in the path of love's subpoena;
Take the first step and enter courageously the field of love's arena.*

O heart! Do not talk about love; it hath such overwhelming powers;
Thou art a droplet; speak not of the ocean with its surging rollers.
Bury this upside-down discourse; for it is but a chimera;
No! On the contrary! Make the lion the prey of the zebra.

Say not another word! The glass has cracked in the parrot's cage;
Now the Face of the Most Beauteous One a myriad mantles swathe.
Moses was veiled despite His skills and virtues, and His innate light,
So be thou wary! With a missing wing, make no attempt at flight.

Thou hast infused excitement with passionate yearning;
The light of knowledge hath dawned revealing the morning.
Thou wert confirmed by God in the Path of thy wayfaring;
Thou wert protected from every danger and suffering.
Until the city of knowledge thou hast entered,
Soaring in every direction, thy wings are spread.

O thou honest one! When thou entered the city of certitude,
Thou became freed from misgivings and every fancied platitude.
O skilled master! Thou hast been relieved from going astray;
By the light of divine Guidance, thou hast now found thy way.
By the light of love, thine eyes have inner vision discovered,
Without need of advisers, thou hast mysteries uncovered.
As soon as, to the bare reality, thine inner eyes were opened,
Thou didst commence communicating and supplicating thy Beloved.
Thou didst become occupied with uttering words of love and prayer;
Thou didst start to commune with God as, with a Loved One, doth a lover.

The wayfarer's inner eye, due to love, widely opens;
So that now he can see Bahá's enchanting Countenance.
He closes the doors of illusion and fantasy
Thus, honoured, to disclose the only reality.
He is content with whatever God for him hath assigned;
So that calamity to him is a bounty disguised.
Self-annihilation, he determines, is life immortal
As, before the eyes of his love, cometh open the portal.
With his inner eye he discovers much wisdom profound;
His eyes enlightened with new vision, he looks all around.

If of love's enchanting spell thou hast never had knowledge,
Find thou its secret from one who with love is besotted.
With no ardour of love, thou art like a cold lump of metal;
For the people of inner knowledge, thy worth is but little.
No one inhales from thee the fragrances of spirit;
Thy loud voice is an empty noise, barren and brittle.
Leave off thine arrogance and thy feigning disdain;

The Valley of Knowledge

Gaze thou on the firebird as it flies to the flame.

The lover knew that fire was his only therapy;
His soul he saw as metal needing forging's remedy.
In that purifying fire hear, the lover's song:
"O Lord! We have, verily, to ourselves done wrong.
O thou, the most excellent Beloved! To our rescue come;
We have given up our worldly fame for the sake of Thy Name."

Let me tell thee a love secret. To me let thine ear bend;
I will narrate thee a love story from beginning to end.
There was a young man in love who was held in high esteem;
His love was truly spiritual; of lust he did not dream.
Outwardly, by a charming face his affections had been caught
But inwardly he was deep in love with the Beauty of God.
The pain of love that young man, for eight years, had suffered;
Thinking of his sweetheart had bent him like a crescent.
His desire for her was on his mind each night and all the day;
Not a moment passed without his thoughts all being turned her way.
Whether he searched amidst the fire, the dust, the wind or water,
He only sought his loved one's face and never any other.
High upon the mountain, in the meadows or the wilderness,
He sought for naught else but a trace of her mystic loveliness.
No matter who sat down beside him for some conversation,
He was distracted; of his love he thought without cessation.
If, to a bird's wing, he had fastened one of his love letters,
Its warmth intense would have scorched the poor bird's pinion
    feathers.
To such a wild condition did love's anguish him inflame,
That constantly he murmured, day and night, his sweetheart's name.

So saith the Prophet: 'if thou wilt knock at a door with persistence,
It will open at last and a face will appear in the entrance.'
If thou keep digging the earth every day from a well,
At last thine excavation will with pure water fill.
When one searcheth for something, whether quickly or slowly,
A true seeker will unearth it, at once or eventually.

While the mysteries of the Valley of Knowledge we investigate,
The tale of the unfortunate lover we will continue to narrate.
For so many years, in the fire of separation, he was burning;
That he lost, in this game of love, all that he had saved from his
    earnings.
He could bear it no longer; his heart was of patience drained;
With each moment, the fire of longing in him higher flamed.
His body could not withstand; it found his soul wearisome;
He was so wholly consumed by love for his dearest one.

His life was nothing save the pain of separation;
To his soul, his body became a contradiction.

Many a night he slept not, in his fancy paying court;
His spirit ever turned toward the one who charmed his heart.
Many a day he dreamt about his love from dawn to eventide,
At his wit's end in ardent yearning to reach his loved one's side.
From the profoundest depths of his heart he oft-times cried:
"O matchless, peerless Sovereign! O Almighty God!
O Thou, the compassionate King! Have mercy on me;
My inner passionate longing is so well known to Thee.
O Thou the Gracious One! My yearning drives me to madness;
O thou, the Lord of the Age! Show me Thy loving-kindness."

When someone is, all of a sudden, with love's fever infected,
He will pace the floor, biting his fist, by excitement affected.
That lover found no rest in the daytime or night season;
With tear-filled eyes, he prayed and searched around for his loved one.
Many a night he could not sleep from the pain of his yearning;
That ardent youth was bewildered at the force of his longing.
His body got so weak that he was worn to a sigh;
His soul was seeking a means from its prison to fly.

Physically weakened from his inner distress,
He was as feeble and thin as a blade of grass.
For just one taste of the nectar of reunion with his sweetheart,
He was ever willing a thousand times with his own life to part.
To attain to his loved one, he entertained such a sacrifice;
Although he knew that, to reach her, it was a hopeless device.
The physicians were bewildered; they could find him no cure;
All their knowledge of medicine could not his health restore.
His companions and friends with him would avoid association;
They were disconcerted and shocked by his alarming condition.

There is not a doctor who knows how the love-sick to cure;
The Beloved's favour is the only remedy sure.
For such a one, the loving-kindness of the Friend is the antidote,
Far beyond the skill and knowledge of the greatest physician of note.
Yea, yea! There is no remedy for a lover's dilemma;
Nothing can heal it save the loving-kindness of Bahá.

By no other measure could he find the way to reunion
Unless, out of His favour, the All-Glorious should summons him.
How much more would Bahá elate him with reunion's bliss!
So enchanting for the lover is that Beloved's face.
The nectar of such reunion would give him life afresh;
He would be relieved of demise from his pain and distress.

*Nothing would remain in his heart except for the light of God
When, by The Beloved's kindness, he has in His presence stood.
When the wayfarer effaces all trace of egotism,
Then God crowns his head with immortality's diadem.*

*O Thou, our Lord! By Thy magnetic power uplift us;
So that we can extol Thee, enlighten and assist us.
Let our hearts be illumined by the mystery of Thine essence;
So our inner eyes can see both visible and hidden realms.*

*O Thou, the one whom God hath purposed! O thou who art Master!
O Thou, appointed by God to expound the Divine verses.
And although Thy countenance hath shed radiance upon the world,
Yet 'the bond-servant of Bahá' is what thou didst choose to be called.
O thou, the protector, the Exemplar for the world!
To see Thy face is, for our burning love, the reward.
Oh! Both the worlds are connected to a strand of Thy hair!
I am a restless lover; Thou dost drag me here and there.*

*Now, I continue the story of the young lover languishing;
His whole body was overcome with this most passionate longing.
Finally, it happened that this most honourable lover
Fell into prayer and supplication, seeking God's kind favour.
In reaching to his inward Self, he became arrayed in selflessness;
As his outer form diminished, his inner self was manifest.*

*At last, one night, feeling wearied by life's wretchedness;
He set out to wander through the city streets and squares.
He had left his home and was strolling round the marketplace,
When a night watchman spotted him and recognized his face.*

*The young man was not much in a mood to dispute
So he ran off; but the guard set out in pursuit.
Then a few other watchmen got involved in the fray;
They lined up all around him and were blocking his way.
They encircled him so every route was stopped by a guard;
From every side now surrounded, from escape he was barred.*

*The poor youth started groaning with heartfelt emotion:
"What have I done to myself with my bizarre notion?"
He muttered to himself: "This devilish night watchman
Is like the Grim Reaper, to take my life he is keen.
Such a torture-monger, lying in wait for the innocents;
A blood-shedding tyrant, in his anger and abhorrence."*

*That weary-hearted youth, already wounded by love's dart,
Being hauled to every side with love's shackle through his heart.
With his sweetheart's tresses like a noose around his throat;*

II THE REPOSITORY OF MYSTERIES: TRANSLATED TEXT

Dragged in all directions, a love-besotted misanthrope.
That poor youth's feet were scurrying while his full heart was groaning,
As he tried to dodge from side to side, panting hard and moaning.
Until the hapless young man reached a hurdle insurmountable;
In front of him a high wall stood, too lofty to be mountable.

With the flames of separation's pain, his heart had long been burning;
For his life he had long since ceased to care, so ardent was his yearning.
Love had scorched his heart and filled it with hopelessness and strife;
He decided he would climb that wall even if he risked his life.
With rigorous exertion the sad lover clambered to the top;
He saw below him was a garden too far down to safely drop.

He risked his life and propelled himself down into the garden;
Then lo! He beheld his sweetheart holding a lighted lantern.
His love was searching in that garden with her lamp raised in her hand;
She had lost a ring there that, now, she was endeavouring to find.

He saw his heart-charmer who, before, had been as if concealed
By a hundred mantles! Now here she stood completely unveiled.
Heaved a heartfelt sigh that faithful young lover
As he raised his hands heavenward in prayer.
"O God! Endear Thou to Thyself that watchman;
Grant to him long life and a lasting fortune.
It seems that, for me, he was a Gabriel from heaven,
In becoming my guide to help me reach my loved one.
As Isráfíl,[1] the angel of life, he was sent to quicken me;
Of the dire separation from my sweetheart he hath relieved me."

In fact, under the night watchman's, seeming, oppression,
A great outcome lay hid; love's wish came to fruition.
Much bounty was concealed in what was strict severity;
Justice was hidden by injustice, in reality.

Oh! How great had been the favour lying hid behind the veil!
He had not seen it previously as it had been well concealed.
For, resulting from that watchman's, seeming, brutal stringency,
Who could have guessed how much there was of unexpected mercy!

O dear one! In like manner, under what seems as oppression,
A mercy may be hidden, only obvious to shrewd vision.

---

[1] Isráfíl, in Islamic tradition, is the archangel who will blow the trumpet to announce the Day of Resurrection. Raphael is the counterpart of Isráfíl in Judeo-Christian scripture.

The Valley of Knowledge

When a person does not realize that, in every painful thing,
There is wisdom hid; he opens his mouth, moaning and muttering.
Justice will follow what apparently is tyranny;
It is what happens in this world; know thou this with certainty.

When thou hast fully grasped the inner meanings of the Holy
  Scriptures;
The station of the Centre of the Covenant thou wilt recognize.
Thou wilt, in the path of Bahá, be prepared thy life to sacrifice;
In return, thou wilt receive the bounty of God's favour and His grace.
This is not tyranny that everyone will understand;
This is not a lesson that everyone can comprehend.

O my friend! Such is the state of the people of rapture;
It is hard to understand if by love thou art not captured.
A hundred wisdoms are hidden in the acts of God;
Save the people of mystery, none can comprehend.
There are unnumbered mysteries within the mysteries;
The Beloved's love-struck lovers are those who can see these.
People with astute vision can uncover secret wisdom;
Those, unaware of hidden mysteries, cannot discern them.

Hearken while an important point I briefly explain;
Thou wilt grasp part of the inner essence of this tune.
After bearing hardship, thou wilt attain to consolation;
God assists thee when thou art helpless and in isolation.

Though the night watchman was a dreadful trouble for the lover,
Yet this trouble was followed by a hundred graces tender.
Though outwardly it was burdensome, inwardly it was kindness;
The lover had never dreamt it would bring such grace and tenderness.
He was not aware that his sweetheart would be his recompense;
After winter, comes springtime with sweet rose-blossoms' fragrance.

Likewise the trouble and hardship of the true believers
Draw on divine grace and attract His tender mercies.
Outwardly it seems to be so much pain and distress;
But inwardly it opens the door to joyfulness.
His grace is secreted under every sore affliction;
Although to outward eyes it appears as retribution.

With their poverty, the Prophets have always been satisfied;
Save the path of His love, no other path have their footsteps plied.
They have seen as their glory their times of vicissitude;
They have detached themselves wholly from all else except God.
If, for the Prophets, love for God was not their driving force,
How could they remain in such a state of rapture and bliss?

II The Repository of Mysteries: Translated text

Detached from all else except God, they were drawn in great exultation
To His undefinable Beauty by its compelling attraction.
Since they took all else save God as being non-existent;
They left the non-existent unheeded and discounted.

O young man! Not a moment should we hesitate,
All the various colours we must obliterate.
Permit only the colour of the one true God;
In truth, that colour effaces every other shade.
That colour from all hues is consecrated;
In 'The Hidden Words',[1] Bahá hath this stated.
The colour of God is a colourless colour;
Any colour other than God's is dishonour.
The colour of God acts like a vat of divine dye;
All hues added to it are of colour purified.
A hue offset by love should be thy colour;
Any colour other than God's doth thee lower.
To be colourless denotes the annihilation of the lover;
Therefore, to be without any colour is the lover's true honour.

When a lover the tint of existence eliminates,
Myriad colours in the divine vat he obliterates.
Love expunges the diversity of colour;
Thus, with a 'non-colour' is tinted the lover.
From the vat of love is poured forth the henna of agony;
As it is said, 'love is accompanied by calamity'.

O noble one! I am seeking that hue of divinity;
If thou art in search of God's colour, come hither and join me.
While black is more powerful than all other pigments;
As a colour, in both the worlds, one's face it blackens.
When love calleth someone to that world yonder
It dyes him a hue that gives him no colour.

O friend! What doth it signify to be thus uncoloured?
It is to be, in the path of His love, undivided.
In other words, all different colours must be relinquished;
One must tread the path of being by no hue distinguished.
Love drives the seeker back to the point of his origin;
For union with God, he removes all added colouring.

---

[1] ... By My beauty! All will I gather beneath the one-coloured covering of the dust and efface all these diverse colours save them that choose My own, and that is purging from every colour. (Bahá'u'lláh, *The Hidden Words*, Persian No. 74)

Yea, yea! He who offers up his life for the love of God,
Surrenders his human traits to attain union with God.
Effacing his selfness, he joins his original source;
His outer form vanisheth; his inner being shines forth.
Learn these secrets of annihilation and illumination;
What a shame that thy soul is draped in such thick shades of
    confusion.

This theme is a long discourse; this we will shorten
And return to the tale of the lover and garden.
A hundred books would not contain the secret of the purging of hues;
So I will remain silent and say no more; God best knoweth the truth.
Narrating more about the mystery of the watchman and the youth—
How love had enabled him to traverse both the worlds in one breath:
When his eyes fell upon his sweetheart by the light of her lantern,
He was released from separation in that beautiful garden.
That delightful youth thrilled with infinite happiness
As, exulting, he gazed at his adored one's comeliness.
"I have found the glorious treasure", to himself he murmured;
"In this game of love, my heart and my soul I gambled."

Indeed, he was immersed in tremendous joy and ecstasy,
So greatly was he gladdened by his sweetheart's proximity!
His happiness was such that if all his limbs had been exploited for
    speech,
He would still have been unable to fully describe his rapturous bliss.
The darkness of separation had been turned into brightness;
When, taking his hand, the Beloved came to his assistance.
Out of His loving-favour, had aided him the All-Glorious,
Thus enabling him to enter reunion's garden of roses.

If the lover could have foreseen the end, he would have been more
    hopeful;
He would, from the start, have recognized the night watchman's act as
    helpful.
Since the faithful lover was not aware of the end,
He complained bitterly both to himself and out aloud.
He had opened his mouth to mutter and moan, and to groan and
    complain
Unaware that God's tender grace and mercy had ahead of him lain.
When the lover attained his sweetheart at the tale's conclusion,
He could see justice and fairness in the seeming oppression.

Whoever sees the end, can better achieve his object;
Shorter is the lover's path to union with his sweetheart.
To see the end in the beginning is in the scope of every seeker;

II The Repository of Mysteries: Translated text

*He, who endeavours, sees the end in the start like every shrewd
    believer.
In each beginning is the end in the eyes of each discerning soul,
Who sees the outer and the inner as different faces of one whole.
Whoever, at the start, could discern the final outcome,
Hath, from the rose-garden divine, gathered a sweet blossom.
To such, the beginning and the ending hath the same identity;
Remote and nearby; outer and inner; all exist in unity.*

*To union with God they have trodden the thoroughfare,
They have gained new vision; they can see peace in warfare.
Likewise, they discern fellowship in apparent dissent;
Because all the veils that hung between them have now been rent.
Of the wayfarers in this Valley such is the state;
They find that, henceforth, for them joy and rapture await.*

*For those, who reach valleys higher than this one,
Rather than see both beginning and ending as one,
More exactly, for them, there is neither end nor beginning;
Though, to the outer eyes, there is both beginning and ending.
The ocean surged, the river and creek merged;
Wonderment came, all direction submerged.*

*To him, who keenly yearns to see the face of divinity,
All save the Beloved is but idle triviality.
Neither non-beginning nor non-ending doth he envision;
All creation is intoxicatingly new to his vision.
In traversing and observing so great is his absorption
That no pen can limn it nor any tongue give it expression.
Observing the new creation, he is transported in ecstasy;
So engrossed in surveying it, he hath no time for philosophy.*

*As wonderment dawned, it swept away any thought or fancy;
The one true God had installed him upon the throne of glory.
How could there be any chance for conceptions and conjecture
When his inner glory had sat him on the throne of grandeur!
How could the lover's mind any fancies accommodate
That on the past, present or future he should cogitate?*

*For him the new creation is so inebriating,
That he becomes all eyes throughout the whole of his being.
There is nothing left within him but the light of perception
To his soul's depths, smitten by the new creation's conception.
The inner essence of the cosmos is now exposed and discernible;
There is not the slightest particle to his inner eyes invisible.
All creation stands before him from the first and to the last;
With nothing from him hidden, he is in scrutiny obsessed.*

The Valley of Knowledge

Thoughts of beginning and end belong to mental speculation;
When one hath gone beyond conception, what remains is revelation.
One becomes so enraptured in discovering God's secret;
Inebriation lasts forever when drinking from that goblet.
Unveiled is the cosmos, as clear as the sun in the sky;
In the face of that sunlight, every dark corner doth fly!

At this stage, thinking is a veil that blurs thine direct vision;
The resplendent sun is shining brightly, O my dearest one!
What can I say of His[1] secrets that bring such ecstasy
So that thou wouldst comprehend His words and His mystery!
All names and attributes are in acquiescence before Him;
They are gazing at that ever-living Beauty and Glory.
How could the created things, in His majestic Presence,
Be able to express a word! They stand astounded in silence!

Yea, yea! Before the presence of the All-Glorious One,
No created thing can speak—it can but hold its tongue.
Whene'er love its majesty's magnificence expresses,
Both the speaker and the silent are left stunned and speechless.
Such is the mystery and the ecstatic state of the lover;
Thou wouldst understand if, from that garden, thou hadst picked a
    flower.

How should beginning and end now have any consequence
In the all-resplendent presence of that Beauty's eminence!
Both beginning and end before Him lie prostrate;
Outer and inner, in His light, can but correlate.

When his soul is immersed in the ocean of reunion with God,
The lover passes the realm of all names, swift as a lightning bolt!
The light of the hidden Essence from six sides doth emanate;
Before it all the names are flabbergasted and dissipate.

On the path of His love are the wayfarers pacing,
To the All Self-subsisting speedily racing;
So completely intent on a glimpse of His Beauty
That they are with devotion filled to satiety.

Ascending beyond, they reach a yet higher plane;
Like lustrous pearls they emit a shimmering sheen.
They are so determined to be with their Beloved as one
That, for them, no form of dualism perchance can remain.
They become so immersed in the ocean of unity,
That no more can they take any heed of duality.

---

[1] Bahá'u'lláh

II The Repository of Mysteries: Translated text

Love requires two entities—the lover and the loved one;
How could duality remain in that state of union?
At this stage, freed from dyads of name and individual,
The lover and beloved are one, and robed in one apparel.
Yet, even at this level, love can be also a veil;
Open thou thine inner eyes so that true sight can prevail.

Love is a mediator between the lover and loved one;
Reaching the inner core, it arbitrates till union is won.
Lover, love, and loved one merge into one at this level;
At this stage, wayfarer, heart and Beloved as one mingle.
The charmer, the charm and the charmed as one become;
Cup-bearer, drinker and drink make the sum.

More than this to portray, I am not permitted;
But, to the eyes of love, it is not secreted.
Henceforth all explanation is inept as time is far beyond
That past constraint, since the morn of knowledge hath now already
    dawned.
The path, at this point, leads beyond intelligence and reason;
The wayfarer's lantern hath been extinguished at this milestone.

Once again my madness doth on me come upon;
To bewitch me, the sorceress speaks of Babylon.
Once more this Junun is annihilated and hath vanished, yallalí[1]
Of a sweetheart's charming eyes he hath drunk and hath been
    vanquished, yallalí.
Once again love's crazy passion hath me wholly overwhelmed;
Once more this homeless lover is a wandering vagabond.
Once again is my heart to its maddening love submitting;
I am plunging in an ocean of yearning unremitting.

O comrades! Love hath intensified its own magnetic power;
It hath enkindled the fire of zeal in this most fervent lover.
Once again she is determined my throbbing heart to break;
Enslaved by her sheer beauty, dragged along in her wake.
Once more around my neck a hawser she is winding;
At times she talks of slaughter, at times she mentions binding.
Once more from her tresses she doth coil up her lasso;
It seems that my heart she wants with madness to endue.
Once more she plans to have me impassioned and bewildered;
She aims to keep me wandering, amazed and dumbfounded.
Once more she wants to render my heart desperate and restless;
She wants to send me wandering the world alone and homeless.

---

[1] Yallalí is an expression in Persian language uttered when a person is extremely delighted, free of all worries, cares or burdens.

Once again she wants me to bewail, in love's lament to wallow;
My heart must languish all alone with naught to ease its sorrow.

Like a lover rejected with no comrade his burden to share,
And no shoulder to cry on, leans his head on a wall in despair.
I long for an intimate friend from amongst the people of heart
To whom I could confide my love, and my soul's sentiments impart.
Perhaps, with no confidant, thou wouldst rather keep quiet;
But, without a friend, the blood is boiling in my heart.

O Junun! How much more must we hear of thy love's ebullition?
How often must thou voice thy passion? Pray, cease this agitation.
For a man of reason all this would appear to be a fairy-tale;
To understand thee, all but another lovelorn heart would surely fail.
The one who knows, as you, the rapture and the passion of love's zeal,
His heart is a treasury of love's gems, if he the same doth feel.

To consort with a love-crazed heart, men of reason would disdain;
What would they know of the Beloved and the all-ensnaring chain?
They whisper among themselves that this man is a crazy lunatic;
What he says of ecstatic joy and passion is a myth fantastic.

The one whose heartstrings have been plucked by love deep in its core
Knows love engenders rapture and brings ardour to the fore.
Otherwise, how should he know what thou sayest, and from whence
    thy source?
How from Bahá's verses thou dost so much of mystery disclose?
Or they would say that these types of words have been often repeated;
The like of this discourse many before have written and uttered.
Of what benefit to us would be such a sermon?
Is it a celestial food descended from heaven?
Likewise, they maintain all sorts of ill feelings and imaginings;
About the people of heart, they express suspicious misgivings.
They have no capacity love's bliss to experience;
How should they ever inhale from love its sweet fragrance?

So, better that I turn to the people of ecstasy and yearning;
I open for them my book of love, its hidden secrets unveiling.
I should share it with those who are the people of rapture;
Aware of such soulful feelings, its force they can capture.

Thus, I wish to bring the discourse to a close at this level;
The journey in the Third Valley comes to an end. So, farewell!
If thou art inspired to hear the rest of this homily,
I invite thee to come with me into the Fourth Valley.

The Fourth Valley
THE VALLEY OF UNITY

O thou honey-tongued parakeet! Speak again sweetly;
Explain in brief the narrative of the Fourth Valley.
O thou echoer of good tidings! Continue then with thy comments;
Limn the Valley of Unity that follows the Valley of Knowledge.

O Thou, the Light of God, the Glory of every faith!
Confirm my description of the fourth vale in brief.
Let me continue; my heart is a fire of ferment;
The sun hath now arisen from the fourth firmament.

I beseech Thee, O Lord! Out of Thy favour assist me;
That, to the end, I can fully portray the Fourth Valley.
O Thou, the Light of the Single One! Out of Thy great bounty,
Assist me to befittingly glorify and extol Thee.
Let the splendours of Thy face fill my soul with illumination,
So that I may depict all Seven Valleys to their conclusion.

Without thy loving-kindness and Thy confirmation,
How should one be able to reach one's destination!
If, in my expounding and extolling, there be defect,
I pray, in Thy sight, make it acceptable and perfect.
O Thou, the Sovereign of all creatures! By Thy bounty
Aid me to bring to a befitting end this Valley.

Now, to portray the Valley of Unity and expound its traits,
I would wish from the chalice of detachment to imbibe a taste.
Since, out of Thy favour, Thou hast every moment inspired me,
The sun hath shone forth from the horizon of the Fourth Valley.

Past the Valley of Knowledge the wayfarer continues,
Thus marking the end of limitations and attributes,
At the Valley of Unity, the seeker of eminence;
Will taste a draught, at this juncture, from the chalice of oneness.
He will be admitted to the haven of the divine Friend's threshold;
Here, the Countenance of the Friend with its dazzling lights he will
    behold.
When he sets foot in that sanctuary of holiness,
He will become intimate with ancient mysteries.

The divine Sovereign told the Prophet Muḥammad:
"Beware! Halt and, at this juncture, make Thou a stand.

II THE REPOSITORY OF MYSTERIES: TRANSLATED TEXT

Stretch out the hand of the Absolute from Thy sleeve;
Behold! Be not concerned about what may harm Thee.
Let Thy hand of power be obvious to everybody;
So that, from every region, the blind may distinguish Thee.
The people are all unaware of the Beloved's mysteries;
Proclaim Thou publicly about Me to make them aware of these.
All over the world, the people are arrogant and confounded;
The Divine mysteries cannot be heard by the narrow-minded.
They have eyes but they do not see;
They have minds but think foolishly.
They have ears but nothing do they hear;
They have hearts but they are unaware.

"O My friend! I am Thy protector and Thy haven;
Behold! Leave not the amazing mysteries hidden.
I will be Thy helper and compassionate companion;
To disclose the subtle mysteries do Thou now hasten.
O My friend! Since Thou art annihilated in Me,
Unveil My mysteries to Thy best ability.
Behold! At all times I am ever Thy intimate friend;
I remain Thy confidant and companion till the end.
Assuredly Thou art in Me and I am in Thee;
With all Thy heart and soul remain Thou ever with Me.
O My friend! Reveal Thou My mysteries publicly;
Not every mean fellow has a share of this bounty.
Unveil the mysteries for the elect of humanity;
Warble this chorus with an all-captivating melody.
Fill the air with the harp and guitar played in harmony;
Let the wicked deprive themselves of this sweet melody.
Let the fool fall behind who hath neither zeal nor any flair;
Of the rapture of ecstatic passion he is unaware."

To attempt such a high pass to traverse, how can anyone dare?
It is a most hazardous adventure, full of danger and fear.
The ardent and animated are able to follow me,
While I pay no attention to the people of apathy.
If of fervent love's lessons thou hast made no study,
Thou art like a stone on the road, a lifeless body.
What I describe of this journey is not for any heedless one
But, rather, for the mystic whose heart is as big as an ocean.

Each and every time the call of God hath been raised: "Return to Me",
The ignorant ignored it, following some false authority.
Such a one is excluded from God for his sinful ungodliness;
He remains an outcast forever, in his arrogant heedlessness.

The Valley of Unity

Tell the person, who is full of self-pride and vainglory,
That his arrogance hath distanced him far from God's Glory:
Say: "Thou hast shown vanity before the Bearer of reality;
Instead, thou makest obeisance to the one who misleadeth thee.
That is why the whole world hath from the right path been turned;
And the divine mysteries so few have ever discerned."
Tell them: "Open your ears of intelligence and listen carefully;
Make your hearts and souls intimate with God's secrets utterly."
Warn each soul to shun the ignorant ones whose hearts are like
    charcoal;
To take refuge in the shade of the King of humans and angels.
Seek assistance from God and give thine heart to the Best-Beloved;
With God's mysteries let thine intelligence become intimate.
Be full of love and faithfulness throughout thy whole being,
Before the threshold of the Master thy soul submitting.

"O divine Minstrel! The notes of inner meanings do Thou play;
The sweet melody of inner secrets let the world enjoy.
O Friend of God! Tell the secrets of My love;
Extend the hand of power from out Thy sleeve.
Demonstrate to all the people the mystery of divine might;
Clad in human form, extraordinary miracles enact.
Thine acts are the very acts of the Beloved;
Thy will is His will—the very will of God."

Hearken unto God's voice through His Manifestation:
Thy glimpse of inner truths will be thine exaltation.
In truth, there is no existence save Divine Providence;
What thou seest other than God deem as non-existence.
Saith He! "My light encompassed the entire cosmos;
It hath made each atom visible as it sheds forth.
Try thou, through Mine eye, the whole universe to observe;
Then, manifest in all things, My light thou wilt perceive.
My light is cast alike on each and every created thing;
To all the names and attributes, its reflection it doth bring.
When truth absolute emergeth, disappeareth all diversity;
The seeker sees no contrasts; no real existence hath variety.
All corners of the world by My light have been illuminated;
Lo! To a fragrant rose-bed, the fertile soil hath been transmuted."

The light of the Essence of Being is shining,
Animating, alike, every created thing.
The light of Divine unity glows in the cosmos visible;
His Being to all entities gives an essence perceptible.
The wayfarer regards the different levels of existence;
In various forms of creation he can observe divergence.

II THE REPOSITORY OF MYSTERIES: TRANSLATED TEXT

Variety vanishes before the original Essence;
A seeker is trapped at a lower stage if he still sees difference.

O thou with good perception! Hearken to this illustration;
Thou knowest that what relates to forms is but variation.
Behold the sun, which sheds its light upon the planet's face;
It shines on all created things with an equal share of rays.
It sheds its light on all creation indiscriminately;
All entities are energised evenly and equally.
Such is the innate quality of our resplendent sun
That it shines unprejudiced upon each and every one.

Likewise, a great Light cometh with awesome splendour shining forth;
The Dayspring of the Sovereign of Revelation is its source.
Its lustrous radiance It bestoweth upon all entities,
Which shine back in accordance with their innate capacities.
Whatever potentialities may exist in any place
This radiant Light makes apparent through its ever-flowing grace.

If a place hath capacity for growing trees or flowers,
Their growth there maketh apparent its hidden innate powers.
On the other hand, where the land is a desert or a salt-marsh,
The sun sheds its light upon it but no flower there can flourish.

Everyone is inclined to talk about his inner qualities;
But never expect from a vicious man other than impieties.
The light of truth torments such a wicked soul especially;
For, like a bat, he hideth from the Sun of Reality.
Like a beetle, he avoids the fragrance of the Rose;
Thus the sweet savour of the Flower he never knows.
He doth not distinguish between shades of black and white,
Therefore, he is left bereft of Bahá's fulsome Light.
Such an evil nature knoweth not the value of that Light;
He is overfilled with waywardness and wickedness and spite.
He is ignorant; he knoweth not the value of God's faith;
With such vain and senseless stubbornness, his life he doth lay waste.

Since he is a wasteful wanton with no yearning for belief,
In his own vainglory futile he hath thus enslaved himself.
Because he does not know what light is, nor discern a conflagration,
Between a devil and an angel he can make no clear distinction.
He runs away from the Light and, just like a mole,
He prefers to seek refuge in the darkest hole.
With no jot of evidence, the new Faith he despises
Instead, getting all entangled in his own misguidance.
Like a silkworm in its tight cocoon, himself he doth swathe;
Therefore, of sunlight's energy he doth himself deprive.

The Valley of Unity

The believers are saddened by this boorish arrogance
While the infidels laugh at the people of paradise.

The light of love hath now been shed upon the world of being;
Upon both the seen and the unseen realms the light of love is shining.
For believers, the rays of His light are like a paradise;
Their hearts have turned into a treasury for His mysteries.
The people of the new Faith know the hidden things of God;
They hearken to the melody—the sweetness of His Word.

The people of hell are absorbed in vainglory and arrogance;
They have dispossessed and deprived themselves of the Light's
  Dawning-place.
Likewise, an unbeliever taketh flight from God;
How strange that, of absconding, he doth feel so proud!
The unbeliever doth boast of his vileness and conceit;
He doth despise and degrade the believers of the Faith.
"The people of fire seek the friendship of the people of fire;
The people of light are attracted to the people of light."[1]

Consider! If a bat can endure a light and does not it shun;
It just proves that this light is not the radiance of the shining sun.
Likewise, if a beetle over a rose doth hover,
Know thou that this blossom is not a scented flower.
A believer turns away from a denier's vile action
And seeks asylum in the shade of the Lord of religion.

The various atoms, which disperse throughout the atmosphere,
Are absorbed, each to its kind, be it chaff or amber dear.
Magic tricks and miracles attract not a true believer;
What absorbs the hearts will demonstrate the same innate nature.
For those who have the taste to enjoy the sweetness of truth,
The prophet's voice and features are a miracle forsooth.
If the Faith's root is in the East and in the West is its limb
By the Will of God, the root and the branch will united become.

About Bahá's effulgent light let us once more converse;
How it hath shone forth and enlightened the whole universe.
Out of His favour and bounty, the lights of justice
Divine have dawned and the entire world have encompassed.
The lights of His essence have bestowed an equal blessing and bounty
On the whole world, to each place as befits its inner capacity.
Whatever potential lies within any atom or particle,
By the radiance of His light, becomes apparent and visible.

---

[1] Quoting Mawlaví (Rúmí).

It depends on the measure and nature of each one's potentiality;
Thus they appear manifested in unnumbered forms of multiplicity.

Every object hath a different potential perceptible;
Through the effect of His light all of them become visible.
The light is cast alike on each created entity;
The difference is due to the recipient's capacity.
For example, when the sun shines in a mirror,
Its reflection parallels the glass's nature.
When it shines within a crystal, it creates heat like a fire;
It looks red or yellow according to the crystal's colour.

The same light appears different in all other matter;
Though there is no distinction at all in light's nature.
The light manifests in accordance to the nature of the objects
On the level of each entity doth depend how the light reflects.
An object's shape is influenced by the primal Source;
Thus are moulded types multitudinous and various.
Whatever potentiality a thing may possess,
It will appear consistent, well-ordered and flawless.

O honourable Person! Let me give you another example;
If in sunlight thou placest of various coloured glasses a sample,
Every glass will reflect light in a colour of its own;
For the reason that sunlight of its own colour hath none.
If thy love becomes coloured, that reflects thine own colour;
Any colour except His, is for you a dishonour.

The yellow-coloured glasses, through being quite depraved,
Follow their corrupt desire which is their yellow shade.
They maintain that, doubtlessly, the hue of God is yellow;
They state that all must love it, and only it must follow.
They say that any hue save yellow bringeth great dishonour;
Everyone should be captivated by this yellow colour.

Likewise, the blue-coloured glasses consider the same;
They proudly show their colour as the best one to claim.
They state that, of all other colours, blue is the exception.
The rest are vain imaginings, fantasy and deception.
This is the colour of God; love it and be not doubtful;
Anyone who acquires our colour is of the faithful.

The red-coloured glasses, likewise,
Display their hue as the choicest.
They say that this surely is the one colour of verity
It should be everyone's aim; all should submit to it only.
Since their actions are determined by their own idle fancies,
They write whatever is prompted by their partialities.

They believe that whatever they do is tremendous
Whereas, they are of the truth completely unconscious.

The tint of the one true God is freedom from every colour;
Any colour other than God's is a shame and dishonour.
That is the reason that difference and disunity appeared;
In vain disputes the entire human race hath become engaged.
For this reason, except for a few, the whole world hath gone awry;
Of the mysteries of the one true God none have become aware.
Each man assumes that he knows the one true God and Him doth obey;
He doth presume that his proceedings are aligned with God's own way.
He is not aware that his selfish desires he follows;
He disregardeth the way of the One, the Bounteous.
He thinks that his colour is the colour of one true God;
He sets his heart to the shade which is his, and not to God's shade.
Instead of being self-effaced; he worships his own colour;
He is brash, ignorant, blind and hostile to his Creator.
Being unseeing and heedless, he doth not try himself to liberate;
He is arrogant; the lights of God he turns from and doth repudiate.

Differing capacities create differences indeed;
So, from the lights of divine religion, do not secede.
Never imagine that God hath created disunity;
There is no place for discord in the court of God's unity.

O comrade! Whatever disputes and clashes thou cometh across,
Not to the Creator must thou ascribe them but to the creatures.
The monotheist who hath comprehended God's Oneness,
Sees absolute unity in whatever he observes.
There is neither difference nor conflict in that unity;
Open thy inner eyes God's unifying lights to see.
That God is far beyond all colours, know thou with certainty;
Any hue, save the Beloved's, is for us ignominy.

Behold! Two men met the Prophet Muḥammad;
One was a good person; the other was bad.
The good man said: "Prophets are the light of justice as is this One;
A wonderful Person hath been born to the Baní Háshim clan!
How handsome He is! What a good character He has and how gracious!
How fascinating He looks and how charming are all of His features!
He is entirely excellent in all His manners;
Sound is His disposition! Brilliant His qualities!"

But of the Prophet the other person spoke unfavourably;
He said: "Any fruit that this tree bears will ever taste bitterly
His face is ugly, His character is unbearable;
His actions are appalling; His speech is insufferable.
What a foul Person hath been born to the Baní Háshim clan!
Nor hath this ancient world ever seen such an ill-mannered Man."

When these two contradicting descriptions were expressed;
Those present there were shocked and their minds were quite
    distressed.
How could two people voice such conflicting views in their portrayal!
One called Him good; the other said the reverse in his appraisal.

The amazed followers asked the Prophet: "O Messenger!
Why such conflicting views? Why such two opposing speakers?
Thou art well-aware of the inner reality of all issues,
Enlighten us: What is the reason for such differing attitudes?
O Prophet! Certainly Thou knowest these varying standpoints;
What is the secret? Explain this mystery? Why such statements?
These two persons described Thee absolutely differently;
One praised Thy goodness while the other said the contrary.
Their descriptions are to each other in total contradiction;
One extols Thee; while the other is loud in his denunciation.

"We are waiting for you to resolve this mystery. So strange it is!
It bewilders us. Please explain it! Relieve our anxieties!
Do not conceal this mystery before us; we are Thine intimates;
We came, as Thy closest companions, to learn Thy hidden secrets.
Our minds are completely confused and totally appalled;
Why about the self-same Light do men such conflicting views hold?

"The sun of truth hath shone forth and all alike hath enveloped;
How, then, could such clashing opinions have possibly developed?
God's light reflected in His Manifestation is One;
Why doth one talk of its goodness and the other condemn?
Our minds are mystified and quite amazed at this incident;
O Beloved! What we have heard fills us with astonishment!

"Thy inner reality to the outer eyes is not apparent;
Why, then, are there such descriptions of what there is and is not
    therein?
Why are there conflicting portrayals about the same Being?
Please answer; about hidden motives Thou hast understanding.
O Thou the most Trusted One! O Thou Sovereign of religion!
Now tell us: What is the secret of this varying opinion?"

Then the King of faithfulness smiled most pleasantly;
He addressed them to relieve them from perplexity.

THE VALLEY OF Unity

He said: "In what those two persons uttered they were both correct;
Now hearken that ye may understand perfectly the secret.
Ye have been tested; listen that ye may uncover the conundrum;
It is that both those two persons naught but their own inner selves did limn.

"When the sun sheds light upon the earth's atmosphere;
All that was hidden is made manifest and clear.
That was the echo of their voice repeated back to them;
When a mirror is clean, it reflects whatever comes in.
When ye look at your faces in a looking-glass,
What ye see is not the mirror's face but yours!
By nature there is neither good nor bad in a looking-glass;
What in the mirrors look good or bad are your own likenesses.

"I am neither this nor that; I am like a looking-glass;
Those two people simply saw in Me their own inner selves.
I am completely beyond being pure or contaminated;
I am entirely beyond being sluggish or animated.
O ye the noble ones! When the sun sheds its light upon
Various glasses, each one reflects a colour of its own.
Though their words were conflicting, both men spoke truthfully;
It was not idle talk; each saw his own self in Me.

"I am entirely beyond any colour variety;
There is naught except for the light of God within Me.
O my dear ones! I am above all kinds of colours;
Open your inner eyes that ye may yourselves realize."

Wherever there is a veil, which blocks the way to light,
How could the sun shed its radiance on that very spot?
Those who are veiled do not perceive the sun's effulgence;
They stay shaded, shutting out the sunlight's radiance.
They have no understanding of the essence of the luminous religion;
They have remained distant from the mystery of the Divine Revelation.
They are destitute of the sanctuary and the light of the Beauty;
They are withdrawn and aloof from the Ka'ba of celestial glory.

Such is the worth of the people of this age, and their comprehension;
They are now being tried with the coming of the new Revelation.
While those people who have been by Bahá confirmed;
Are redeemed and, from all else save God, have been freed.

The Manifestation of God, as the celestial Nightingale,
In the heart's rose-garden, a divine descant doth warble and trill.
At times, in the Arabic tone, He chants the heavenly melodies;
That Great One intones unceasingly the mantras of love's mysteries.

He warbleth the anthem, out of His love for all humanity,
That expresseth the hidden mystery of love and unity.
Then, he starts singing in the Persian tone with great fervour;
All who hear him are raised to bliss and celestial rapture.
When he writes of the path and the station of the enlightened ones;
One single letter from his written Word revives the mouldering bones.

His Word doth give new life; the dead it doth quicken;
It delivers all to the joy of salvation.
It stirs up great ardour; it inspires love in all hearts;
It breathes new life; it revives bodies that were lifeless.
It renders withered trees and grasses freshly verdant;
It illuminates the eyes with its lights effulgent.
On the earth and its peoples the Holy Spirit it endows;
Upon them all the lights of the divine Essence it bestows.
He desires to confer new life on the whole human race;
He sings the melodious songs of the hidden mysteries.

The jealous chase after him with their myriad sharpened claws;
To their utmost power, they are intent on his demise.
In this era, such is the worth of the people;
They have not remained from tests insusceptible.
Thousands of beaks of hatred, all filled with malice
Prey on the Nightingale, ready to assail it.
Their intention is to show evil hostility and hatred;
They call upon their corrupt desires as if calling on their God.
They murmur amongst themselves that they follow God's command;
And that, in worshipping their God, all people they transcend.
They reassure each other that they have the right path found;
They say that they are on the way to where all ills will mend.

They do not know that they obey their own base inclination;
Hence, they call themselves the followers of the best religion.
They cannot bear seeing the new Faith's followers;
The sight of them heightens their hatred and malice.
Alas! This is the worth of the people of this epoch;
Save us from severe tests and liberate us, O God!

The infidels think it easy with God to do battle;
Of their malicious actions such hostile ones are boastful.
In their hearts, those arrogant people have no fear of God;
The Manifestation of God they hang on the scaffold.
They execute Him by firing squad out of their sheer ignorance;
They persecute His disciples with brutal acts of violence.
Such are the acts of corrupt people who have sold their souls!
Thou dost realize that this is belief without godly goals.

The Valley of Unity

Thou dost recognize God's Representative by His absolute purity;
Be thou wary of the reckless felon with his evil and duplicity.

O God! Guide us to the right path to attain perfection;
Aid us to distinguish between good and evil action.
With all our hearts and souls, hither come we, turning unto Thee;
We implore Thee ceaselessly, in public and in privacy.
So that by Thy light our inner eyes may be illumined;
And our hearts, by Thy love, may turn into a rose-garden.
By Thy beauty inspired, we join the nightingale's song
To praise 'Abdu'l-Bahá, the much loved One, and extoll.

If we use our reason, discernment and intelligence
We know that nothing save God hath any real existence.
O Sovereign of the world! Without Thy loving-kindness,
We are nothing; for are not our minds and souls worthless?
Our minds and souls are in dire need of the ocean of Thy bounty;
They ever take refuge in the protection of Thy potency.

Would that on us be showered Thy bountiful benediction!
Out of Thy mercy, wouldst Thou not fulfil our supplication?
O compassionate God! Of our own selves we are not aware;
How then can we locate what is for us the right thoroughfare.

O my Beloved! The whole world is in dire need of Thine assistance;
Give us a portion of Thy grace out of Thy loving benevolence.
O Bahá! We need to borrow an inner eye from Thee;
So Thy Face through Thine own Eye we might be able to see.
Otherwise, even our own selves we do not perceive;
Unless Thy loving assistance our hearts could receive.
After all, without Thy tender favour, who are we really?
Thou Thyself dost state that we are utter nothingness merely.
With every breath, we hope that Thou kindly assist us;
We crave that our hearts by Thy lights be made luminous.

O my Lord! We beg Thee to let us shelter at Thy portal;
We implore Thee: Aid us to stay to Thy love ever loyal.
We turn our very hearts towards Thy mighty Covenant;
We yearn to gaze with inner eyes upon Thy Countenance.
O Sovereign! We desire in Thy Cause to be ever steadfast;
With the utmost love and faithfulness, we would be Thy servants.
We would attach our hearts to Thee in every situation;
We would eschew all empty noise and vain imagination.

Love is needed to draw our hearts along Thy path to pace;
Love is called for to inspire us and perception to induce.
We pray that Thy love's light to our hearts enlightenment may bring;
We know well that Thou dost assist Thy servants in everything.

Then succour all Thy bondsmen, we earnestly beseech Thee;
Let them learn to know Thee on gaining their maturity.
Thy light will help their growth as more saintly and refined;
In treading Thy love's path, they will together be aligned.

O my Lord! Thou art the refuge of the world and its only resort;
O Thou, the best Helper! Fulfil Thy promise as its aid and support.

Before finishing this stage of wayfaring's description
More of the secrets of this valley I will expand on.
If a Divine Nightingale starteth to warble the secrets of love,
And with the sweet strains of celestial amity fills the air above,
Intent upon His annihilation all the people arise;
Out of envy, they employ every ruse for His demise.

Fragrance is no use to those with a catarrh congested nostril;
Even the sweetest aroma of the rose does not please them at all.
That is the reason why Rúmí, that great man of wisdom,
Hath given such good counsel for the guidance of humans:
"Cleanse thou the rheum from out of thy head
Then breathe thou the breath of God instead."

It hath been made obvious and clearly demonstrated
That all difference is to the nature of each place related.
Therefore, the whole world is teeming with worthless disputation;
All heads are dulled with fancies vain and useless aggravation.
Among the various factions, are vehement disagreements;
Thus, controversy and dispute obstruct mankind's achievements.

Forget this negativity in affirming His reality;
With thine inner eyes His verses scan to ascertain their verity.
O brother! A pure and stainless heart is a mirror;
Do not defile it; instead, cleanse it and keep it pure.
With the fire of the love of Bahá, hone and burnish it;
So that it is cleansed from the world's tarnish and detritus.
That, in thy stainless mirror, the sun of truth may shine;
And thus may dawn within it His guidance divine.

To illustrate His glory, grandeur and majesty,
Thus saith that Sovereign, the Source of all mystery:
"Neither the earth nor the heaven can Me contain
But the true believer's heart—I abide therein.
The heart is immense beyond measure. It is God's domain;
How could earth or heaven encompass Me though under My reign?
The heart of the believer is vaster than the universe;
Therefore, My dwelling place is in the hearts of the believers.
Any heart, which is stainless and radiant, therein am I;
So search thou in a spotless heart if thou wouldst Me espy.

In the heart of a true believer I am reflected and manifest;
Likewise I am discernible and manifest in the whole universe."

When, upon a heart, the radiance of His lights God doth impart,
The throne of the Knower of the unseen becometh that heart.
He perceives that unto God he himself hath always been nigh;
In loving God, he holds precedence over others thereby.
There never was an hour that God was distant from his heart;
Not even for a moment hath God held Himself apart.
So continuously with it hath God been intimate;
Not even for a second hath He from it been remote.
God hath it escorted with his every little stride;
Not for even half a breath hath it been cast aside.
God is, throughout this world, his close Companion to the end,
His confidant, his intimate and sympathetic Friend.
He will be his loving Comrade in this material realm;
For as long as he exists, God with him will always dwell.

God hath ever been kind to him to such a degree
That no tongue can describe it and no pen can portray.
He hath been so ever-loving and compassionate to him;
No word can define His favour or His tenderness to limn.
But of God's kindness human beings ever are neglectful;
Whereas, that Friend most excellent is of loving-favour full.

About such similar mysteries the mystic doth hear,
Which he hath already heard some thousands of times before.
A Countenance appears before his inner eyes;
He sees the Face that he hath seen hundreds of times.
Through his own inner ears such secrets he hath heard
How can he then describe that for which there is no word!
He sees a Face, though invisible, in an obvious vision;
Thousands of times before hath he perceived this apparition.
Being ardent in his learning, he hears mysteries untold;
Such secrets for his ears those sugar-shedding lips unfold.
God, throughout all time, hath been his companion ever kindly;
With God he is in tune, harmonized in song melodiously.

When, on his heart, the Supreme Being doth shed His radiance;
The mystic doth see, as he hath oft before, His Countenance.
With effulgent light his heart becomes illuminated;
All of his being with love and faith is satiated.
Now that the Lord of the household Himself is in attendance;
With that Being's lights he feels himself arrayed in abundance.

The pillars of the dwelling with His lights are brightly shining;
With zeal and ecstasy enthused becometh his whole being.

Since, in His home, His Beauty's lights have shed their rays abroad;
The lights of the All-Glorious now fill the whole abode.
The entire inner reality, God's light doth now illumine,
In utmost beauty all is transformed into a rose-filled garden.

As the heart, in which God dwelleth, is with His radiance glowing,
Like a rose-garden it seemeth with charming blossoms growing.
The mystic is a shining lamp and like a fragrant flower;
He enters a vale in which he feels protected and secure.

Thus the wayfarer is shining with radiance all because
From the lights of Bahá's glory enlightenment he draws.
To the splendid lights of the one true God, he is very close;
He doth, in his enlightenment, now the world entire surpass.
He is so nigh to God that now God's Beauty him is tinting;
His whole persona seems aglow with sparks of light all glinting.
He is intimate with mysteries in the Beloved's own pavilion;
His body is permeated with the love of God through to the very bone.

The uncovering of mysteries doth him to raptures raise;
His eyes, his mind, his heart, his soul are elated by God's grace.
The universe before his eyes seems but a blade of straw;
Filled brim-full with the lights, he is, of all God doth bestow.
He is so near to God that, face to face, His Beauty seeing,
He is inundated by God's light, surging through his being.

Steadfastly, in his love for God, he ever grows more faithful;
How could he, even for a breath, now be of Him neglectful?
He fully observes the universe through the Beloved's eye;
The Dayspring of God is as the lens through which he doth espy.
He perceives what all the atoms are, with his God-seeing vision,
Of His brilliant Face, he knows, they are the signs and the reflection.
He sees that, to His existence, the whole cosmos testifies;
Everywhere he doth observe the pearls of wisdom's mysteries.

From this, the spring celestial, those nigh to God do quaff;
With all their hearts and all their souls they drink their fill thereof.
Love can help thee recognize the divine Reality;
Thy whole heart will be enamoured with that Visage of Beauty.
His light is spread throughout thy heart and thy companion it will be;
As thy intimate confidant, to thy path's end it leadeth thee.
The sun of His Countenance unveils its image luminous;
It doth manifest in thy heart with no obstructing hindrance.
Thou wilt become enlightened fully with His radiance;
Thou wilt be stirred by ardour that robbeth thee of calmness.

The Valley of Unity

Thou wilt feel such utter rapture that sends thy heart and soul a-
    dancing;
This state of ecstasy will free thee from flaws of vain imagining.

The sun of His Countenance hath shone with effulgent radiance;
How could the shadow stand against the sunlight's surging ambiance?
O thou noble one! This is the path that the wayfarer treadeth;
So thou might know what the ancient mysteries are that he seeketh.
In observing His effulgent lights, thou wilt become totally attracted;
From seeing His enchanting Face thou wilt be entirely intoxicated.
By His luminous Face thou wilt be infatuated and absorbed;
Thou wilt settle in the neighbourhood of the celestial Friend's abode.
Thou wilt attach thy heart to the fragrant tresses of the Beloved;
From inhaling the scent of those locks thou wilt be inebriated.

May my life be offered to a strand of hair of that Essence;
The whole world is in love, engaged in adoring Its Presence.
Lovers are inebriated with so sweet a fragrance;
The heart of the world hath been ensnared in those tresses.
Their hearts are intoxicated when at Thy Beauty they are gazing;
They are hoping, with their every breath, new light to be receiving.
My eagerness for Thee keeps me alive in this realm;
I am all enchanted, obsessed and overwhelmed.

The souls are tied to the strand of Thy tresses;
To Thy locks every heart is firmly fastened.
When Thy Face shineth forth, all the hearts are illumined;
In their enthusiasm for Thee, the souls are impassioned.
Every person is enthused when he discovers Thy mysteries;
When it seeth Thy signs, the soul starts dancing in its rhapsodies.

Where can the heart survive save in the shelter of Thy Covenant?
Where is the one who, seeking Thee, is not baffled and indigent?
O Thou Best-Beloved! My soul is astonished by Thy Countenance;
My body is entirely spellbound by Thy magnetic influence.
O Thou my heart's desire! How well Thou didst ensnare
Myriad hearts with but one strand of Thy perfumed hair.
Thou draweth me to every place and in each direction;
I have no choice, being dragged against my own volition.
O Thou of the fragrant locks and braided tresses!
How well Thou hast united the hearts to oneness!
The splendour of Thy Face hath enlightened every heart;
Everyone, young and old, seeketh a home near Thy hearth.
They see, as the sign of Thy countenance, the whole of creation;
It is the mirror in which Thy image appears in reflection.

II The Repository of Mysteries: Translated text

O noble one! Listen to the wayfarer's experiences of mystery;
More of the stages of wayfaring, expressed in words, I would show to thee.

The secret of union with God is an omni-present reality;
But not every ear is able to hearken to that inscrutability.
O dear one! Thou hast heard of this union being a secret verity;
Listen again to fathom it in accord with thy rational faculty.
Through thy inner eye, behold the wayfarer's path and the mystic vision;
See thyself in union with the Beloved at the end of thy mission.
Of these words about the union with God be thou wary
Lest thou interpret them such that God enters into thee.

From all limitations of ascent and descent the one true God is free;
He hath ever been, and will remain, on His lofty throne eternally.
Countless thousands of mirrors reflect Him in the universe;
In all the various forms, the light of His Face is manifest.
When to the Day-star of Divinity a mirror turns its face,
Every part of it will scintillate with celestial radiance.
It indicates that the mirror reflecteth His Beauty;
All over it is saturated with the lights of glory.
He neither doth ascend nor descend, that Beauty most heavenly;
For He is Placeless and beyond all restriction or boundary.
From location and limitation He is free entirely;
While each position, by His light, displays its reality.
When a mirror becomes worthy to reflect that Beauty,
Then on it will shine the light of that glorious Sovereignty.
He is peerless and incomparable in His eminence;
He is the unborn Potentate not subject to renaissance.
It is only He Who is unborn and Who doth not beget;
He, only, is the Placeless, Peerless, and He hath no limit.

Anyone who is begotten and might beget another one,
He is a worshipper; thus he cannot be the Worshipped One.

The Essence of God from all attributes is sanctified;
By His dazzling lights, creation is effaced and mystified.
Any Personage Who is the Manifestation of God's Beauty
Is, in every case and all matters, the Guide of all humanity.
He is the Dayspring of all Divine attributes, and their Fountainhead;
All else are but mirrors that reflect the lights of the Dayspring of God.
If thou seest His Face thou hast seen the Face of God;
If thou hast heard Him speak thou hast heard the Word of God.

Of all the Divine attributes He is the Manifestation;
The mirror of His heart showeth God's Essence in reflection.

Since that mirror is turned towards God and is reflecting His Beauty,
Seek out the Manifestation, if God's Face thou dost desire to see.
He manifests every wonder and marvel in all their reality;
He is unique in the world; He is God on earth in His Divinity.

The sun, the light and the mirror are combined;
They are one, although at three levels they stand.
The light is the sun and the sun that very light itself;
Open thou thine inner eye to see God reveal Himself.
If we know God, we recognize His Manifestation;
As the Source of all healing, towards Him we will hasten.
If we seek Divine grace, we must supplicate at this threshold;
He is the sole Leader who guideth the peoples of this world.
Otherwise, from all created things is sanctified His reality;
But whatever His light shines upon becomes a place of safety.

If myriad mirrors are turned towards the Manifestation,
His effulgent lights shed radiance on all with no exception.
If thou were to turn thousands of mirrors to face the sun,
Sunlight would be found reflected in each and every one.
The reflection neither increaseth nor doth it decrease His light;
Neither in quantity nor quality can be measured His might.

If you say that He cannot perform anything that is impossible,
Know thou that, in the field of His might's control, everything is possible.
O my friend! Read: 'I was a hidden treasure', [1] *and meditate upon it:*
Ponder on it to understand what the Sovereign of that age meant by it.
God hath said: "I was a hidden treasure and I desired to be known;
I wished My splendid glory to manifest and apparent become.
'Therefore, I brought into being the creation, so that
The world of being, as a mirror, would reflect My light.
'Thus, the creatures recognize Me when they see My reflection;
They perceive My mystery hidden in My creation.
I was a hidden treasure, unseen by the creatures;
So I wanted to make known My inner mysteries.
I brought creation into being to reflect My secrets;
So that, through My marks and traces, I would be made manifest.
'The reflection of My beauty I wished to see it and observe;
Thus, I desired to make Myself manifest in the universe.
'Therefore, I made Myself a mirror for My own benefit;
So I could see My image like a sun reflected in it.

---

[1] This refers to a holy tradition uttered by Prophet Muḥammad about God: "I was a hidden treasure. I liked to be known. Wherefore, I created the creation to be known." *The Mathnawi of Jalalu'd-Din Rumi* (E. H. Whinfield tr), Book 4.

When My beauty shone forth in the mirror of My cosmic creation;
Every created thing became a sign of My manifestation.

"O noble one! Whatever in creation thou canst trace,
Know thou that the whole universe is the sign of My Face.
That thou wouldst become aware of My manifested mysteries;
Thou must see all the signs as the reflection of My Countenance.
As soon as the Sun of My Beauty shone forth,
Its reflection brought to being countless works.
Being free from any limitation, and incomparable,
I created everything matchless and inimitable.
So that thou seest the world of creation as My effects;
My light is displayed in the universe by all that exists.
O noble Junun! To thee I have made known My mystery in full;
So continue thou to expound the rest of the valley. Now, farewell!"

The worldly intellect is not able to comprehend this mystery;
Of this luminous Face and fragrant hair, it is totally unaware.
How, by the limited mind, should this splendid glory be recognized?
Both the speaker and the silent are left dumbfounded and stupefied.

"He that desireth to see Me must use Mine own eye;
Without the acutest vision, none can Me espy!
'One needs to have My eyes to be able to see Me;
My character can only be understood by Me.
'Otherwise, how could the eyes of a stranger see Me?
That eye can see Me that hath been illumined by Me.
'The outer eyes can see only the outer realm;
The outer ear can hear only a worldly timbre.

"Whatever a mortal eye can see is mortal;
Whatever it sees is worldly and temporal.
Wherever thou dost observe radiance, it is from Me;
Wherever thou seest purity, it cometh from Me.
Wherever thou seest intelligence, it is from Me;
Wherever thou dost observe a light, it shineth from Me.
Wherever thou seest faith, it radiates from Me;
Wherever thou seest contentment, it is from Me.
Wherever thou dost observe knowledge, its source is from Me;
Wherever thou seest patience, it is inspired by Me.
Wherever thou seest fondness, it emanateth from Me;
Whatever love thou seest, hath been emitted by Me.
Any good attribute thou seest cometh from Me;
Any good essence thou seest, it cometh from Me.

"Since I am the source of all goodness and nobility;
How should anything save goodness be emitted from Me?

The Valley of Unity

O thou trusted one! I am as the orb's aureola;
Naught radiates from My essence save My light's corona.
O My dear one! I am an ocean of light entirely;
O thou the esteemed one! All the hearts are My Mount Sinai.
O My dear one! I am Joy and Bliss entirely;
How should sorrow, pain or poverty be in Me?

"I am beyond the intellect of the whole of humankind;
All the minds are baffled in attempting Me to comprehend.
I am unconditioned, absolute, free of bounds and hindrance;
For the entire humanity, I am the source of guidance.
What thou sayest, out of love, in praising Me, the reality is more
That the entire cosmos compriseth My signs while I am the hidden
    core.
Being unconditioned is an attribute of My hidden Essence,
And of My innate reality, one of the qualities and signs.
That is the reason the mystics are baffled when trying to know Me;
The chosen ones are bewildered in attempting to understand Me.

"I have disclosed to thee a glimpse of the features of My reality;
I now retreat into the invisible realm, veiled in obscurity.
O My lover! Again behind the mirror My face I am concealing;
Begone, and explain thou to others how they must tread the Path to
    reach Me.

"O Junun! From time to time I draw back the veiling curtain
To offer to thee a hint of My secrets that are hidden.
I am the same invisible treasure as I have ever been;
I am the same visible shining sun as I have ever been.
Thou art a smitten lover and by My beauty spell-bound;
A ringlet of My fragrant hair around thy heart is wound.
On the face of 'Abdu'l-Bahá, My beauty is manifest;
More and more in the world, It becometh clear and obvious.
Otherwise, My Essence from all attributes is sanctified;
The minds, in their attempt to comprehend Me, are mystified.
To attempt to grasp My Essence, the Universal Mind[1] was bewildered;
The people of the world are left entirely wondering and astounded.
No imagination is able to sound the depths of My Essence;
Here, it is as a fathomless ocean of dazzling lights most intense.
How is it possible for a mote to fathom the depths of the oceans?
How could a gnat soar with a phoenix to the zeniths of the heavens?
The Chosen Ones are bodies and I am their Soul;
As Lover and Beloved, We are clothed in one robe.

---

[1] A title of Prophet Muḥammad Who said, "I have not comprehended Thee [God] as a true recognition."

Their dispositions are the image of My own disposition;
Their faces are the true mirrors of My very own reflection.
Their condition is the reflection of My condition;
What they would utter is of My own words the expression.
To obey Me exactly is to obey Their instruction;
They are as the mirrors in which can be seen My reflection.

"The Chosen Ones reflect Me as a mirror;
They are the treasure-house; I am their treasure.
Other than by this door, there is no way to reach Me;
Their hearts are the only hearts that truly mirror Me.
The eye of every Chosen One is by My light illumined;
His heart is a rose-garden where My mysteries are enshrined.
For My beauteous Countenance He beareth a love most intense;
Whether it be day or night, to see My face He is athirst.
Save to attract My good pleasure he desireth nothing;
His heart and his soul are ceaselessly with Me communing.
For him to be away from Me is a death agony;
It is energizing life for him when he is with Me.
His life is totally destroyed when He is separated from Me
He is, then, neither aware of His household nor of His home-country.

"He wandereth at times in the mountains, at times in the wilderness;
My love maketh of Him a vagabond, ever restless and homeless.
He is at his wit's end in His eagerness My words to hear;
To see the effulgence of My face, He is crazed with desire.
He is not aware of time or of the place where He is;
He knoweth neither what voice He hears nor what noise it is.
He knoweth not when the morn dawns or when cometh nightfall;
He distinguisheth not between the grain and the pitfall.
To whichever side He turneth his eye His purpose is to see Me;
Along whatever passageway He goes He desireth to find Me.
He sniffeth not a flower but to inhale My fragrance;
He gazeth not at a face but to see My Countenance.
Whatever he is observing, He seeth naught except Me;
For that, he hath trod the Path, to be reunited with Me.
In the entire world, He perceiveth not anything save His Beloved;
In seeing Me through His inner eye, He is amazed and enamoured.
As a moth becometh totally absorbed into the light,
So, too, the world fadeth away to disappear from His sight.
The two worlds turn into one before His inner eye;
No more is he now concerned with worldly grief or joy.
For whatever He is searching throughout the seen and unseen world,
And at wherever He glanceth, he seeth nought but His Beloved.

The Valley of Unity

"Between belief and unbelief He seeth no distinction;
For Him, the river hath become the equal of the ocean.
No difference doth He find between honour and humiliation;
For Him, people come from just one stock regardless of their nation.
Day and night, to the curl of My hair, His heart is tied securely;
So, it is not surprising that He should feel His love so keenly.
The outer form and the inner reality interwoven have become;
The spell is broken; now He seeth the inner meaning in the outer form.
His eyes become freed from seeing anything other than God;
He soareth high throughout the heavens like the phoenix of love.

"All at once, My love hath raised Him aloft, from all else refining;
Towards unity Divine and My presence, He is hastening.
He becometh a shining candle when He attains unto My company;
After union with Me, He then returneth to the world of humanity.

"When I disclose My mysteries to the people of bliss,
Their schooling is to peruse the manuscript of My face.
I uncovered My mystery for thee as a token of My love;
Begone; Teach thou others how to attain Me by the wayfarer's Path.

"O thou my lover! Portray in words the Path, and each wayside
    station;
Teach wayfaring's stages, My secrets and the final destination.
Explain thou the byways of the valley leading to spiritual growth;
O enlightened one! Tell of the twists and turns of the spiritual Path.
I have once again hidden My face behind the mirror of the cosmos;
Tell thou the secrets of wayfarers who, to reach Me, are treading their
    course.
To thee, in a brief description, My mysteries I did tell;
Hasten to explain the secrets of the valley. Now, farewell!"

O comrades! Once more is flaming high the fire of rapture;
It raiseth this passionate lover to intense fervour.
The hidden Beloved unveiled His face and, then, He faded away;
My heart was kindled by the sight of His face then went its lovelorn
    way.
Once again my heart is foundering in love's storm-ridden ocean;
I am plunged in a sea of sorrow and yearning every moment.

Though many a madman is joyful and free from care and anxiety;
The companion of this maddened one is the grief of love-longing only.
The pain of love is my destiny; I was educated in love's longing;
Throughout my life, I have become accustomed to the agony of
    yearning.
Welcome O thou love-longing! Thou art ever my most intimate friend;
From the beginning of my life thou hast always been my confidant.

II THE REPOSITORY OF MYSTERIES: TRANSLATED TEXT

If thou wert not, who else would be my companion!
Who could comfort me in my so woeful condition!
From my start in my mother's womb, thou wert already my comrade;
Until now thou art still my attendant, my friend and intimate.

O my Lord! Enkindle the fire that refines and unto Thee draws us;
Thus is heard my cry: O Lord we have been to our own selves malicious.
Once again my heart writhes in the pain of this passionate love;
Once more my soul smoulders in the flames of this consummate love.
Once again my pen hath inscribed the word 'fire';
Its flame hath lit in my soul a blazing pyre.

Once again I inhaled the heady fumes of love's fragrancy;
I heard love's call and it roused my mind to utter ardency.
Once again the lion of my zeal broke loose the fettering chains;
It breathed the fresh and intoxicating air of distant mountains.
Again and once again the lion of my rapture roared and roared;
It broke the fetters, and the shackles into fragments shattered.
My lion was drunk with freedom; in frenzy its restraints it tore;
It frightened near to death all those who heard its awe-inspiring roar.

O friends! Come quickly! Please hasten! I desperately need assisting;
My elephant is out of control; towards India it is racing.
I have no power to curb it; it has snapped my handler's rope;
There is no chance of restraining it; I have abandoned hope.
My mind is at a loss what to do; it is baffled and helpless;
O thou, my good man! Come here to assist me; I am powerless.
The lion of the soul hath broken the chain of my ties to the world;
It hath charged out of its cage, towards open space it hath itself hurled.
This is the fire of love blazing up; be alert and step aside quickly;
It can conflagrate all the land and the ocean within an eye's twinkling.
Hearken: it is the roar of a maddened lion rumbling in its fury;
If thou art prudent and responsive, thou wilt move aside in a hurry.
Behold! A drunken lion hath broken the chain and hath burst out of its cage;
Guard thy self; such a lion cannot be blamed for what it does in its rage.
Beware! This is an enraged lion; it is quite ferocious;
O dear! Please get out of the way to save thy life! Be cautious!

The fire of my turbulent passion is once again blazing;
I know not if it is a road or a bridge on which I am pacing.
This mad passion hath sent me wandering far out in the desert;
Hard granite is the pillow on which my head seeketh comfort.

The Valley of Unity

My love for my Heart's Desire hath now rendered me homeless;
I cannot resist being chained in those rippling tresses.
Where is my Beloved to whisper the secrets?
Where is my jailer who would place me in fetters?
If I say: "Come thou prison-guard to fetter me!" it is duplicity;
For a mad lover like me is trussed up, chained and shackled already.
A wild lion that is stricken by a love so passionate,
The more thou wouldst fetter it, the more thou wilt madden it.

O Thou Charmer of my heart! Thy flowing locks are my fetters;
Behold! My heart is agitated like Thy rippling tresses.
I know not what road to follow, or which bridge to cross;
My helpless heart cannot find its way. It is quite lost.

I heard a celestial Voice calling this crazy lover; it was sufficient
For me to leave behind all my property, my town and my residence.
I am neither worried for my comfort or any worldly matters;
O my Beloved! My heart is tied up in Thine enchanting tresses.
Since Junun hath attached his heart to a maddening passion;
All the time, he is plunged in yearning grief deep as an ocean.
O Thou Branch of God! I am devoted in my love of Thee;
By the light of Thy face, I peruse the book of mystery.
O my Beloved! For three days of each month, madness overtakes me;
As today is the first of these, Thou seest me at present happy.
I endeavour to restrain myself. I am striving to stay silent;
But still for Thee my yearning keeps me stirred up, bubbling with
  excitement.

O Thou who art sanctified from all created entities!
Thy Essence is exclusive of attributes and qualities.
How would there be any way to fathom the depths of Thine Essence?
To grasp Thy reality lies beyond the mind's intelligence.
Thou art verily beyond attributes and descriptive utterance;
How, then, could knowledge fathom to the profundity of Thine
  Essence?
The knowledge, which we can access, is to the attributes related;
But, when Thine Essence doth appear, all knowledge hath been
  dissipated.

The Prophet Muhammad, for whose sake came into being the world;
Hath labelled the knowledge man hath of God, as 'precious as a pearl'.
O Thou, the Possessor of all the attributes divine!
As true knowledge should ideally be, Thee I have not known.
For, whatever be the realm that the Prophet may be dwelling on,
He speaketh at the level of the limits of our acumen.

The Point advises the non-seekers that a line it is;
The sea tells the non-initiates that a stream it is.

At times He speaketh of the path and at times of the reunion;
At times He speaketh of the root, at times the shoot doth mention.
At times He speaketh of unity infinite;
At times He speaks of diversity limited.
At times He doth spur His steed onto outer Reality's ground;
At times the path that a wayfarer treads is what He doth expound.
At times He speaketh of a point; at times a line He doth mention;
At times He talketh of the sea; then, to a stream makes allusion.
Whatever He sayeth, He hath divine authority to define it;
At times He speaketh as a Wayfarer, at times as the Reunited.
At times He appeareth as the Lover and at times He is the Beloved;
Whatever He sayeth is absolute Truth, and His expression is perfect.
His words, 'I have not known Thine inner Reality' no one disputes
For such comprehension cannot pass beyond the sphere of attributes.

Once again, in the field of outer Reality, He doth gallop His steed;
He signaleth to me, meaning: "That is far enough; go no further, indeed!"
Further on, no word can be uttered; there can be offered no description;
Further on, there is no room for concepts, and no place for speculation.
There are footprints on the shore to the edge of the ocean;
Lo! Beyond that, the wavelets smooth out the indentation.
Beyond, is but an endless sea reaching the horizon;
Only the ocean knows the mysteries of the ocean.

O comrade! Who knoweth the nature of the ocean?
Only he who hath plunged in for total immersion.
Of a sea's quality only a sea hath conception;
The eye of an ocean is needed to see the ocean.
It is not possible the sea's volume to quantify;
One should only drink of water one's thirst to satisfy.
Hence the reason for the statement of the Ancient Sovereign:
No scale is capable to measure the weight of an ocean.
None can determine how much water an ocean comprises;
But one should reflect on the river that from it vaporises.
For, otherwise, how can the ocean be placed on a scale?
To know and understand that hidden truth, one must not fail.

When the clouds of diversity have been cleared;
The shining Sun of Truth will then have appeared.
Or when all vain imaginings and fancy disappear;
The sea of truth appeareth with its water sparkling clear.

The Valley of Unity

When, by the lights of love, the inner eye becomes illumined;
Then the mysteries of love become unveiled and determined.
The mystery 'if the veil is removed' then becomes apparent;
The outcome is the uncovered truth that in the heart is evident.
The two worlds become perceptible before the inner eyes;
Thus manifest and visible are the hidden mysteries.

Open thine inner eyes and behold thou the light resplendent;
It is light upon light; shadow can no dazzling glare withstand.
Thou seest the whole cosmos as a sign reflecting His Face;
Around that central Orb revolveth the entire universe.

O parrot of our mind! Echo what thou dost hear from us;
Reflect our mood and feelings from inside the looking-glass.

When the enamoured mystic had gone apart from his companions,
While traversing the vale of wonderment, what did he experience?
Of his existence there remained no longer any trace;
He had plunged into an ocean of great and rolling waves.
He became enamoured; wonderment upon wonderment!
His selfness faded; of existence was left no remnant.
In that state of wonderment, he acquired new inner eyes;
What he saw was beyond sound or speech for him to analyse.

At times he sees diversity as true unity;
At times he sees eyes to be the hearing faculty.
At times he sees humiliation in glory;
At times he sees darkness in irradiancy.
At times he sees majestic glory in humility;
At times he sees effulgent lights in dark obscurity.
At times he sees a Persian as an Arab veritable;
While the instigated shows the instigator visible.
At times he sees the earth as the celestial paradise;
At times he sees the hidden One before his very eyes.
At times he sees the loved One in utter indigence;
Unveiled is the Beloved's alluring Countenance.
He sees captivated lovers standing in a circle round Him;
In such terms of joy and rapture all their love they strive to limn.

The hearts of the lovers are fastened to the strand of the Beloved's
hair;
They are in an ecstatic mood, impatient to their Loved One to adhere.
That intoxicating Eye hath the effect of wine in barrelfuls
It inebriates the lovers who then become like drunken fools.
The lovers are holding out their hands with their lives ready to offer;
Inebriated by that Eye, their heads at those Feet they would proffer.

How strange! That alluring Beauty elevates the spirits ceaselessly;
How is it possible not to love One of such joyous quality?
The lovers are willing to sacrifice their lives, nay the entire world;
For a glance of their Beloved Who is enchanting their hearts and souls.

O my heart! Be thou steadfast in thy servitude;
Exert every effort thy love to demonstrate.
Peruse thou the signs in which His Face is reflected
So that, to thee, might be disclosed Its every secret.
The religion of lovers is not the same as that of others;
God is both the religion and the entire tribe of the lovers.

A sweetheart said to her lover: "O my young man!
Thou hast travelled the world and many cities seen.
Tell me, then, which of all those cities seemed the best to thee?"
Quoth he: "Where my love resideth, that city is for me.
Wherever thou art with me, there I am in bliss;
Even were it in the depths of a black abyss."

O my Beloved! To be with you in hell would be as if in heaven;
Thine entrancing Countenance is both my Eden and a rose-garden.
Thy luminous Countenance is to us our paradise;
For us a loving-favour is the shadow of Thy grace.
The sheer radiance beaming from Thy Face is our breaking light of day,
Turning this world into a garden of roses in sweet array.
Thy tresses are the night season and Thy face is our daytime;
Thy beauty illumines our hearts as a blazing sun sublime.
Reunion with Thee is the Lote-tree; while Thy lips do reveal
The living waters of heaven, pouring forth ruby and pearl
Thy towering stature is the Lote-tree of paradise;
Oh! Thy breath gives life to the peoples of all the nations.
O Thou charming Countenance! To be with Thee turns hell into heaven;
Happy the soul that cherisheth the love of Bahá in his bosom!

Once again blazing up in my heart is my love's passion;
It is drawing me to the vale of the Ancient Sovereign.
This rapture is provoking me to move onward once again;
It driveth me to the dwelling of the Ancient Sovereign.

O Bahá'u'lláh! O Thou, the Lord of the Age!
All are illumined by the light of Thy Face.
O Thou whose Beauty by all the created things is praised!
O Thou whose Essence from all attributes is sanctified!

The Valley of Unity

No one hath ever comprehended Thine hidden Essence;
In observing Thy signs all minds are left speechless.
Thine Essence is unrestricted by limiting confines;
By Thy light came into being the world of existence.
If Thy light in the visible world had not been made manifest,
How, without Thy light, would any soul have ever come to exist?
O Thou the Ancient Beauty! If Thy light had not shone forth;
We would have been in the land of the dead forevermore.

Many a Moses is crying out in His heart's Sinai,
Supplicating: "O Lord! Reveal to us Thy beauty."
Many a Jesus, dwelling in the celestial sphere, hath come down
To earth, and is left astounded observing Thine exalted throne.
Myriad sweet-natured 'Muḥammad's feel that their wings are too
    flimsy
To soar to the heights of the firmament of Thy might's potency.
Unnumbered of Thy Chosen Ones have their eyes upon Thee fixed,
Their hearts unto Thy curling locks inextricably affixed.

O Thou celestial Guide! Many a heart-stricken mystic
By Thy beauty is amazed, enchanted and left love-sick.
Countless lovers, spell-bound and fascinated by Thy beauty,
Would fling their severed heads at Thy feet in sacrifice to Thee.
O Lord! Unity and diversity are both immersed within Thy Sea;
Both the higher and the lower worlds are mixt before Thy unity.
To Thine Essence it is impossible for us to gain access.
Thine hidden Reality left the Universal Mind speechless.

Intellect is unable to reach the depths of Thy Essence;
Reason and speech are drowning in the Ocean of Thy Presence.
The road to Thine Essence is completely barricaded;
In seeing Thy signs, both the worlds are intoxicated.
Thou art forever sanctified from the arc of ascent;
Nor dost Thou stoop to descend; on Thee there is no constraint.
Thou art hidden from the outer eye yet, in the heart, apparent;
Thou, the Eternal Reality, entirely self-sufficient!

Nay, nay! Before the outer eyes, Thou are not concealed;
Indeed, the men of insight see Thee in the outer world.
How could Thou be unseen, O Thou, the Soul of the universe?
Save in the eyes of heedless people in sinful thoughts immersed!
Heedless is one who of enlightenment hath no experience;
The heart of that one is deprived of the bounty of God's Presence.
A wayfarer with true perception of Thy lights sublime
Doth see Thee manifested at all points in space and time.
Any person who Thy lights doth truly understand;
Sees Thy presence evident and obvious all around.

O Thou, Who art our Sovereign! O thou, our sweet soul-stirrer!
I can see Thee manifest, unveiled and present everywhere.
Who am I to open my mouth in Thy Presence,
Proclaiming Thee to be hidden or manifest!
With all my soul and heart, to my shortcomings I do admit;
Thou art my Lord, the Object of my love; help me, I beseech.
Thou Thyself dost point to the reality of Thine hidden Essence;
Thou makest Thy Self to be known through Thy signs and Thine evidences.

The mystics are astounded trying to obtain knowledge of Thee;
They are baffled attempting to comprehend Thy reality.
The way leading to Thine Essence is barred, verily;
The most eloquent tongues stammer in describing Thee.
Thou art beyond all description or discussion;
Thou art beyond imagining or allusion.
Of Thy Revelation, Thy verses are the proof;
Thy very Being doth bear witness to Thy truth.
Thine Essence alone doth indicate Thine Essence and show;
Thou art above the creatures, which are the shadows below.
The outer world with the names and attributes, the body and mind,
All, enshrining the treasure of Thy Essence, are the talisman.

Who am I? A mortal speck to be a treasury of mysteries?
Who am I? Only a fleeting shade who the lights of love portrays!
How can an utter nothingness, a mere non-existent thing,
Gallop his steed to the arena of Thine Ancient Being!
How can an evanescent shadow glimpse the Orb of Love above?
Ah! One can see the Face of Love only with the eyes of love.

He is the Everlasting, the Imperishable Sphere,
And sanctified from vain illusions and all fancies mere.
The Prophet Muḥammad referred to this mystery;
This was the reason that He said: "I have not known Thee".
He said: "O Thou embodiment of every attribute!
I know Thee not in any way that knowing is in truth."
That means there cannot be any comprehension beyond that echelon;
The Universal Mind hath been astounded by Thy Face, O Radiant One!

An example crossed my mind that might clarify the meaning;
I will share it so that thou canst gain a deeper fathoming.
When the heart faces the Sun of Unity with Its dazzling brilliancy,
It becometh baffled, immersed entirely in profound perplexity.
Oh! Thy most beauteous Face is my conjecture's mystery;
It is the leaven of my love and inner ecstasy.
Oh! Thou makest to be baffled every mind;
Oh! Thou art for any comment far beyond.

The Valley of Unity

The ocean of Thine Essence is of wonderment a verity;
The essence of all things is a mirror that reflecteth Thee.
If all the minds were to acquire a great Platonic wisdom,
They would, nonetheless, not understand the essence of an atom.
How could a mere mind comprehend the kernel of a particle?
Of one feather of Thy love, the cosmic vault is but a barbule.
All of creation is a mirror that reflecteth Thee;
Each atom testifies to Thy Being's certainty.

It is proven that the Sun of the All-Glorious is a field where wonder lies;
Beware! Such an area of astonishment all theories of men defies.
So, the statement: "I have not known Thee" is perfectly sincere;
His luminous Face doth amaze and baffle every scholar mere.
May my life be a sacrifice to the lips that said: "I have not known Thee"!
The minds are beguiled with the lips that have given such a testimony.

A gentle gazelle doth hunt the raging lion in this analogy;
For similar is the profoundness of meaning of "I have not known Thee".
Behold! "I have not known Thee" implieth "I have known Thee" actually;
How surprising! Pick a flower from this rose-garden of mystery.
The statement "I do not know Thee" is the veritable knowing;
It indicates awareness. It is the proof of understanding.
This statement "I do not know" is true knowledge and glory;
Open thy inner eyes! See how His Beauty will dazzle thee.
That chief of the Messengers [1] stated: "O Lord! Increase my wonderment";
To denote the Lord's majesty, the chief Messenger made this statement.
"I have not attained Thy presence", was what the Loved One said;
Thus He shed a light on the path His lovers had to tread.
He clarified the path and the stages of the soul's hard journey;
It was true for its time and place, what was said by that Sea of Bounty.

Every statement hath a special place and a special stage for each;
On this pathway there are stages before the Primal Point we reach.
Our knowledge is but the knowledge of the rays emanating from the Sun
Of Divinity, which reflect in the mirror as either five or one.
That divine light doth manifest in the mirrors; it doth shine
Upon pure hearts; shedding rays from the Utterance Divine.

---

[1] Referring to the Prophet Muḥammad

II The Repository of Mysteries: Translated text

Celestial lights are shining forth—in every heart are mirrored,
Save where Divine Reality is by screening veils obscured.
Buried under worldly things and limitations' shroud;
His light cannot be seen by those who stand beneath a cloud.
For this light doth not force its ways through veils of self-defilement;
The Beloved's Face will not be seen for all its great allurement.
Neither doth His Face gaze through conditions non-essential;
He stays unseen just like a lamp with a masking shield of metal.
When a lantern's cover is removed, like darkness swept away;
Then its light is visible; there is nothing in the way.
Thus, in every open heart, God's light becomes apparent;
In our beloved Master's face that light glows ever present.
Wherever the veil that masks our hearts is all asunder rent,
Then the light of Bahá will be manifest all-radiant.
Thus too, when, from thine own heart's face, the veil is torn apart,
The light of Bahá's sun reflects resplendent in thine heart.
The light of unity shines forth from such a heart transparent;
And mirrored is in all pure hearts till all gleam luminescent.

Worldly limits and conditions are but an impediment
Because the light of God is ever shining, independent.
If worldly limitations do not block the way;
The light of Bahá's Sun doth, in the soul, hold sway.
Whenever His effulgent rays within the heart appear,
The secrets of the universe become explained and clear.
There is no dawn or setting of His Sun's illumination;
Both rising sun and sunset are but earthly limitations.
Whenever the clouds disperse and the veils are rent asunder;
Like sunlight His light shineth forth in all its glorious splendour.
Not subject His celestial light to exit nor to entrance;
Raise thine eyelids to perceive His Manifested radiance.

Egress and regress both relate to the world of God's creation;
Neither condition doth apply to His Manifestation.
His light is beaming with a most great lustre irresistible;
This light is glimpsed whenever His Face becometh visible.
The Sun of the one true God hath no setting and no dawning;
His radiance always sheds its light upon the world of being.
When, from the inner eyes, the clouding veils are once torn off,
The light of the Beloved's Face will then come streaming forth.

Remember how it is that when thou closest tight thine eyes;
Thou canst no longer see the sunlight's penetrating rays.
Then, when thine eyelids thou dost raise like the raising of a shroud;
Thou dost behold the sun come forth as from behind a cloud.

The Valley of Unity

Know thou, the same applies when seeking God's illumination;
Remove the veils and raise thine eyes to His Manifestation.

O brother! Thou must needs probe deep if thou wouldst gain perception;
Forsake thou, then, and put aside all blinded imitation.
Negotiate this valley, observing all with focus sharp and clear;
Open thine eyes to the aid of His lights and new vision will appear.
Then thou will grow enamoured and so absorbed in thy Beloved
That no stone or thorn shall halt thee on the path thou hast discovered.

The person who doth fall in love—enchanted by his Loved One—
Beyond that beauteous Countenance, the lover seeth no one!
Being thus absorbed by his Beloved's fascinating Face;
Dashing headlong to his Heart's Desire, he recklessly gives chase.
Being plunged beneath the billowed seas of his Beloved's Essence
He pays no heed to the gruesome howls of ghouls and screeching phantoms.
Not even Alexander's wall can block his way, pursuing
His Best-Beloved's Countenance—its beauty all-alluring!

All the veils have been burnt by the light of that Face;
The lover's heart is consumed in a flaming embrace.
Between lover and Beloved sparks a friendship so magnetic
Only lovers true experience such a feeling all-ecstatic.
While the lover is enthralled by the light of Divine Essence,
How can he attend to the clamour and uproar of ignorance?
He has left behind the phantoms, the dragons and the devils;
Enchanted and beguiled, it is his Loved One that he follows.

He is aware of neither unity nor diversity;
In the lights of the Beloved, he is submerged completely.
He is so rapt by the verses and the Lips from whence they flow;
He just follows his Beloved or runs besotted to and fro.
He is enchanted and amazed in learning of such countless mysteries;
He hath passed beyond discussing the various puzzling old philosophies.

O my dear one! Here there are many mysteries upon mysteries;
But those who are not able to discern and grasp them are numerous.
Whatever I say is according to the level of thy perception;
I would die in grief if I found none endowed with comprehension.
Yet, if all the inner mysteries I could record in written word,
Forty camels would not have the strength to carry such a load.
And however hard I struggle these mysteries to limn;
The Beloved's myriad secrets are beyond an earthly pen.

II The Repository of Mysteries: Translated text

It is said that knowledge, in its essence, is but one single point;
But the ignorant see it as multiple, various and different.
In their eyes, the single light of the Beloved's unity
Appears as myriad entities of endless variety.

That is why a person who is cross-eyed and of a narrow-mind,
Being unenlightened, is to the first stage of the Path confined,
The light that manifest in Adam to him is not the light of Noah;
For to inner vision in his heart of hearts unopened is the door.
From the dawning-place he knows of, he identifies the sun,
To him the sun is but a sham if elsewhere it doth dawn.
Since he only doth consider the sun's one-time dawning-place,
When, next time, from another point the sun doth shows its face,
He doth contend that if the light cometh from the self-same sun,
Why should it rise elsewhere? This must surely be a different one!
Having arrogantly argued that the self-same sun it cannot be;
Like a bat, avoiding sunlight, into the darkness he doth flee.

When, from the horizon of Jesus Christ, the Sun rose in the sky,
The infidels said, "With their constraints, it is He Who must comply.
If He follows not our every law and tradition's expectation,
We will suspend Him from a cross by way of execution.
Either He must be, like us, self-righteous, proud and prejudiced,
Or He must be excommunicated from our very midst.
We will not abandon our old faith and all its known traditions;
We will neither heed Him nor accept His brazen admonitions!"

Thus salute such people the new dawn of every spiritual age;
They are descendants of Satan and like the devil they behave.
They ever show enmity to God's new Manifestation;
They persecute His followers in every dispensation.
They thought it would be easy the new Messenger to vanquish;
In fact, they battled God Himself, His divine Truth to extinguish.

Once again the eternal Sun of Truth its shining radiance shed,
And a new Day was dawning from the horizon of Muḥammad.
The deniers of His claim said: "Our Promised One, we know,
Must come down from heaven and, only thus, fulfil our law.
He will be riding on the clouds with supreme majesty;
And singing angels, rank on rank, will Him accompany.
Both the moon and the sun must dimmed become
While the world's peoples all to turmoil succumb.
When the stars fall from the sky to the earth;
We will know the Son of Man cometh forth.

"Riding on the clouds, attended by angels in cohorts,
He will descend towards the earth from the heavenly heights.

The Valley of Unity

Our beliefs He will propagate and spread throughout the earth;
All the world's peoples will carry the banner of our Faith.
To the four corners of the planet will our religion spread;
Except for our Faith, there will in the world no other creed."

Idolaters said: "This youth is the son of Abdullah;
We know him, and his family are all well-known as well.
How claimeth He to converse with some heavenly denizen?
He is our contemporary and a fellow-citizen!
He is our associate and speaks our vernacular;
He is subject to hunger and thirst just like we all are!
Firstly, his appearance doth not fulfil our expectations;
Secondly, he doth abrogate the laws of past religions.
The earth and heaven may both have perished and vanished;
But our faith will never be annulled or extinguished."

The believers retorted: "We know Him as our Promised One because
Just His Light is sufficient testimony to the Truth of His Cause."
So what was it that descended to the believers from heaven?
It was the Holy Qur'án, from on high revealed and then given.
Also, from heaven did come the spirit of the Prophet;
The faithful believers were the angels of His cohort.
And, because from heaven the verses of His Scripture came;
His Words were abundant proof to authenticate His claim.
He quickened the lifeless that rose from spiritual death;
For from that 'pride of prophets' life-giving was the breath.
He blew aloud the trumpet to quicken the whole world;
Many were the kings who bowed down before His threshold.
This is the inner meaning of the terms 'might' and 'sovereignty';
It is clear for people of knowledge and perspicacity.

Once again the Divine Sun dawned from yet another horizon;
It shone forth with such dazzling lights that the veils were torn down.
Once again the Sinai and the burning bush appeared;
His face shone forth; he declared: "Verily I am God!"
When that divine Guide drew aside the veil from His Beauty,
The whole world was filled with Bahá's radiant lights of Glory.

When a new Revelation comes, the deniers, like the shades of the dead,
Are moribund, unaware of the quickening breaths of the Beloved.
But behold, when this celestial Revelation occurred,
By the Divine light the entire world was left enraptured.
His radiance enriched and elevated the whole of humanity;
A hundred Prophets Moses knelt to pay Him homage in His Mount
    Sinai.
He gave to a particle the potential of the light of the sun;
He made a droplet prosperous with the capacity of an ocean.

If, within a particle, was hidden a sun's potentiality,
He made it become magnificently manifest, shining forth brightly.
If the mystery of an ocean was concealed in a droplet,
Then the Ancient Beauty brought it forth so it became apparent.

When for this new Era was made manifest its Solomon;
Intellect was as Servitude and selfness was as Satan.
Bahá was Love celestial and 'Abdu'l-Bahá His highest Agent;
Oh! May my life be a sacrifice unto such a faithful Servant!
May my heart be for that celestial Face a sacrifice!
May my life be an offering for that ringlet's fragrance!

The being of the Master hath branched from out that Ancient Root;
He was the intimate and helper of the Beauty of God.
The Mother Earth to such a Sovereign hath never given birth;
In the Kitáb-i-Aqdas, God named Him, 'He whom God hath purposed'.
The heart of the world is captivated by His luminous face;
Wandering in search of Him, every heart looks to His dwelling place.
Infatuated by the rose, love's nightingales sing in their bower,
All warbling in their adoration at the beauty of the flower.
The blossom of His face in its full bloom the world did grace;
The light that from it beamed brought joy to the whole human race.
From the cup-bearer of His Covenant take the vessel;
Drink from the chalice of love to thus stay to Him faithful.

Now I wish to broach another theme in our conversation
To disclose to thee the mystery of each Revelation.
There is a hidden wisdom in each religious dispensation;
Each Prophet's Revelation doth focus on a certain question.

Know thou that Adam's dispensation was the era of the earth;
So, the earthly elements were the axis of Adamic Faith.
The qualities of earth are contentment, patience and submission;
And, overtly or covertly, caring, love and comprehension.
The quality of fire is rebelliousness and power-lust;
Out of its arrogant pride, it doth intimidate and boast.
Since Satan sought, in his conceit, complete supremacy;
He belittled the earth, and held it in low subserviency.
Out of jealousy, he would not show submission and compliance;
His being was completely filled with selfishness and arrogance.
He refused to genuflect before the light in Adam manifest,
Being full of pride and jealousy; and with ambition too obsessed.
He weighed his nature of fire against Adam's puny earthly nature,
And, then, broke the covenant, displaying total enmity and rancour.

Of course, Satan did not realize that Adam was of light celestial;
So, he disobeyed. O God! Save us from enduring such a testing trial.

The Valley of Unity

Now, Adam and Satan exist in every Revelation's advent;
Therefore, beware with whom thou dost shake hands in making an agreement.

Every Revelation displays its own distinctive sign;
Do thou investigate if thou dost wish them all to find.
There is a secret wisdom enshrined in every Revelation;
And around a special theme revolveth every dispensation.
A beginning and an end there is in each religious cycle;
In its start and its conclusion a wisdom is discernible.

Remember that the theme of Adam's dispensation was the earth;
But for earth is needed water its potential to bring forth.
If there were no water how could plants shoot up and bring forth flowers?
How could trees bear fruit and fields grow green without life-bringing showers?

Though each Revelation holds within it every aspect in potential,
That each doth emphasize one aspect shows a wisdom special.
The tale of flooding rain and Noah's ark is special to his Dispensation;
The story in Abraham's Dispensation is about divine attraction.
He taught people not to deify the sun, the stars and moon;
We know how God the fire cooled saving Abraham from harm.

As water, earth and fire combined, the temperature was lowered;
The fire cooled to a safe degree when Abraham it entered.
That Friend of God[1] sincere attained love's most exalted station;
Thus, 'the father of all prophets' became his designation.
Each and every prophet of God from celestial love is born;
It is for this reason that Abraham as 'father of all' is known.

O noble man! Those who nurture divine love in their hearts,
One and all are recognized as Abraham's descendants!
Since in the time of Moses, those four elements were thus combined—
Hark, O people who hear! 'The final dispensation' it was named.
The four elements were combined and a perfect body was formed;
But, when you consider this closely, the body needeth a soul.

When Jesus came He declared: "I am the Spirit of God;
I am the Holy Spirit; I breathe spirit on the world.
One who is quickened through me, with a spirit new is reborn;
Thus the door of seeing the Lord becometh open for him."

---

[1] Title of Abraham

We described earth, water, fire, wind; and, then, the soul we did depict;
Now hearken attentively to the account of the need for intellect.
We have mentioned the four elements to which was admixed the soul;
But, to these five entities there must be need for intellect as well.
Though basically perfect and complete is the stage of each revelation;
For growth, the four elements must have soul and intellect in addition.
An embryo grows into a foetus of flesh and blood and bones;
First the soul is manifest then the mind to develop begins.
An embryo potentially possesses everything within its essence;
As the child matures to adulthood all its potentials become manifest.
Uncountable mysteries are potentially present;
In stages they will manifest, becoming apparent.
Whatever is hidden in an embryo's reality,
All becometh evident as it reaches maturity.

When Muḥammad came, He said: "I am the Universal Mind;
All creation is My realm and all of it I comprehend."
The need for an intellect in man is undeniable
While the crowning component of the elements is the Soul.
The Prophet Muḥammad said: "My ascension unto the high heaven
Cannot be compared with the descent of Jonah into the ocean.
Approaching God, Mine is upwards while downwards was his."
Closeness to God is quite impossible to assess.
When a seed is buried and in the soil is hidden;
Its potential doth rise in the treetop apparent.
Lo! What do you need after the reasoning power?
No doubt love will be thine intellect's crown.

The dispensation of the Qá'im [1] is the era of love for humanity;
It is the epoch of man's reunion with God and the day of world unity.
The promised Qá'im appeared and for love He raised the call;
His was the voice of God, chanting a psalm of love for all.
When that hidden One His enchanting Countenance unveiled;
The world by Him was mesmerized and totally enthralled.
The era of this Beloved betokens the age of love hath dawned;
As the unveiled Face of the Heart's Desire hath from love's horizon shone.
That eternal Sun dawned and the entire world was illuminated;
With the lights of the unlimited One all hearts were satiated.
The Mouthpiece of God on earth the song of love chanted;
To the whole world the secrets of love He imparted.

---

[1] The Báb

The Valley of Unity

Now hearken carefully to another mystery;
This I wouldst fain disclose in my communion with thee.
Since the Manifestation of God is with God in close liaison,
He doth act as the intermediary between God and every human.
That pure and holy Soul, from God receiveth grace,
Then transfers and extends it to the human race.
As divine grace to every soul He is ceaselessly vouchsafing,
He embodies all divine attributes; His grace is all-sufficing.
The Manifestation, through God's command, the Covenant imparteth
To His authorized successor to whom Divine knowledge He granteth.

This book cannot encompass more than what is here propounded
Despite the myriad mysteries as yet to be expounded!
The people of God know of uncountable mysteries left untold;
These are secrets of love that are derived from the Best-Beloved.

Move on! The Fourth Valley is now getting close to its end;
Well is it with him who, for love of Bahá, hath listened.
Were I to write one hundred tomes, they never could contain
All the secrets of mystic wayfaring, or of love divine.

The Fourth Valley hath almost reached to its completeness
By the confirmations of Bahá and His loving-kindness.
Myriad thanks to the sovereign, 'Whom God hath purposed'—
That king of righteousness who hath my work assisted.
In my efforts to describe and extol Him, He hath helped me,
Though my pen was unable to portray Him as He should be.
That majestic Beauty, out of His loving favour,
Caused this nightingale to warble songs of love's ardour.
So that you may discover the ways and the rules of lovers
From this book; that, in thee, fervour and rapture it engenders.

Whether publicly or in private, He is my intimate companion;
He is the Loved One of my inner soul and of the entire creation.
The pleasant discourse about this Valley is now drawing to a close;
It was achieved by the help of the effulgent Day-Star Glorious.
Also, 'Abdu'l-Bahá, the Centre of the Covenant of God
Assisted me out of His loving-kindness—my faithful Beloved.

The date—if thou shouldst wish to know this—of the composition of this lyric
Was one thousand three hundred and twenty nine of the Hegira Islamic.
According to the new Bahá'í Era it was the year sixty eight[1]
From the time the Báb's effulgent Face did first the world irradiate.

---

[1] AD 1911

Of the coming of the Father, the Son of Man[1] *brought joyful tidings;*
He prophesied that the Ancient Beauty would with glory be descending.
He predicted that the Father would the whole world come to conquer;
That the vineyard He would take back from the hands of the grape grower.[2]

If, with a heart full of His love, thou wouldst sincerely take one step to advance;
The veils would be torn down and thou wouldst gaze upon His luminous Countenance.

Lo! The entire world by His light will be illumined;
Every heart that loves Him, will become a rose-garden.
His face sheds radiance upon the East and the West;
Like a lightning flash, from east to west it doth traverse.
His commandments will ultimately govern the whole planet;
All mankind will be safeguarded by His love, and protected.
The entire created cosmos is in His radiance immersed;
The bonds of unity in diversity are by Him expressed.

Try thou to discover this secret, by the light of His face made clear;
That thou shouldst to the mystery of beginning and end be brought near.
Detach thyself from this world of shades and imaginings;
To soar high, inspired by His love, spread out fully thy wings.
Those personages who, on the wings of erudition,
Are flying high above the world of names and condition,
Therefore, to the relative world, attach no importance,
Soar far above the limits of fleeting forms appearance.
Since they pass high above the plane of imitation,
They are leaving behind all forms of limitation.
They are entirely light, all immersed in light's ocean;
To the realm of diverseness they pay no attention.
There is no trace of worldly attachment left in them;
They have passed through all the stages and reached to the end.

Meditating on the mysteries of this realm doth bewilder the mind;
Leave mind; mystical reality is beyond what mind can comprehend.
The mind is for discernment and discrimination;
It maketh out between the forms every distinction.
At times it calleth water a droplet and at times an ocean;
At times it calls Earth a temple and, at other times, a tavern.

---

[1] Referring to Jesus Christ
[2] Referring to Christ's parable of the owner of the vineyard who sent his servants to collect the grapes.

The Valley of Unity

Bravo O love, well-done! Thy language is with the heart in harmony;
Thou dost not make distinction between unity and diversity.
For thee, other than the Friend, there is no beginning and no end;
For thee there is neither seen nor unseen world other than the Friend.

Since far above the plane of limits the wayfarer hath now passed,
He beholdeth in Thee the realm of divine unity at last.
He will dwell on that enchanting plane with unimagined delight;
He will sojourn in the pleasure of Bahá's radiating light.

They soar in the sphere, which hath neither bound nor limit;
In the world of the Absolute They will pitch Their tent.
Since, in the realm of divine authority, They erect Their canopy,
From every other thing, except the love of God, Their hearts are ever free.
They burned off all attachments in a single flare of flame;
From the fire of His love, Their hearts and souls ablaze became
They entirely blotted out every meaningless phrase;
All vain imaginings They did totally erase.
They swim with pleased delight in the ocean of transcendence;
They find open on all sides the portals to His Presence.
They soar high in the holy air of unmeasured mystery;
They bask in the lights of God all ashine with irradiancy.

Lo! How could words carry any sense of existence
In the plane of light of the All-loving God's radiance!
In this realm, but a breath is the beginning and ending
When, full of grace, the captivating Face is appearing.
In this realm the first is the very last itself;
And the very last is the very first itself.
On this plane all the nations are seen as one nation;
Hundreds of thousands of years and one hour are as one.
Though the forms are manifold, but one is the Source;
Though the paths are various, they all lead to one course.

Enkindle in thy soul of love a fire;
Burn away all the thoughts and words entire.
Raze all the veils by the fire of love of the Beloved;
Then advance just one more step to enter the lovers' abode.
That thou mayest become aware of the mysteries ancient;
And incinerate all the blocking veils of the non-existent.

O my friend! Meditate for a moment upon thy self;
That the hidden mysteries become for thee unearthed.
O dear! Hadst thou not become a father in this world,
How wouldst thou, then, be able thine infant to behold?

II The Repository of Mysteries: Translated text

Likewise, if words had not come into being,
How couldst thou, then, the various psalms be hearing?
How couldst thou, in that case, hearken to all those phrases
That indicate all the various forms and images?
How could there be various tongues—Italian, Arabic, Turkish;
How could you listen to all the different songs and melodies?

Lo! Put aside and forsake every veil-creating word
So that thou seest only the heart-ravishing Beloved.
Hearken to what the All-Knowing saith of God's Unity,
That thou learnest the lessons of each splendid mystery.
Hearken faithfully to what the Knower of love teaches;
With such studies the mysteries of Bahá thou learnest.
So thine heart be touched and, like an organ, doth sound
The sweet song: 'We verily return unto God'. [1]

This melody reminds thee thy covenant to reaffirm,
That back to the bosom of thy Beloved thou canst return.
Thou wouldst be released from the bonds of earth's soil of illusion,
Exalted in attaining with thy Beloved reunion.
In the ocean of reunion with the Loved One thou art immersed;
Within the shadow of His tree of knowledge thou dost take thy rest.
Thou wilt dwell under the Lote-tree of His divine wisdom
And, thus, attain the mystic Path, exploring His kingdom.

Love of God hath ever been servitude's loftiest station;
To attain eternal life drink from love's chalice thy portion.
O dear one! Subdue thy craving and make a treasure of poverty
So that, inwardly and outwardly, rich will be thy reality.
Thus thou wilt obtain divine wealth and from all want be free,
Marvelling at the mystery manifested in thee.

O my dear one! Humble the body and tame every wild passion;
So that, like Joseph, thou wilt be freed from the fleshpots of Canaan.
Drink thou from the grail of the well-spring of glory and honour
Thus unchained from the chimera of the pitfall of nature.

Since all the various stages have been made clearly manifest,
Open even to the outer eyes, they should now be obvious.
Unravelling the mysteries depends on the wayfarer's own progress;
For, hidden in his inner self, reunion's treasure he doth possess.
He hears celestial melodies in every meadow that he passes nigh,
Not even stopping for one moment's rest at any caravanserai.

---

[1] Referring to Qur'án 2:156, which can be translated as: "*We come from God and we verily return to Him.*"

The Valley of Unity

A new voice he hears in every pasture through the inner ear,
Urging him along his journey with glad tidings and good cheer.

Many secrets come to light that were to him concealed;
Many hidden mysteries now manifest, unveiled.
With his sharpened eye, he doth behold uncovered mysteries;
With his inner ears, he listens to once secret melodies.

The celestial Falcon knoweth all the mysteries of this stage;
Such secrets as these cannot be set down in words on any page.
Such melodies divine that are coursing through His heart
Are not made to be portrayed by any form of art.

A melody of notes divine is enshrined in our beings innermost:
It is a melody that brings great fervour and elation to its host.
In the inner chamber of my soul this celestial song is playing
Its unknown harmonies are new; it is melodious and compelling.
It is a fascinating song of the Adored One's mysteries;
The loving glance of our Hearts' Desire it so lyrically portrays.

He beckoned me no more to speak; with silence me did task;
"How long must thou fermenting be like wine doth in its cask?"
Thus many wondrous secret things concerning my Beloved,
And His illustrious utterances have remained untold!

To divulge further mysteries I am now forbidden;
But, to the inner eye of love, they are not all hidden.
A mystic descant is enshrined in my heart's inner core—
The secret of reunion left unheard forevermore.
It must continue undisclosed, at all times left concealed;
For wisdom rules which mysteries of Being be revealed.
Many a mind would be maddened, if more I were to utter;
And if I were further words to write, every pen would shatter.

I have spoken and scribed the words of all that I could convey;
The Fourth Valley is near its close; I will soon bid thee 'adieu'.
My ever-living Lord hath communed with me last night;
With His all-compelling eye, He bid me to be quiet.
With His noble brow that Beloved did unto me beckon:
He is the One for whom both the worlds yearn to be in union.

That Beauteous One from Whose lips pours the sweetness of molasses,
He glanced at me; His smile was fond, and fragrant were His tresses.
Out of His favour, that Sovereign of all the world's nations opened
His sugar-shedding lips, sighing to His smitten lover, Junun.
Thus that honey-tongued One spoke—His voice was mild and
    pleasant:
"Now thou must expound and limn the Valley of Contentment."

II THE REPOSITORY OF MYSTERIES: TRANSLATED TEXT

If thou art interested to imbibe more of this discourse;
O dear one! Please follow me along the Fifth Valley's course.

The Fifth Valley
THE VALLEY OF CONTENTMENT

Now of the Valley of Contentment, I would converse with thee;
My Sovereign Lord hath bounteously continued to assist me.
The confirmation and favours of Bahá, and the light that shineth
From the countenance of 'Abdu'l-Bahá, will aid me to define it.

In the Fifth Valley, the light that hath ever spread its emanation,
With all its effulgence, hath shed forth in the kingdom of creation.
Beyond the Vale of Unity, where Divine light bestows its radiance,
The spellbound wayfarer is drawn onward by the Adored One's
  ambiance.
He enters the Valley of Contentment filled with rapture and zeal;
The force of the fervour flowing throughout all his veins, he doth feel.

In this vale a breeze doth waft over from contentment's arena,
Refreshing the wayfarer with the loving-kindness of Bahá.
The lights of divine contentment, emitted from the Countenance
Of the Beloved, from every direction shed their luminance.

The wayfarer burns off the veil of poverty, and dearth he feels no
  more;
He doth ignite the candle of contentment deep in his heart's inner
  core.
He is illumined by the radiant lights that emanate from God;
Bound only to His Being, he is freed from the mortal world.
His sorrow, grief and anguish are transformed into bliss and joy;
He is drunk on light and energy that in his soul alloy.

The wayfarers who set out and through this valley pass,
Outwardly, appear to dwell upon this earthly dust.
But they are established on the throne of the spirits' heights;
Intoxicated and immersed in Bahá' s radiant lights.
They enjoy the plentiful bounties of innate reality;
They become the denizens of the summits of love and amity.
Outwardly, of the planet earth they are the citizens,
But, inwardly, they soar in the space of inner meanings.
To them is proffered mystic wine that to their fill they quaff,
Inebriated by the bounty that doth flow thereof.
They enter a dewy rose-garden of beauty glorious to behold;
There they find shelter from both the burning heat and from the bitter
  cold.
They associate with the concourse of souls spiritual;
Words are unable to portray that assembly celestial.

II THE REPOSITORY OF MYSTERIES: TRANSLATED TEXT

I admit my words do not succeed to limn that lofty space;
O Junun! Do not try onto that plane thy foot to place.
The nightingale of the heart hath in its repertoire another psalm;
The bird of holiness aspires to spread its wing in another realm.
The heart ferments with excitement in this realm of mysteries;
On this plane the soul thrills and calls aloud in its ecstasies.
This hidden enigma must be whispered from one heart to another;
It must be kept concealed and only be from breast to breast passed
     over.

Between the lovers are sent heart to heart communiqués;
With no murmuring they transmit the hidden mysteries.
Of the state of the people of love this is the picture;
The state of the enraptured ones hath a gemlike lustre.

If thou dost not enter the rose-garden of the inner Divine,
How, then, canst thou taste the sweetness of rarefied celestial wine?
If thou shouldst taste the immortal draught of faith from that crystal
     chalice;
Thou wouldst see nothing except God in thy state so rapturous.
Quaff thou the nectar quickening from the chalice of contentment;
Let self be turned to intellect from its contents fragrant.
That, save for the love of thy Beloved, break thou all binding tethers,
Leave the musk filled locks of thine Adored One as thine only fetters.
Thou wouldst willingly throw thy life at His feet with delight;
And, instead, fill thine entire being with His living light.
Thou wouldst offer up thy soul in His path with eager ecstasy;
None in either world but thy Beloved can evermore suffice thee.
At this stage, only thy Sovereign fills the canvas of thy mind;
Whether thine eyes are open or closed thou art no longer blind.

He hath ever been and will ever be alone in His dominion;
Without the least doubt, there is none other to share with Him His
     Kingdom.
Alone He rules His whole domain for none can share such Majesty;
He is seated on His ancient throne wielding sole Authority.

The eye of the mystic seeth nought except the Loving Friend;
Finding his Beloved's signs that guide him to the journey's end—
The Manifest and the Hidden, at the same time apparent and veiled;
There is no doubt that in Divine unity no diversity doth prevail.
His sublime dignity alloweth of no partner or equal;
For He is, in Himself, both the Hidden and the Visible.
How could duality be possible in that world of being?
On this level, there is neither thou-ness nor we-ness existing.

He Himself is the vendor; and He is also the vendee;
Pouring bounty upon all around and hearing every plea.
At times He billows like the waves; at times He is Himself the ocean;
If thou hast an inner eye, carefully observe its endless motion.
He is directionless; at times there is no way that leadeth to Him;
He is sanctified above any trait that might be ascribed unto Him.
He is the very Essence, beyond any name or quality;
How can the human mind conceive the breadth of His Reality?

Love hath five hundred wings; when it is outspread, each wing,
From heaven above to earth below, is extending.
When both heart and soul are intoxicated from the cup of immortality,
In that state one is the wine, the chalice and the cup-bearer in totality.
The wayfarer sees the reflection of the Face of his Heart's Desire
In all things; whether it is water or the earth, the wind or the fire.
He hath found the secret of inner reality in the outer sphere;
Grace openeth wide her portals for him and his way is clear.

The secret of inner Essence, in outer attributes expressed,
He perceives with ease in passing through inner eyes that God hath blessed.
Released he is from the spell of the world of limitation;
On his head the crowning diadem of insight's consecration.
He hath burnt away all obstructing veils with just one heaving sigh;
O dear one! He hath lit love's candle in his heart, now flaming high.
Naught remains of the previous path, not even of dust a trace;
With one single glimpse, the blocking veils he doth instantly efface.

He journeys on, beholding the entire world of creation;
He doth gaze on this new universe with all-penetrating vision.
In but a single glance, he hath traversed from one end to the other;
He now sees all created things with the clear eyes of a lover.

If thou wouldst listen raptly to what a mystic sayeth;
His outward speech to his inward state strongly testifieth.
In the mystic's utterance thou wilt find the key
To the door of his insight's reality.
And if thou shouldst care through his eyes to look;
Thou might peruse the page of his mystic book.

The pen of Majnún expresses his love for Layla;
The nightingale warbles to extol the rose flower.
The mystics are dedicated only to their Hearts' Desire;
With the love of their Beloved their hearts are brimming over.
Day and night they are employed in extolling their Adored One;
They are engaged in their communion with their Best-Beloved One.

II THE REPOSITORY OF MYSTERIES: TRANSLATED TEXT

I am as a nightingale that in the springtime is warbling;
I cannot stop singing for my heart with love is roiling.
At times I disclose the mysteries; at times I am taciturn;
In either of these states I have no aim but searching for Him.
The more I drink from the cask of extolling my Beloved,
The more from my cup-bearer I desire another draught.
I must now return to the main subject of my thesis;
My eager heart is never filled when our God it praises.

O Junun! Once more tune up the harp of the Seven Valleys;
Come now! Play thou a chord from the secret of love's mysteries.
The people of mysticism believe there are seven valleys;
They beseech God to assist them in their spiritual odyssey.
The wayfarers whose hearts are flooded with the lights of sincerity
Have all spoken of the seven stages of the spiritual journey.
The song of seven valleys each true wayfarer sings
Whose forehead God hath crowned with the diadem of kings.

Out of His love, God hath opened wide the gates of divine mysteries;
Out of His love, the King of lovers to them unveiled His radiant face.
Love drives the wayfarers to reach their desired destination;
Love doth nourish their faith to flourish, blooming in perfection.

Now I wish to speak again of the inner essence and the outer form;
About this hidden secret, Mind hath no capacity to be informed.
He is our spiritual Leader in His outer form;
While, in His inner essence, He is the Judge Divine.
In the outer form, our spiritual Guide He is;
But in His inner essence He is God Manifest.
In the outer form it is the utmost servitude He suffers
But in His inner essence, the cup of immortality He offers.
In the outer form He demonstrates complete humility;
In His inner essence His is the most Ancient Sovereignty.
In the outer form He passes down ordinances and laws;
In His inner reality He talks of nothing else save God.
"I am a servant and He is God", in the outer form He doth decree;
In the inner essence He maketh the statement: "There is no God but Me".
In the outer form He maketh claim that He is God made Manifest;
But in the inner essence He says He is the All-Forgiving, God Himself.
In His outer form as our human Guide Bahá'u'lláh appeareth;
But Bahá'u'lláh is God Himself in His inner essence.
He is certainly our Guide in His outer form;
But, in Bahá's inner essence, He and God are One.
Likewise, with the Servant of Bahá—His outer form doth belie
That, in his inner essence, the universe doth him glorify.

Though in the outer form He is the Branch of God,[1]
His inner essence is the Mystery of God[2]
In outer form He is the most perfect of humanity;
But in the realm of names, He is of God's names the treasury.
If thou art able to rupture tradition's standard's bond,
In the depths of thy heart, His inner reality is enthroned.
In the limit of His duties, He is the authorized Interpreter;
But, in fact, He is of His works the producer and originator.
In the limit of His servitude, He is Bahá's foremost servant;
While He is the Branch of the Ancient Root in His inner essence.

These statements illustrate the effulgent lights of Bahá;
I am explaining this innate light in terms particular.
No doubt, thou art not conversant with the terms that here are used;
Therefore, think thou in more familiar terms this to comprehend.
The lovers use a tongue that differs from that in common usage;
To the people of no insight, it is like a foreign language.

The beauty of the Loved One is the instructor of the lovers;
His beauteous Face is their lesson and the course book that it covers.
These lessons are of rapture, excitement, passion and joyous dilemma;
And not like reading tedious books such as "Ádat' and 'Báb-i-Silsilah'.[3]
The 'Silsilah' book of this people is of those tresses scented;
Whatever dialogues they hold, are around the Loved One centred.
In the limits of this world, He obeys the laws and rules;
He is concerned with ethics and values principles.
While in His sphere the Absolute, He soars beyond all ties and limits;
Like a dervish wandering, He is unrestrained and free of fetters.
Praise to Thee! O thou, of all the liberated ones, the Sovereign!
Hurrah! Thou Lord of all those freed from their shackle and their
        clanking chain!

To Thy summons raised its voice the heavenly phoenix;
The birds heard it and all started trilling their lyrics.
With whatever praises I extol thee, far above them Thou art;
Thou Thyself canst see the devoted yearning within every heart.
However we describe Thee is according to our limitations;
But Thou art above our comprehension and all evaluations.
My pen cannot adequately describe Thine inner reality;
Thou canst not be gauged by any scale of quantity or quality.
Thou art light upon light, radiating with light within light;
Thus we must hail Thee as the Sovereign of Revelation's might.

---

[1] One of the titles of 'Abdu'l-Bahá
[2] One of the titles of 'Abdu'l-Bahá
[3] 'Ádat is "custom" and Báb-i-Silsilah is "Chain Gate". Publications unknown.

The souls are exhilarated by a sip of the wine of Thy chalice;
The hearts are fastened to a strand of Thine tresses of enchanting fragrance.

O Thou Who art the King of kings, the Sovereign and Lord of munificence!
The leaven of both seen and unseen worlds is the light of Thy Countenance.
O Thou, Lord of humanity, Cache of the mysteries of the Kingdom!
Thou hast tuned Thine harp to harmonize the melodies of divine wisdom.
Although Thou dost serve God to the fullest with all of Thy heart and soul;
Save for the one true God, Thy inner reality surpasseth all.

And Thou, 'Whom God hath purposed', Thou the potentate of bounty!
Boundless is the description of Thy inner reality.
O Thou, 'the Mystery of God' and the 'Branch of the Ancient Root'!
Of thy innate reality's nature Thou art more cognizant.
Thou art our beloved Master in the field of servitude;
Thou art our guide to show us the way to the court of Godhood.
We bow down before Thee as Thou dost bow down before the Ancient Beauty;
No one can adequately describe Thy fascinating qualities.
In proclamation of truth, Thy voice in the world Thou didst raise;
While the hidden secrets of God, thou didst with Thy pen disclose.
If Thou wert not the divinely-appointed successor of Thy Father,
How could Thy pen by its marvellous writings perform such feats of wonder?

How is verity to be from falsehood distinguished?
One is light; the other is in darkness extinguished.
On the first night in the lunar month only a crescent is evident;
Just a small part of the moon is in light, the rest is in darkness hidden.
Little by little, is removed the obscuring gloom;
As from every corner the covering veil is torn down.

O thou who are wrapped up in the veils of arrogance!
Tear down all thy veils to see the Loved One's Countenance.
The curtain covering the chamber of thine heart must be drawn aside
That, by the revealing light, thou canst see the Face of Beloved.
So long as thine heart hath not been released from its veiling cover,
How wouldst thou be able to see God's light shining from all over?

A Manifestation of God is needed to rip apart the wrapping veils;
Only He can revitalize the faded hearts and quicken the withered souls.

Superstitions can only be purged by the Manifestation of God;
Only His heart hath been entirely illumined by the Radiance of God.

Likewise, no one is able to do what the Master attained;
If, to thee, the Father and Son are as two, thou art cross-eyed.
As the Master breathed the spirit of searching for the truth;
So, little by little, the obstructing veils were removed.

As the moon gradually becomes visible a little at a time,
The dark part turns into light, and the crescent into the full moon.
What happens in the higher realm is reflected on the lower plane;
Thus the Beloved's Beauty becomes known like the beauty of the
    moon.
The spirit is in the higher level, and the body is its semblance;
In the physical world, the body is seen as a tangible substance.
What is in the higher realm has a form in the lower realm;
Know thou that the physical is a mirror of the kingdom.
The spiritual kingdom is by the entire universe being mirrored forth;
The living body to the reality of the spirit testifieth.
The spirit dwells in the realm above and the body lives in the world
    below;
The spirit is immortal while the mortal body is a passing shadow.
The human spirit comes from neither a father nor a mother;
Unlike the body that is its image in the world of matter.
Whatever relationship in the physical world the body can claim;
The spirit doth neither a relationship nor counterpart maintain.
In not having a father or mother, the spirit is unique;
It stands upon its heights of dignity and loftiness of rank.
The spirit neither descends into the body nor ascends out of it;
It neither doth enter into the body nor make an exit from it.
Both entry and egression are physical qualities;
Physical form is the talisman of divine bounties.

The various physical forms are the veils of innate unity;
The physical world stands mounted on the pillar of fantasy.
Once the covering veil hath been removed from thy vision,
Thou wilt become restless, inflamed with fiery devotion.
What thou wilt see will render thee a homeless, aimless vagabond;
Seeing the realm of the spirits will leave thee bewildered and stunned.
Thou wilt become totally attached to the Adored One's Beauty,
Having now been chained to the love of the Heart's Desire completely.

The people of faith are those who are blinded by no covering
And can see, in the deepest core of their hearts, the Sun is shining.
The people of profanity are those who in veils are all covered;
They are not at all conscious of God; they are spiritually dead.

II THE REPOSITORY OF MYSTERIES: TRANSLATED TEXT

That was the reason that the Sovereign of Ḥijáz[1] *said:*
All the veils will gradually from the hearts be removed.
Little by little, the obstructing screen will be eliminated;
The mystery of 'If the veil be removed'[2] *is thus explicated.*
That sugar-tongued Beloved, by tearing asunder the veil
Of one secret, the sense of faith and blasphemy did reveal.

If thou canst fathom this as the meaning of 'splitting the moon',
Then, indeed, thou art a man of true knowledge and comprehension.
Otherwise, thou art enveloped in the veil of vain imaginings;
Do thou try to grasp this, if thou art a man of inner meanings.
Otherwise, thou art ignorant of the innate reality;
No wonder thou art not able to unravel the mystery.
Anyone who is shrouded in vain imaginings and illusions,
Is in darkness, in thick darkness, in the pitch black darkness of delusions!
In the same way that the unwise person does not act with sagacity;
Likewise the people of true faith do not indulge in immorality.

The lovers do not express anything but affectionate words;
And sweethearts do not behave in any way but to charm the hearts.
Whatever the chosen ones do is also of goodness outstanding
Because, in each of them, the lights of God glow throughout their whole being.

Nothing ever emitted from Bahá but Bahá's effulgence;
Nothing ever came out of Azal[3] *save his dark evil actions.*
Likewise from the Branch of Bahá nothing emanates but light;
Nothing but faithfulness emanates from the people of faith.

In joyful mood thou canst not sleep through thine exhilaration;
When grieved, thou liest wakeful in thine couch of agitation.
One is from joyfulness awake, the other due to grief;
Behold! Both have the same effect: that of keeping you from sleep.

O thou informed one! Examine carefully both grief and exultation;
Observe this with thine inner eye to gage the effect of each condition.
When thou dost feel great joy, thine eyes will fill with tears of emotion;
When deep in grief thou dost moan with gushing tears of lamentation.
What is this secret and how to explain the strange enigma!

---

[1] Referring to Prophet Muḥammad Who is recognized as the Arabian Prophet.
[2] Referring to Qur'án 50:22.
[3] Referring to Yaḥyá surnamed Azal, the half-brother of Bahá'u'lláh, notorious for his evil deeds and plots to kill Baha'u'llah. Yaḥyá succeeded in poisoning Baha'u'llah. From then on Bahá'u'lláh suffered from shaking hands when writing.

How can the same effect come from two conflicting criteria!
Likewise, in the soprano and the bass voice, there is a strange connection;
If I were to unravel it I would plunge the world into commotion.
If I had a bosom friend with whom my secrets to confide,
I would blow into a hollow reed, telling all to be conveyed.

Well is it that the secret state of the lovers
Be narrated through the love-stories of others.
Behold, both brightness and darkness are rebellious;
One is caused by light; the other by fire is caused.
The light of faith is rebellious because love its flame doth fuel;
The fire of envy is rebellious, being kindled by evil.
One stirs thee to alertness; the other lulls thee to a false sense of security;
The light of the one true God is not limited by either peculiarity.

Know thou, that there are myriads of examples like these ones;
Try to figure out the others by using thine own sense.
One is obstinate in being self-seeking and haughty;
The other is unyielding in his love for the Beauty.

O comrade! Behold there are mysteries within mysteries;
Thou art becoming aware of the subtle intricacies.
Many a devil in the guise of a human appeareth;
Therefore, one should not shake hands with everyone that one meeteth.
God, the exalted One, hath awakened thee to watch out for the baited snare;
So, open thy eyes; walk not blindly lest thou fall into the pit; do be aware!

O my dear! Let thyself not be deceived by the seemingly pious divines;
Do not be confused by this bold statement; listen and this thou wilt recognize.
Thou art well-aware of how much the Chosen Ones suffered;
What shameful words vicious people against them uttered.

Lo! They demanded that the Absolute Ones be constrained;
That the Chosen Ones were but men like themselves, they maintained.
They argued that the Chosen Ones should meet their expected conditions;
They insisted that They appear in accord with their expectations.
They told the Chosen Ones: "You are not better a creature than us;
If you are, then you must prove it by performing miracles."

God hath said that the Prophets are established on the highest throne;
God hath opened the door for us to realize Their high station.

II The Repository of Mysteries: Translated text

The wise Sultan hath made this patent to all of humankind:
God created men and angels and, to worship Him, designed.
The aim of man's creation was for man to worship God;
To know God was its purpose, and its fruit was love for God.
But, not having seen in the Divine Envoys the pure inner reality,
They saw in Those, for Whom the world came into being, only mortality.
O God, help us to acquire awareness, courtesy and graciousness;
For, of the favour of the Lord, are dispossessed the discourteous ones.

O my dear! I would like to narrate to you a tale
To warn you that people will be tested without fail.
A farmer had a dairy cow, which he tethered inside his barn;
A lion ate the cow. Then, in its place, for a rest it lay down.
The farmer returned to the barn later when it was already dark;
Quite unsuspecting, he fearlessly started to rub the lion's back.
The lion smiled: "He rubs my back with no fear
As he thinks I am the cow lying here.
If there was more light so that he could see my tawny back,
He would get such a fright; he would die of a heart attack."
To pat a lion, no farmer would have had the foolhardiness;
He never guessed it was a lion's back he had dared to caress.

O my friend! The lion may well pretend to be slumbering;
Be wary; thy life by rash deeds do not be endangering.

To test humankind, that most sanctified Soul, the Prophet,
May appear helpless, poorly clad and greatly afflicted.
When Tartar horsemen set out to raid a village, ere their attack,
They nail their horses' shoes on back to front so as not to be tracked.

Here is the reason the King of Power, Might and Kindness
Hath said that His pleasure is in the pleasure of His creatures. [1]
If thou dost desire to have a pleasant character and charming nature,
Behave in a gracious way and never indulge in a sour-temper.
O son! Know thou that this is the way that each true wayfarer hath trod;
With such sweet manners thou, too, canst follow the spiritual path to God.
O my comrade! Treat the people of the world with genuine love;
Open thine inner eyes; walk with clear vision on this subtle path.

O Thou, the Absolute One! O Thou, the Ancient Sovereign!
My impassioned love for Thee brimmeth over in my being.

---

[1] Referring to the statement of Bahá'u'lláh in *The Hidden Words*, Persian No. 43.

The heart of the world is radiant from Thy light's conferral;
The souls of the Chosen Ones are nourished by Thy bestowal.
Aid us so that we are able the nature of Thy light to recognize;
To follow Thine Elect Ones both in our private and in our public lives.

Hearken to this, O thou who, on the spiritual path, art journeying;
That thou mayest uncover the hidden mystery of the Sovereigns.
O thou who, with all thine heart and soul, dost seek the love of God;
Hearken well to the secret that sugared lips have spread abroad.
From the outer eyes of man the Chosen Ones are hidden;
Thou must open thine eye of discernment to perceive them.
In the visible world a hidden mystery is borne on every forehead;
Every single atom of the world of creation is a sign of Godhead.
Behold! Moses received a Revelation from Almighty God;
To disclose to Him a secret, the Knower of all mysteries said:
"O Moses! Beneath the ruins of an allegorical wall, concealed,
A treasure is buried, which is in fact the secret yet to be revealed."

Every non-essential is for the inner essential an emblem;
Likewise, every transient form enshrines within it a hidden wisdom.
When, in the outer form, the Original Cause we come across,
The outer form fades; we see only the Original Cause.
The Original Cause is that, which bringeth life abundantly;
The form is the bridge that leadeth to inward reality.
The Original Cause, being the living waters, thus life giveth;
The form is the veil covering the face of the hidden Spirit.

The Manifestation of God is, of the Primal Cause, the sign;
He hath taken the outer form and freed it from all that doth confine.
That was the reason that the Most Holy, Righteous Spirit of God
In the garment of a human being upon the earth hath trod.
Since God wisheth to have intimate communion with us;
Repeatedly His Spirit robes Itself in human guise.
It is not mere human though the human form It hath put on;
He befriends all the creatures while looking just like other men.
The All-Glorious God created man in His image and own likeness
That is why, in a Perfect Man, God on earth becometh manifest.

But do you know that, not so long ago, the Voice of Love was raised
In Shiraz, the city of love, where He unveiled His radiant Face?
He uncovered his luminous Countenance in Shiraz;
The entire world thrilled to the blazing forth of His visage.
He is the One Who, in all Scriptures and every Age, was promised;
To the people of innate wisdom, He this secret had disclosed.

How pleasingly He hath unveiled the Face of hidden mysteries,
That heart-ravishing Beloved, the Soul of souls, the Beauteous.

II The Repository of Mysteries: Translated text

He tuned up His harp to play the chords of Love's celestial melodies;
He filled to the brim the whole creation with His unveiled mysteries.

Not to fail to recognize the coming Revelation, He made emphasis;
He, Whose innate reality hath surpassed the universe entire, spoke thus:
To recognize the Sun of Bahá when it rises and shines forth,
It is sufficient that you hear His call when it is raised on earth.
His call sufficeth all as soon as raised between the earth and heaven;
To that sweet celestial Voice resounding, all give your ears and hearken.

When a thirsty person hears a call saying; "Here is water!"
He cannot help being eager; towards it he will hasten.
O ye who have ears to hear! Know that the people of love do likewise;
Every lover hastens to join the lovers of God in their congress.

There are certain common features seen with every Revelation;
Those elements thou wilt perceive with sharp eyes of observation.
There are four signs with every Manifestation of God;
These signs are the proofs of the reality of each Lord.
Hearken attentively to the explanation of these four signs,
Thus to understand the mystery and secret of the Loved Ones.

Firstly, to proclaim His message, He raiseth a clarion call;
His voice echoes from heaven above to the earth down below.
He claims: "Lo! I am the representative of the heavenly Father;
Behold! Observe ye God's effulgent lights that from my Countenance glitter.
The light of the unity of God beams from My whole Being;
Truly, My words and My voice are all His, not of My doing.
Rejoice! I am vouchsafed upon humankind as the hidden Paragon;
I am He Who infuseth new spirit at the start of each new eon.
I am the treasure of the unity of God, bathed in light perpetual."
The coming of a Revelation is a new era's sign inaugural.

So, the first evidence of the truth of a new Revelation is
The call that He raises; the second is the new Scripture that He brings.
This is for life's protection and for the redemption of all humans;
It doth illumine all humanity with its celestial guidance.
Thirdly, He stands steadfast in the face of opposition and persecution;
He delivers his message in the spirit of great love and dedication.
Fourthly, many people become His devoted believers;
He doth breathe the Divine spirit into all the world's peoples.

He is the celestial authority for the entire human race;
His Revelation inducteth the Day of righteousness and justice.
When the Day of Resurrection and Divine Justice us assembles

The Valley of Contentment

At the threshold of the Creator of human beings and angels,
I bring into His presence my heart that is scorched with love's passion;
I will cry out: "O Thou, the central Orb of the new Revelation,
O Thou the Full-moon of Beauty! This scorched heart that I have
Beareth me witness that I have been faithful to Thy love."

Now, I wish to speak again of the beginning and the end;
About the Beloved of Shiraz a point I would extend.
Be careful! Do not say to others that God, the All-righteous,
Hath taken the robe of one member of the human species.
Since, as our Guide, He wished to associate with us more closely;
His Spirit hath, therefore, put on a human garment repeatedly.
It is a test for humans that the Most Pure Spirit should here dwell
In penury, clad in ragged clothes or with a torn shirt lapel.

The Lord of the New Age, for a reason, said this:
"My good pleasure is the pleasure of my creatures."
For this, in the spirit of unity, the Sovereign of Righteousness,
In the art of showing love to all men hath, therefore, instructed us.

Thus the Manifestations of God unfurl and hoist love's pennon;
And sow the seeds of love in the inner soul of every human.
Love doth relieve thee from double-vision and every doubt;
It doth smooth thy way into the valley of certitude.
Love transformeth an enemy into a friend;
One becomes, as Abraham, reliant on God.
Love made the very breath of Christ quickening and life-giving;
Love transforms a ruling king into a servant attending.
Love is an elixir; let it touch thy soul with its transforming potential;
Thus thou wilt know not just the nature of thy body but of thy soul as
*   well.*
The only healing medicine for lovers is love itself;
Love doth slay the lover, therefore, from whence cometh all that grief?
O wise man! To say there is anything other than love is a myth;
If thou dost possess anything more precious than love, give me a
*   glimpse.*

Once again the fire of separation from Him hath blazed up high;
How long should this handful of dust stay smouldering as love's sigh?
Another tongue of fire hath leapt within my inner soul
So fierce, it could the whole world burn as but a lump of coal.
The flame of love consumeth the dales of a hundred 'Mount Sinai's;
Through love's blaze, myriad well-built fire temples rise as smoke to
*   the skies!*

Gaze upon thy self through love's eye of observation;
Thou wilt be filled with grief at thine inner condition.

Thou wilt see in thy self mountains of shortcomings so gross;
Their corrosion leaves thine associates riled and harassed.

Love doth elevate thee to the heaven of righteousness;
Love carries thee safely past the pit of ungraciousness.
What is of greater value than love on this earth?
Nothing is better than love; know thou its great worth.
Love raises thee to the summit of the soul from which to gleam,
For it sends thee soaring high above into the placeless realm.
Ponder on the preordained and certain human destiny;
Love renders thee ever-mindful of mortality's mystery.

The truth of thy love grows together with good character development;
Abandon thou empty words, then, and let good actions be thine adornment.
Love doth assist thee to enter into the valley of trustworthiness;
It purges thee from the defilements of perfidy and deceitfulness.
Love doth save thee from the degradation of arrogance;
It makes thee comprehend the reality of justice.
The fire of love purifies thee from all unseen corruption;
Like aloes wood, thou art ablaze with fragrant emanation.
Love opens thine inner eye to the secrets of the universe;
Love helps thee grasp the meanings that lie hid within a sacred verse.
Love makes thee hear God's Voice calling thee to return to Him;
So that thou might be completely freed from this mudhut grim.
Pass beyond the mausoleum of earthly life for but a moment,
So that in God's domain of reunion thou canst soar in wonderment.
Love assists thee to attract the good-pleasure of the Beloved;
From all else save the one true God, it instils in thee detachment.
To break free of the chains of thine existence, Love doth bring thee aid;
Towards the court of joyful reunion with God it doth thee lead.
So deeply doth Love absorb thee, that thy free will is lost entire!
No one else dwells within thine inner being save thine Heart's Desire.

The fire of His love doth render thee blissfully exuberant;
But do not, then, disclose thine inner feelings to the ignorant.
Love opens thine inner eyes to discern the Manifestation of God;
It enables thee to perceive the divine Friend however He be robed.
Love leadeth thee to the threshold of the Best-Beloved;
Faith shines forth within thine heart as love's path thou dost tread.
Love enables thee to give thy life, and thine existence forfeit;
Then, thou wilt be honoured in the presence of the Lord Exalted.
Love lets thee leave the world behind, with all thine heart to cry:
"O Source of my love-pangs! O Lord of my heart's agony!"

The Valley of Contentment

Love makes thine eyes a window to disclose the secrets in thy soul enshrined;
It maketh of a hundred worlds a rose-garden of mysteries divine.
Love leads thee to the fountainhead of eternal life to quaff;
It relieves thee from the distress of grief and the pain of death.
Love directs thee onward beyond both the worlds to pass;
It draws thee on into the field of foolhardiness.

If, to this theme thou hast been drawn to know a little more,
Then hasten! The Sixth Valley read to find what lies in store.
O thou noble one! The Fifth Valley hath come to its finale;
Peace be unto thee. Now is the time to traverse the Sixth Valley.

The Sixth Valley
THE VALLEY OF WONDERMENT

Hail! O Thou, most wondrous Mystery and Guide;
Hail! O Thou, Who art the lovers' loving Friend.
Hail! O Thou, our Lord; the Object of our wish Thou art;
Hail! O Thou, Healer of every lacerated heart!
Hail! O Thou, the Sovereign of both the land and sea;
Hail! O Thou, the Leading Light for lovers seeking Thee!
Hail! O Thou, the Sanctified above all signs and traits;
Hail! O Thou, Who granteth life to the entire human race!
Hail! O Thou, the Burning Torch in the mystics' gathering;
Hail! O Thou, the Lord above the whole domain of being!
Hail! O Thou, the Lodestar of all the people of devotion;
Hail! O Thou, for those of faith, their Point of adoration!
Hail! O thou, the Nightingale that warbles in love's garden;
Hail! O thou, who yearneth for the rapture of love's heaven.
Hail! O thou, who art drawn hither to Bahá's radiance;
Hail! O thou, the wayfarer who seeketh Bahá's Countenance.

O wayfarer! Further mysteries of God give ear thou to unearth;
Peruse the mystic book, a rose-garden of the poetry of truth.
If thou art of the meaning true of the word Bahá aware,
Why hast thou closed thy God-seeing eye that meaning to forswear?
Since the word Bahá denoteth an illuminating, glorious light,
Enter thou this flower-garden if its nightingale thou art by right.

The Sacred Leader of the entire human race is Bahá;
The Heavenly Sovereign of all humans and angels is Bahá.
Our Divine Cup-bearer offers thee the chalice of eternal life;
O comrade! To attain immortality, hasten a cup to quaff.

My inner ear of a sudden heard love's celestial Voice call from above;
I packed my bag, being resolute to go to the dwelling-place of love.
O my friend, if thou wouldst follow me unguided on love's path!
Know thou that any clamour, confused and void, must be bypassed.
O my comrade! Now is the time to take this taxing journey;
If thou shouldst wish my company, I beg thee, come and join me!

Whilst thy free will thou still dost wield, the need for zealous deeds is dire.
Gird up thy loins, then, if to glimpse the Friend divine thou dost aspire.

II THE REPOSITORY OF MYSTERIES: TRANSLATED TEXT

Hearken to His voice, which ringeth in the ears; 'tis God's own harmony;
The voice doth spring not from the reed but from Him Who pipes the melody.
Instantly, thou wilt be trapped in total fascination;
So, exert thyself while thou still canst claim thine own volition.
In the next hour, mayhap, thou wilt not know whether it be night or day;
In this all-important Day of God, seize thine opportunity.
But as long as thou art in the noose of earthly fancies caught,
How canst thou trek with ease this path, which is so with hardship fraught!

When the venerable man[1] *spoke of seven scrolls,*
The words that he expressed were like most precious pearls.
Through the seven cities of love, Attar his way did wend;
He followed every bend of every lane of wonderment.

The Prophet of Islam referred to seven heavens, and said:
"I traversed them all while the divine mysteries were unveiled.
My ascension to heaven brought me to the threshold of the God of Might;
Many mysteries are treasured in that Sanctuary of Absolute Light."

If thou hast not experienced how spell-binding is love's power,
Find out this secret from the one who is a fevered lover.
Dost thou aspire to join the ones, who speak of secrets mystical?
Then shut the door on scholarship that is false or superficial.
O pen, disclose the mysteries of the vale of wonderment;
Again narrate in detail of the beginning and the end.

The person who plunges into wonderment's ocean,
Marvels, and is ever amazed to stupefaction.
Whosoever in this most great ocean hath been all immersed,
He becometh adept, creative, virtuous and well-versed.
He is in wonder; his wonder grows with every moment;
His wonderment renders him besotted and dumbfounded.
As the effulgence of the Ancient Beauty flashes with dazzling lustre,
His astonishment and his amazement are increasing ever faster.
He observes with inner vision; his amazement multiplies;
A multitude of vistas appear before his inner eyes.

---

[1] Referring to Faríd al-Dín 'Aṭṭár', a great Persian mystic poet who composed The Conference of the Birds *(Manṭiqu'ṭ-Ṭayr)*, an epic poem in which he beautifully describes how a group of birds travel seven valleys to reach their destination. He might have been the first to use the allegory of seven valleys for treading the spiritual path.

In the utmost poverty, he sees the essence of prosperity;
He finds no trace of destitution in weakness or humility
He observes it is the wealthy who, in fact, are those deprived;
And the essence of privation doth control the world entire.
At times, in diversity, actual unity he spies;
At times, as the very ears, he perceives the actual eyes.
At times he sees abasement in what counts as earthly majesty;
At times the brightest light appears to him as dark obscurity.
At times discredit seems to him as but the highest reverence;
At times he seeth darkness naught but as a dazzling radiance.
At times neither diversity nor unity—nor his own self—he sees;
With utter humbleness, engrossed he is in only the All-Beauteous.

I have lost my mind; henceforth, I am quite as one besotted,
To myself I am estranged—my ego obliterated.
Beyond the grasp of intellect, lovers are soaring high above;
Therefore, do not criticize those who are so crazily in love.
Once again this wonderment hath made me surpass the boundaries;
I am immersed in madness, and caught in love's all-fevered frenzies.
At times in leaping flames I see the glowing Face of the Beloved;
As from before my inner vision myriad veils have been removed.
To whichever region I gaze, I see the Loved One scintillating;
The light of His true knowledge is my inner self illuminating.
Since, in the unity of God, all the distinctive features disappear;
The light of inner Essence is, from every aspect, manifestly clear;

Wonderment is unclouded vision, not speculation nor mere notion;
It is all ecstasy, blissful joy, with neither toil nor irritation.
The highest level of servitude is to love God with devotion;
A true lover attains eternal life by self-annihilation.
The lovers of His Face have no desire but to meet their Beloved;
They have no other thought but to be with the Loved One reunited.

The personage who attains the most great ocean and into it plunges,
Is the embodiment of all attributes, and is utterly matchless.
In humans and in angels, God's mystery is everywhere;
The story of His secrets from all created things we hear.
His mystery is apparent everywhere and in every assembly;
Gracious God! O Thou our Lord! Enshrined in all hearts is His mystery.
Even when His lips are sealed and He speaketh not,
His story is well-known, and everywhere is told.
Day and night, all the creatures are engaged in praising Him;
He is omnipresent but most people cannot grasp Him.

We are as caged and hooded birds, deprived of distant vision;
Thus for the Solomon divine we have no recognition.

II The Repository of Mysteries: Translated text

The divine Solomon is present before the eyes of all;
But like a prestidigitator, He veils our eyes at will.
We strive, out of our utter blindness and utmost ignorance,
To persecute the purest souls who are God's dearly-loved ones.

This world is like a mountain full of the echoes of His Voice;
His call, which from Him proceeded, back to Him reverberates.
He is the ultimate desire of the world and every creature;
Know thou: the entire cosmos echoes back to Him His overture.
He encompasses the entire universe yet is apart from all;
For the wayfarer He is, at once, the yearning and the final goal.

When heart and soul are inebriated by the wine of eternity;
He is the Wine, the Cup and the very Cup-bearer in all unity.
His loftiness alloweth no other being as His partner;
So we know He is the only One both hidden and apparent.
"To turn away from God it is a deadly sin", a mystic said;
It is a great transgression to see anything else but God.

O dear one! How could duality exist in the world of creation?
There existeth neither thou-ness nor is there we-ness at this echelon.
He himself is the One who is attracted and He is the One who attracts;
He himself is the One who is seeking and He is the One being sought.
At times He billows as the waves; at times He is the very ocean;
If thou hast an inner eye, look through it to see the waves in motion.
At times, being directionless, there is no way that leads to Him;
He is sanctified beyond any attribute that is ascribed to Him.
He is the very inner Essence, beyond any name or quality;
No one can ever obtain knowledge of the depth of His reality.

Once again the wonderment aroused in me an ardour all-intense;
A hundred 'Mount Sinai's start to blaze from this celestial heat immense.
Once again, astonishment hath carried off my reason and my soul;
The celestial Cup-bearer hath poured a fiery wine into my bowl.
Once again, it sent me soaring into another heaven;
It breathed another life into my body's frame to leaven.
Once again, within my heart, a whirlwind of wonderment began to brew;
Beyond the radius of speech or hearing all the mysteries withdrew.

Wonderment hath caused my mind and intellect to dissipate;
Once again, my blood is broiling from love's heat so passionate.
For me there now remaineth neither rest nor patience nor endurance;
A rushing torrent swept me up and washed away my residence.
Being mesmerized, entranced and now driven quite to madness;
I am heading for the wastelands to wander in the wilderness.

Love robbed me of comfort and rendered me a vagrant;
For the aching of my love, there is no healing treatment.
Thinking of my Loved One, my very being doth inflame;
The shaft of love from my Beloved broke my heart in twain.
My broken heart so many tears of blood hath shed for Thee,
That even mine own heart-ache feeleth sympathy for me.
Bravo, O painful yearning! Thou art my healing cure-all;
Thou art the close companion of my life, my heart and soul.

Of painful yearning for Thee, a tiny share for me sufficeth;
Anyone who hath felt no pain of yearning hath deprived himself.
The anguish of yearning robs the lover of all patience and quietude;
The pain of longing for God is better than any other saintly good.

A breeze from Thy vineyard brought its fresh intoxicating odour;
The broken-hearted lovers were drunk with it and linked together.
When the lover tasted but a droplet from the chalice of Thy wine,
So intoxicated was he that his life he did, to Thee, consign.

Take a sip from His chalice; remove the garment of existence;
Enkindle a fire in thy heart; let tears of blood gush from thine eyes.
O my heart! Break thyself free from every fettering bond;
Thus a heart can be inspired by the compassionate Lord.
Enter thou this garden to behold its beauteous flowers;
Lo! With what blazing ardour circle round Him the lovers!
Each one heaves a heart-felt sigh and utters words of great intensity:
"O Thou Beloved of the world! Make my life a sacrifice unto Thee."
The burning heat of love touched the heart and caused its life's blood
     to be shed;
The wise man experienced such inflaming love that all his wisdom fled.

O bleeding heart! Raise thou thine head up out of thine amazement;
Inspect thy self with care to diagnose thy serious ailment.
Describe again how much thy yearning causes thee dire agony;
Thou art mounted on a steed that can to the heavens carry thee.
O my heart! Why dost thou endlessly heave such ardent sighs?
How long can this handful of dust seethe in this scorching blaze?
O heart! Burn in the fire of love; then gather up the ash;
Hold it in thy hand and inhale the sweet fragrance it has.
The shirt that came from Egypt, full of Joseph was its redolence; [1]
O heart! These are ashes but they bear the Loved One's fragrance.

---

[1] This refers to the story of Joseph who, unknown to his family, became the ruler of Egypt. Jacob, the father of Joseph, had shed so many tears when separated from Joseph that he was blinded. However, when Jacob smelled the fragrance of Joseph on his shirt, Jacob's sight was restored. See Qur'án 12:69, 84, 93–6.

Use it as a collyrium for thine eyes, thus, insight thou might gain
Thus to an image of the King thine inner vision may attain.

Once again, the King appeared with the greatest splendour and majesty;
O my bleeding heart! Take heed; this is a rare and prized moment for thee.
Oh! What a wondrous Countenance! It shineth with dazzling light;
Oh! What a blazing glare! It could set all Mount Sinai alight.
Oh! What wonderful ashes! From the pure Spirit cometh their energy;
O my heart! Say it again: "May my life be a sacrifice unto Thee."
O my heart! Exert the utmost effort; a ceaseless call doth beckon;
This is the summons: "A lover hath no choice other than to hasten."
O! What blessed embers—redolent of the Beloved!
Gushing from out mine eyes are relentless tears of blood.
Oh! What fragrant ashes! Both musk and ambergris are put to shame;
Oh! What precious residue! Like a prized pearl, its equal none can claim.
Oh! How fortunate thou art! Thou art dust but reflecting light of purity;
O heart! Cry out again and say: "May my life be a sacrifice unto Thee."
It is wonder upon wonder; it maketh me totally enamoured;
On this level, nothing can be depicted or even be imagined.

Observe thine insignificance and heave a sigh from thine heart's inner depths;
Be humble and see thine own self as nothing more than a handful of chaff.
Let the hindering veil of thine egoistic self be razed from all existence;
And thine essence be annihilated, being as naught before His Essence.
O my heart! Burn thou! How pleasant it is to burn in love's conflagration;
How wonderful! This blazing fire is the daily bread of my nutrition.
Lo! Thy fire is flaring up in a spectacular performance;
How joyfully the blazing flames play as they leap around and dance.
Make haste in thy search for the Beloved, and be prepared to be astounded;
Let thy soul melt away until with the Beloved thou art reunited.

O my heart! Do not refuse thy neck to be lassoed by love's lariat;
Thou wouldst not to be deemed utterly worthless by the people of insight.
Let thy breast be the target for the Divine Archer's dart;
Enshrine the pearl of yearning, as in its shell, in thine heart.

Abandon thy free will and submit thy self to His will fully,
So that the fire of thy love for the Beloved might redeem thee.
Augment the light of thine eyes with the light of the people of
*   perception;*
That, freed from thine ego, thou canst see the reality of creation.

Firstly, be speedy and agile in the path of thy spiritual quest;
Thou must soar like a phoenix to reach the heights of the firmament's
*   crest.*
O intellect! Be astounded and silent in that arena of wonder;
Roll up thy book of intellectual concepts! Be free of them! Fly yonder.
O thou, uninitiated one! Turn thy back unto thy lower self;
So that thou canst spread thy wings high in the celestial sphere of God
*   Himself.*
O heart! To be touched by love for the Beloved thou art blessed,
Neither by mind nor by imagination can He be expressed.

My heart cherishes Thee and my inner eye wishes to gaze upon Thee;
Reason is diving deep in the ocean, searching through the sea-bed for
*   Thee.*
Thy black ringlet hath turned my bright daytime into night-time
*   darkness;*
My body sickens in its longing for Thy beauteous Countenance.
Like a moth drawn to the flame, my heart is circling around Thee;
In its keenness to fly to Thy Face, it circles frantically.

My beloved Joseph was abducted from Canaan and brought unto
*   Egypt;*
In separation from him, my eyes shed tears of blood and were of vision
*   stripped.*
O friends! I cry for help, my heart is in anguish and I keep weeping;
The flood of grief has devastated the foundation of my being.
Let my head be covered in the dust; let my house in ruins be;
I have no hope that anyone will hear my cry or can help me.
Then, His light again shed its radiance on me and my heart hath
*   become blessed!*
O Beloved of heart and soul! May my life be unto Thee sacrificed!

O heart! Thou art bleeding; thou art stunned and bemused!
Thou hast become adorned with the breath of the Beloved.
O my bleeding heart! Out of thy maze of wonderment, raise thine
*   eyes;*
I implore thee to look at me that thou might with me sympathize.
O my heart! Wearied to the point of death, I am chasing after thee;
Remember! In the end, naught but a handful of paltry dust are we.

II The Repository of Mysteries: Translated text

Take heed! Where has thine intelligence fled; art thou bereft of reason?
Why, with every passing moment, doth seethe and simmer thine emotion?
Thou hast been my close companion in every situation;
I ask thee to look at me, and judge my piteous condition.

This sore-hearted one doth shed tears, and doth groan in his torment;
Why seemeth he more besotted with every passing moment?
My weeping and wailing is of no use; no result doth it produce;
By my groaning and tears, his roiling and raving are only increased.

O reason! Be quiet; this passionate love hath quite besotted him;
Leave him! Let him go; he cannot be fettered; he is a vagabond.
He is so love-struck by his Beloved that his free will hath gone astray;
It is better that thou desist from thine advise; let him go his own way.
He is so spellbound that he cannot distinguish between friend and foe;
How long wilt thou waste thy breath calling to this mad lover! Let him go!
So drunken on love he is that, to rules, he payeth no attention;
He is not willing to give ear to surrogate, synthetic contention.

When a heart hath become besotted in a passionate love;
The entire world with all its artifacts becometh a myth.
"Love's a stranger to earth and heaven too;
In him are lunacies seventy-and-two." [1]

O heart in quest of God! Hearken to the celestial melody;
To detach thyself from all else save God, it is summoning thee.
Gird up thy loins to exert the utmost efforts in thy quest;
Like a phoenix, soar on wings of love in the heavens' compass.
Make such haste in thy search so that thy feet touch not the ground;
As thine own ego doth fade, thou wilt be ever more spellbound.
Release thy feet from the stocks that keep thee earth-bound, and fetter thee;
Remember the counsel of thy Lord, Bahá, to soar high and free.

If thine interest hath been aroused by this book's titled designation,
O wayfarer! Hearken thou attentively to our explanation.
If thou dost cherish within thine heart an ardent love's anxieties,
Then pertinent to thee is "The Repository of Mysteries".
Of "The Repository of Mysteries", I am not the author;
Who am I? Only an impassioned lover, thrilled and filled with ardour.

---

[1] Jalálu'd-Dín Rúmí (AD 1207–1273), called Mawláná (our Master), is the greatest of all Persian Sufi poets, and founder of the Mawlawí "whirling" dervish order.

How would I be able to expound the inner mysteries of love?
How should I, a fleeting shadow, illustrate the effulgence of love?
It is the repository of mysteries of all else save God;
Know thou, it is the celestial melody of love's ardent path trod.

O Bahá! Thou Who revives the hearts, and the souls revitalizes!
Thou hast unveiled and made perceptible all the hidden mysteries.
O Bahá, the All-knower! Thou art aware of the mystery of the heart!
O Thou, King of Generosity! O Thou who dost cover our every fault!
A grain of Thy loving-kindness is sufficient to heal the entire earth;
Bestow upon us Thy favour; Thou Thyself dost lead us on the straight path.

O son! How shouldst thou know of Bahá's inner reality?
Alas! Thy heart is bereft of His effulgent lights' bounty.
Anyone whose heart is purged and illumined by His radiant aura,
Cannot help but cry out from the very depths of his heart: O Bahá!
Thou hast not understood the mystery of His Manifestation;
Thou hast not trodden the path of love leading to His Habitation.
Thou hast heard the name of Bahá without knowing its implication;
That is why thou art still meandering away from His Revelation.
Seclude thyself and, in the innermost core of thy heart's penetration,
Ponder, to discern the inscrutability of His Designation.
Then thou wilt cry out of the depth of thy heart: O Bahá! Thou art my Lord;
On me, the light of Thy love a true understanding of Thee hath bestowed.
His Being hath given life to our being and substance to our existence;
Our entity is less than a small spark in its transient insignificance.
We are all but puny mortals; while immortal is His inner essence;
All creation undergoes death and decay save His shining Countenance.

Hast thou never heard through thine inner ear that the angel of death
May, at any moment, come to thee to remove thy life in stealth.
As we do not think 'we' hath no reality, we say 'we' proudly;
But, since, 'we' must pass away, why do we even mention the word 'we'?
We do not realize that our arrogant ego will eventually
Bring us deprivation of our potential bliss of joy and ecstasy.
We must take heed to avoid all egoistic arrogance;
The mouth that boasts through selfishness—let it stay closed and silenced.
Chop down and totally uproot all unbecoming selfish arrogance;
Look at thine acts; ask thyself if they conform to God's Laws and Ordinance!

II THE REPOSITORY OF MYSTERIES: TRANSLATED TEXT

No man can root out his ego without experiencing the pain of yearning;
A person so deprived cannot be regarded as a true human being.
Blessed is the soul that, from its lower self, is set free;
He hath learnt self-annihilation's innate mystery.
Without the loving-kindness of God, it is impossible to achieve this;
So thou must ever yearn to receive divine confirmation thee to assist.
One drop of God's divine grace with which one hath been favoured
Is better than a sea of knowledge that one hath acquired.

If, to a soul, God should, out of His favour, His divine grace bequeath
That one could traverse from the beginning to the end in one breath.
Nine firmaments appeared like a light diffuser before his inner eyes;
For this reason, a door was opened in his soul, filling him with awed surprise.
Hundreds of thousands of light years, in just one breath, can be traversed;
The lover can, at once, cross that span as if riding a Pegasus.

O Thou, the Absolute One! O Thou, the Sultan of every mystery!
Both the worlds are ever engaged in supplicating and praying to Thee.
O Thou, the peerless, the incomparable, the matchless Sovereign!
Thy grace is ceaselessly energizing the whole world of being.
O thou, the All-Forgiving! O Thou, the Main-spring of Generosity!
O Thou, the Ocean of Light! Do not deprive us of Thy loving bounty.
Oh! Thy love doth motivate the entire world and fills it with ebullience;
Hearts are enchanted; and astounded is every mind and intelligence.

Oh! Once again, I inhaled the intoxicating fragrance of Thy love;
It made me totally forsake my own self and in Thee be all absorbed.
Once again, my passionate desire for Thee hath utterly destroyed me;
Once again, I have lost control of my heart and my mind for want of Thee.
No more do I hold the reins of my life; I have no free choice
Except to expose the secrets and rend the covering shrouds.

I wish to uncover the hidden secrets and speak of these;
I desire to entirely disclose the ancient mysteries.
Love hath completely absorbed and enchanted me—and to such a degree
That it seems I have never lived in the world and have no identity.
I am neither conscious of my state nor of the world around me;
No one is my intimate friend, and no one seeks my company.
Neither with unity nor with diversity am I cognizant;
Neither with the East nor yet with the West am I at all conversant.

I am aware neither of the descending slope nor of the rising hill;
Neither do I distinguish what is real from what is only virtual.
I am detached from all else save God; my ego is obliterated;
I feel wonder upon wonder; I am totally annihilated.
Lo! I know not what I am saying or of what realm I am speaking;
I am lured by enchanting eyes that disturb the calm of my being.
Do I draw near Him by my own will or am I drawn involuntarily?
What the secret attraction of my Beloved is, I can tell nobody.

Wonderment hath dawned! Whither hath reason disappeared?
Yea, yea! Reason runs berserk when wonders have appeared.
This hath nothing to do with reason; it is the work of wonderment;
Other than wonderment, there are also limits of mind and judgement.
Sell off thy reason and, of wonderment, make acquisition;
Reason is but supposition while wonderment is vision.

If thou wishest to partake of the pleasure of love's excitement;
Leave behind reason; enter thou into the dale of wonderment.
O man of insight! Open thy inner eyes to wonderment's realm;
Then let all those dazzling flashes of wonderment thee overwhelm.
Close thou thine outer eyes and open, instead, thine inner eye;
Then, in the seed, thou wilt see the grown tree, reaching to the sky.
Since, in thy wonderment, the entrance door is opened to thy very
    soul;
Thou wilt see, in a tiny atom, the sun and the solar system whole.
In wonderment, the beginning and end are but one moment;
Thou wilt find the secrets of an ocean within a droplet.
Nay, nay! In wonderment, there is neither beginning nor an end;
Beginning and end are seen by outer eyes in the outer world.

The sea billowed, the creek and river merged into one;
Wonderment flashed; 'hither' and 'thither' were in unison.
Reunion with God dawned for duality had gone;
Love had stepped in; freedom of choice had no place thereon.

O dear one! Thou hast observed at many a break of day;
That, when the sun's orb starts to shine, the stars just fade away.
When wonderment manifests, it takes away one's breath;
When the drum beats, the buzz of a fly cannot be heard.

Once again, wonderment simmers, bubbles and ferments;
Once again, the Cup-bearer offers His cup's contents.
The Cup-bearer hath increased my wonderment with His chalice;
The intoxicating wine hath rendered me yet more zealous.
Once again the Musician hath tuned up His harp to play an anthem;
That celestial melody opened another door to wonderment.

If thou art searching out the secrets that fill thee with astonishment,
Open thine inner eyes to the marvels in the dale of wonderment.
Then, in apparent oppression, thou wilt find that justice abides;
Thou wilt discover a hundred wisdoms in such justice disguised.
Out of divine wisdom, myriad doors of grace have been flung open;
Many offered their lives so that divine grace should flow to all men.

Behold! In the humble words "I do not know" much knowledge is concealed;
In the midst of apparent darkness, an ocean of light is revealed.
O Bahá! In some knowledge there lieth wisdom prodigious;
It is not hidden; indeed, it is infinite and obvious.

If thou art at all familiar with wonderment's mysteries,
Thou wilt see divine truth hidden in religious ordinances.
Behold! The inward truth in the outward form is discernible;
To understand hidden secrets divine love will thee enable.

Therefore, know thou that even some wars are, indeed, but peace in disguise;
In self-annihilation, thine immortal life thou wilt realize.
Open wide thy discerning eye to perceive the actuality;
My dear! Conflict doth not exist if thou dost see the reality.
Seeming peace or war is the product of the mind's creation;
As fame or shame is the product of our imagination.

If thou art eager to see the reality of the mystery of God;
To see Divinity manifest, observe the Manifestation of God.
To grasp the mystery of return, search thou with thine eyes inward;
Thou wilt see that all created things and humans move towards God.
Behold in a drop of water the mysteries of an ocean;
Bear in mind that in a droplet of water the sea can be seen.
If thou split apart the tiny nucleus at the heart of an atom;
Thou wouldst see a whole sun manifested in its innermost atrium.
Thus thou knowest that, except the Beloved, nothing else exists;
When the Absolute His reality displays, all else desists!

Since the Sun of God doth shed the energy of its light on all creation,
If thou study it with the eyes of justice, thou wilt find all things in motion.
Close thine eyes to all non-essentials and illusive existence;
Ascend high to the celestial domain of the mystic compass.
Out of the wings of love make thou a ladder reaching to paradise;
Thou wouldst then traverse an unmeasurable distance in just a trice.

If, with thy Beloved, thou desirest to come into union,
Then leave thou behind both the worlds and whatever lies within them.

The Valley of Wonderment

When thou art wandering all alone in the valley of His love,
Lo! Thou wilt find the entire world also seeking the Beloved.
Observe the lovers through thine inner eyes and carefully watch them;
Thou wilt see all are searching unceasingly after the Loved One.
Jacob-like, all are searching after their cherished Joseph;
All are instinctively eager to find their Best-Beloved.
Since the lovers receive assistance from the invisible realm,
No chain can fetter them and no obstacle can them overwhelm.
Love doth make a lover so anxious in the search for his Loved One,
That his worldly ties and his existence are swept away and gone.

He removeth his heart entirely from the outer world;
He plants the love for his Beloved in his heart and soul.
With great zeal he doth set out towards the abode of his Heart's
 Desire;
He closeth his eyes to all fettering ties and every worldly snare.

If the ultimate goal of a lover is to meet his Beloved;
Then, into "The Repository of Mysteries", he should delve.
"The Repository of Mysteries" is a gate to the world of love;
In this book are portrayed the traits of true lovers along their questing
 path.
If thine heart doth beat with love and thou art a perceptive person,
To the melodies of "The Repository of Mysteries" hearken.

O thou with insight! Open thine inner eye to truth's domain;
Forsake thou the world and disentangle thy self from its chain.
The Face of the Heart's Desire is seen manifest and resplendent;
The lover hath no other desire than to see his Beloved.
Other than to behold his alluring Loved One, a lover hath no fancy;
He is smitten with the Beloved and yearns to see His Beauty
 entrancing.

As his Loved One removed the veil from His luminous Face;
The lover's selfness melted; the veil was torn and displaced.
When the central Orb of divine unity shed its effulgent lights;
It burnt away the veils of divers forms and put fancies vain to flight.
When the attributes of the Ancient of Days manifested;
Then Moses reduced to ashes all the earthly qualities.
When a droplet hath fallen into a vast and billowing ocean;
Its traits are annihilated and the traits of the sea it doth gain.
When a man's human traits are burnt away by love's own quality,
He is transformed; his deeds are coloured with God's divinity.

II The Repository of Mysteries: Translated text

With divine mysteries, the Beloved of God[1] is innately intimate,
He doth stretch His hand out from His bosom as the Hand of the Absolute.
To the people, the mysteries of divine power, He doth portray;
He performeth miracles, though in a human form He is arrayed.
Everything He doeth is the very deed of the Beloved;
Everything He willeth is a reflection of the Will of God.
Since within Him are reflected God's qualities and attributes,
Though He appears in human form, He manifests the Absolute.
Since totally annihilated is His every earthly quality,
God doth, therefor, crown His head with the diadem of immortality.

O Thou, the Absolute One! O Thou, the Sovereign of All-kindness!
There is no existence save Thine in the seen and unseen cosmos.
Let our hearts be illumined by Thy light resplendent;
We pray Thee; heal us from our cross-eyed vision's ailment.
By Thy favour, apply collyrium to our bleary eyes to help us see,
Rather than seeming diversity, only a single Reality.
Thou hast the remedy to cure our selfishness and haughty conceit!
Thou art our Physician; Thou art our Plato and our Galen, indeed.
A small portion of Thy favour can heal the whole world;
Out of Thy Grace, do Thou guide us to tread the right road.

O Thou, our Messiah! The life-giver of every body, mind and soul;
O Thou, Divine Physician! Thou dost heal our grave ailment and make us whole.
O Thou, our spiritual Guide, our Master and our Beloved Friend!
I have no refuge save Thee; all my affairs are in Thy hand.
No shame, no shame if the ignorant call me infidel or otherwise defame!
Who else, who else, other than Thee, is my Beloved, the One I adore and esteem?
Whether I am intoxicated or sober, I revere Thee;
Even if I were godless or worshipped idols, I adore Thee.
What is it to me to be an infidel or godly, to be naive or shrewd!
What is it to me to be considered safe or feared, to be cultured or be crude!
What is it to me to be wise or unwise, to be skilful or untrained!
What is it to me to be learned or untaught, to have fame or be shamed!

The path of worldly-wisdom is a long and imaginary boulevard;
The lovers experience no rapture save through reunion with their Beloved.

---

[1] One of the 99 titles of Muḥammad.

The Valley of Wonderment

Tied to reason, thou seest here a compatriot and there a foreigner;
When wonderment arrives, thou seest no difference between Cathay and China.

Once again the flame of love blazes in my heart's inner chambers;
Once again love's kindled fire is scattering wide my dying embers.
Once again the flames leapt high in both my heart and soul;
The veil was rent and, into view, there came another world.
Wonderment hath struck; abandon thy reason and intelligence;
Close thine eyes to all the changing forms of the world of transience.
Only those who are unconscious know the higher consciousness;
Only the attentive listen to the celestial summons.
Though language portrays and clarifies the inner condition,
Love wordlessly conveys more clearly the inner emotion.

Oh sweet-tongued parakeet! The veil is rent; speak with erudition;
My heart is inebriated from the chalice of reunion.
O parrot! Once again spread out thy wings in the heaven of utterance;
Repeat what thou dost hear from the One that speaketh behind the looking-glass.

When the enamoured wayfarer left his friends, and on his path went,
Describe to us all that he experienced in the realm of wonderment.
Of his existence and his egoistic self no trace doth remain;
He found himself totally immersed and floating in a great ocean.
He went from astonishment to astonishment and was captivated;
Neither remained a sign of his existence, nor even the concept of it.
He gained a new-born inner vision in the realm of wonderment;
What he saw was beyond reason, could not be heard or spoken of.
Journeying, he gazed with inner eyes on wonder upon wonder;
He observed many things; his amazement grew deeper and deeper.
By the Beauty of the All-Glorious, at times, he was dumbfounded;
Then, with light eternal, his entire being would be pervaded.
At times, with his body and earthly life, he felt restless and wearied:
Now detached from existence's fetters, he longed to be finally freed.

Many people of ecstasy were struck down in the tempest of wonders;
For lightning flashes in wonderment's valley amidst the rumbling thunders.
Many a mystic tree was snatched by the root within that dale;
The rushing gale of wonders blew at full blast throughout this vale.
Many people were unshackled from the chains that had them held;
To reach the realm of glory's liberty, they were thus impelled.

In this valley the wayfarer will have passed through many a vicissitude;
Now, astonished and astounded, before the open mystic door he stood.

The wayfarer is in a great amazement; his state is revolutionized;
As he journeys through this wondrous realm, the core unity he doth
   recognize;
Such marvels flash before the eyes of the wayfarer along his way;
They are a great blessing, filling him with discovery's blissful sway.
At every moment, he beholds a new and wondrous world;
His whole being with dazzling lights is filled and overwhelmed.
And all the time, he doth observe yet another new creation;
Glad tidings ring through his inner ears in resonant vibration.
Greater and greater grows his astonishment and amazement;
He is endlessly immersed in an ocean of wonderment.
He becomes absorbed in the work of God as seen by His very light;
His whole being overflows with eagerness and prodigious delight.
Discovering divine mysteries leaves him stunned in stupefaction;
With his sharpened vision, he beholds the breath-taking new creation.
The Lord's handiwork amazes him with all its wondrous marvels;
Illumined brightly by this spirit realm, onward he still travels.

O dear one! We must deeply ponder over and meditate on
All phenomena and their meaning in the world of creation.
We will see the door of knowledge on every side is open;
This leads to the mysteries within every atom hidden.
As every created thing holds for us a scientific lesson,
We will rejoice to see ajar the door to all such treasured wisdom.

Consider, for example, the dreams of every human being;
Lo! So many mysteries a simple dream may be concealing!
While we are asleep our five senses are inactivated;
Yet many divine mysteries are in that state secreted.
Lo! Within a dream how much wisdom there is treasured;
Look! How many worlds in a dream remain unmeasured!
The door of knowledge opens and permits thine exploration;
Though asleep thou dost converse and engage in supplication.
Though, at thine home, the entrance doors are locked and barred
   securely,
In the twinkling of an eye, thou art in another city.

With no movement of thy feet thou dost find thyself in rapid motion
Then, in a trice, thou hast reached a town at some faraway location.
Without troubling thine ear, thou canst hearken;
Without using thy tongue, thou hast spoken.
Perhaps what thou dost dream tonight may yet happen later,
When some ten years will have elapsed, in the world of matter.

O brother! Indeed, what a lover dreams becometh reality;
For into the future, with the eyes of the Beloved, he doth see.

The Valley of Wonderment

O brother! How long wilt thou, in thine ego, thyself envelop?
How long wilt thou dream of what will never in truth develop?
Like a dream, the outer form of religion is a sign
But its treasured inner meaning is as clear as the sun.
When appears, with lustrous glory, the new Revelation,
The dreams of former faiths come to pass with great precision.
There are several inner wisdoms within a dream concealed;
Only to the people of insight is the meaning revealed.
Only the people of this Valley can understand the significance;
With the aid of His pure light they have traversed much that is of relevance.
Without using their ears, their eyes or tongue, they have explored the valley;
In the realm of hidden mysteries, they have observed it all clearly.

The things thou seest plainly in the outer world today;
Thou hast, with thy inner vision, already passed that way.
What, in some dream ten years ago, thou saw, now long-forgotten,
Thine outer eyes, in present time, observe the same things happen.
Behold! Much secret wisdom is treasured in a dream;
This is a trust of God placed in every human being.
Lo! This sign of the realm is of divine unity; it invites thee
To pick from the rose-garden of wonders a blossom of mystery.
Therefore, know thou that all the kindred and nations are one;
Think of a hundred thousand years or one hour—it is one!
Although the forms multiply, but one is their origin;
There are various paths, yet all lead to one destination.

Meditate on the difference between Divine unity and variety;
Thus wilt thou comprehend the mystery of unity in diversity.
The realm of diversity means both the worlds of the unseen and seen;
Whereas, Divine unity doth the dazzling lights of the Being mean.
Ponder over for a while the diverse forms and central unity;
Mayhap thou wouldst become immersed in the light of the Ancient Beauty.

Contemplate both these realms through thine inner vision;
With thine Heart's Desire, thou wilt surely reach reunion.
Observing the divergence of the two worlds and their mystery;
Now see the Beloved's Face, which will send you into ecstasy.
With clear vision thou wilt make distinction between these two realms;
O dear one! Only with thine inner eyes, thou canst it discern.
Creation is the world of diversity, Godhood is Divine unity;
By the guiding light of His sun-like Countenance, the right path thou shalt see.

II The Repository of Mysteries: Translated text

Lo! Study all by His light, bright as a sun, and thou wilt clearly
    fathom:
Unity is the Oneness of God; diversity is creation's spectrum.
All the hidden mysteries will then to thee be revealed;
Thou wilt see the Beloved Beauty entirely unveiled.
O dear one! Thou dost discover the celestial realm of holiness;
While with thy discerning eyes, thou dost traverse throughout the
    hidden realms.

Some, for comprehending, cling to reason and, on it, totally rely;
Thus, whatever cannot be grasped by their limited minds, they will
    deny.
When their reason cannot identify a phenomenon's reality,
They hesitate to accept it, doubting the simple truth's actuality.
They do not see the hidden mysteries as their inner eyes are closed;
We can but hope that they will grasp the enigma of the one true God.
They do not know that the human mind is too narrow to discern
The abstruse meaning of such a delicate and subtle concern.
Since they have not comprehended the hidden mystery,
They have only observed some foliage and twigs on this tree.
They are not aware of the tree's concealed fruit;
Seeing hidden fruit requires deep inner sight.

A Divine mind is needed, which is able to see
The hidden fruit on every bough of this mighty tree.
How can feeble human reason comprehend the Holy Scriptures?
How can the limited mind discern the infinite mysteries?
How would any fragile, earth-bound spider ever manage to ensnare,
In its web, a flying phoenix, soaring high up in the stratosphere!
That is the reason that the King, the Honour of the world,
Was the Diamond-mine of Life, and the Master in both realms!

Aḥmad, Who was the Pride of Religion—its scintillating Star;
He, Who was the Abode of certitude for every wayfarer,
When he was immersed in deep meditation, His longing He expressed;
It was like a flower from the rose-garden of the vale of wonders.
In His state of wonder, that King of Bounty uttered His plea,
Speaking thus: "O God! Increase in me my wonderment in Thee."
By the words "Increase in me my wonderment", the Prophet meant:
"Increase my inner vision so that I can see Thee with Wonderment!"

So, if thou wouldst reflect and meditate deeply on the world of
    creation,
Thou wilt find the world of being all-inclusive and in utmost
    perfection.

Lo! How the creation of the human being is flawless to the extreme;
The mysteries of both the worlds are concealed within the depths of him.
Contemplate thou the world of being; in the entire cosmos, thou wilt admit:
Both the visible and invisible worlds are most perfect and consummate.
Behold! How perfect and complete hath been the human being's mould,
—Enshrining the secrets of the physical and spiritual world.
Man is exceptionally perfect, endowed with great potentiality;
In man is the manifestation and image of God Almighty.
So, man is a crystal grail in which can be seen the whole creation;
Man is the highest manifestation of God, tooled to perfection.
It is an actual fact that so many worlds have been folded up in man;
O my dear! Look at him with the inner mystic eye to discover them.
Man looks a meagre being in his outward fleshly mould;
But, within him, a whole universe doth itself enfold.
Whereas, merely like a crescent, is man's apparent form;
Within him is enveloped, in its beauty, the full moon.
On the tablet of the human being is the greater world engraved;
The mystery of both the seen and unseen worlds is in him portrayed.

So, even shouldst thou reckon that man is a puny creature,
Nonetheless, folded up in him is mystery unmeasured.
He may seem such a weak and wretched creature in his physical form;
But a delicate and subtle mystery is treasured up in him.
He appears restricted and encompassed in his material mould;
Yet, with his innate potential, he can encompass the whole world.
Therefore, one should exert the utmost efforts in progressing;
So, that this encompassed one becomes the one encompassing.
When to effort is added the Divine Being's confirmation,
All trace of what is animal must yield to elimination.
Unless the animal qualities have been totally effaced,
How can the innate lights shine forth and become fully manifest?
When man is purged from defilements, is polished and made pure,
Then, the true meaning of being human becometh clear.
Thus, the Divine mysteries become unveiled and evident
Through the light of that loving Beauty, the Luminescent.
Then the inner mysteries of God become to thee perceptible;
As, for all the Chosen Ones, the Divine mysteries are visible.

Having passed through the Valley of Wonderment, the wayfarer now doth enter
The Vale of Self Annihilation, where true poverty he will encounter.

II THE REPOSITORY OF MYSTERIES: TRANSLATED TEXT

O thou who art keen to know! After the wayfarer's journey
Through the Vale of Wonderment, he doth attain true poverty.
This is the meaning of true poverty—to be, of all save God, divested;
The path's ultimate goal, for the sake of which, mystics have their all
    invested.
Without God's aid, how could anyone succeed in self-annihilation!
Yet, within the reach of wayfarers, this is their final destination.
Henceforth, in the lights of reunion, the wayfarer is immersed totally;
He shines all over, decked with attentive ears and an eye of acuity.
When thou dost meet His shining Sun and see it face to Face,
Everywhere is filled with lights; for no shadow is there space.
The seeker is intoxicated, blissful in union with Divinity;
How think of diversity? Behold! It is unity upon unity!

Were he to descend from unity's realm to the plane of diversity,
Then, he might talk of 'me' and 'we', and use the words 'limit' or
    'boundary'.
While, in the realm of unity, there is but one ultimate Reality;
Who would not be overcome by it, left staggering in inebriety?
How could within His sunlight a shadow exist?
Light itself hath no shadow nor will let one persist!
He is immersed in the lights of unity to such a degree
That he payeth no attention to the world of diversity.
In the ocean of lights, he is so profoundly immersed and fully absorbed
Neither thought of Divine unity nor world's diversity him doth disturb.

Wonderment came and swept away all imaginings and thought;
His whole heart was rapt in the blissful light of reunion with God.
How should anything cross his mind other than God
When his whole being is filled with the lights of God?
He is obsessed by the light and circles around it like a moth;
He is full of ebullience and, for Him, with excitement doth throb.
In that ecstatic state, how could he think of beginning and end?
How can what is the outer or inner of things engage his mind?
How could he even consider what the hour, what day or what year it
    might be!
Wonderment came and unity within unity—this is eternity!
The light of the Central Essence from every aspect doth shine;
Thus all attributes are excluded by Unity Divine.
The men of insight have expressed a pearl-like estimation;
They have called attributes non-essential marks of creation.

After so much explanation, thou must surely grasp the argument
That all else except God is non-essential and non-existent.
These 'I' and 'we' words are veils that obscure our vision of His Face;
Tear asunder the blocking veils to see His shining Countenance.

Take steps to overcome all distracting physical desires;
So that uncovered for thee will be the ancient mysteries.
Close both thine outer and inner eyes to what thy lower self doth
 demand;
For behold! Then thou wilt find thyself in reunion with the Beloved.
As long as thou art wrapped up in thine illusive existence;
How, from that noose, wouldst thou catch a glimpse of His
 Countenance?
Then, let thy self-ness, thine I-ness and thy we-ness be effaced in total
Self-annihilation is the criterion for thee to become immortal.
When effaced are egoistic qualities and every trace of selfness;
Then thou wilt see nothing else save that the one true God is manifest.
If all thy 'thou-ness' is abolished, thou art annihilated in Him;
Thou art then the creek, the river and the sea, all merging as one
 Ocean.

O Junun, repeat thou what the Centre of the Covenant hath referred
 to;
Break the shackles of limitation; soar high in the sphere of the
 Absolute.

HE IS GOD

O dear one! Thus far I was trying to break the talisman's seal;
Now the hidden treasure is completely uncovered and revealed.
Up to now the attributes of God I was describing and extolling;
Now I am going to make some comments about the Absolute Being.
Lay aside every written or spoken word, every speech or colloquy;
Then bring thou an attentive ear, instead, to learn of Divine Unity.

In "The Repository of Mysteries", up to now, my main pursuit
Was the mystery between this world and the realm of the Absolute.
Henceforth, the profoundest inner Reality we will be exploring;
With this verse, we have now touched upon the theme of the Essence
 of Being.

The Essence of God, which is that Existence ineffable,
Is called by mystics the Absolute Being, Unconditional.
Although this unconditional Being is the Mainstay of the cosmos;
He is, likewise, totally independent of all names and attributes.
To say 'unconditional' of the Essence of God is paradoxical;
Rather, He is beyond being termed conditional or unconditional.
There is no fettering chain to restrict and tie this Being;
His Essence is free; nothing is binding Him or confining.
He is free; He is far beyond calling liberated or restricted;
He is totally above being portrayed as detached or connected.
He is beyond the limitations of the human mind and its conceptions;
He is exalted above the grasp of either common man or Chosen Ones.

Although, of His inner Essence, there can be no restraint;
At times He manifests Himself in attributes' constraint.
Yet, as in the bonds of attributes His Essence is not chained,
It is as if He breaks the bonds to remain the Unconstrained.
Because He is entirely unconstrained and His freedom is total;
He hath of the Absolute Being all the qualities essential.

When He bestows His attributes on a common or a Perfect Man,
That is respectively termed a prophet of God or a Chosen One.
Because He is independent from any quality that is limiting,
We do not call His Essence anything other than the Absolute Being.
When God's attributes are manifest in a prophet, they are bound by limits;
God, in His Essence, is Unconstrained; He is beyond the bounds of attributes.

The One Who is constrained we call a Prophet and a divine Guide;
The One Who is the Absolute, we can, in fact, in no way Him describe.
He, Who is embodied in a physical form, is bound and fettered;
While of the Absolute, we remain silent; no word can be uttered.
The One Who is bound is, at once, the Wayfarer and the Desired One;
At times He is the Worshipper; at others He is the Worshipped One.
As the Unconstrained He is neither the Servant nor the Lord;
How strange! Not God; not creature! He is Unknown by either word!

O Thou, the Protector of the world! O Thou, its Fashioner!
O Thou, Whose bright Face is the Core of my love so passionate.
O Thou, the Lord of the people, of loving favour the Sovereign!
O Thou Whose Countenance is the Treasure of the seen and unseen!

O Thou! Thy being[1] hath branched out from the Ancient Root;[2]
O Thou, companion and aide of the Beauty of God!
Through Thy speech and the movement of Thy pen unerring
Thou hast in the whole world raised a tumult amazing.

O Junun! O thou crazed lover who in chains are tied secure!
Break thy fettering shackles and like a raging lion roar.
Beware! Now bring to an end thy dissertation for thy time is running out;
Bravo, that love hath effaced thine existence, which to thee is of no account.
Desist from admonition; the ocean hath started its surging and seething;
The mystery of the ecstasy of lovers to its climax is speeding.

---

[1] Referring to 'Abdu'l-Bahá
[2] Referring to Bahá'u'lláh

The Valley of Wonderment

Hush! Do not speak; the sea of Divine Unity is billowing and foaming;
Sense, reason and intelligence have been sucked into its depths and are drowning.
Be silent; there is no room for outer forms of display;
Begone; the inner meanings, too, are left in disarray.
How could a mere outer form speak of the yonder realm?
How, by God's Ocean, would a droplet not be overwhelmed?
While thou dost rely on reason, thou perceivest but forms and vocabulary;
When the ocean of wonderment surges, it is unity upon unity.

Once again, in my heart, a few more verses fermented in their ecstasy;
The listener to that melodious song became all ears in his entirety.
Though the souls of the audience are athirst enough to drink an ocean;
The more they imbibe from this sea, the more it fills up in proportion.

This book of rhyming couplets is a fountain, flowing love;
The more its waters are consumed, the more it gusheth forth.
May God assist thee each moment that thou dost peruse this book,
To see in it a surging sea and not just a babbling brook.
God opened for us the door to the hidden mystery;
No one is able to close this door because of jealousy.

I beseech God that He showers upon thee His confirmations and favour,
That the door leading to ancient secrets is opened wide to thine endeavour.
I hope and pray that the effulgent lights of Abhá are cast upon thee;
That, being immersed in His abundant lights, thou wilt feel all ecstasy.

Out of His loving-favour, Abhá hath assisted His loved ones;
So that their hearts became illumined by the light of Bahá's suns.
The Centre of the Covenant also showered His loving-kindness;
He is a unique pearl in the whole of the world, a gem most priceless.
He hath surpassed all human beings in His servitude to God;
Ceaselessly He offers the grail of eternal life to the world.

Man hath a limit and that is to serve God and His laws observe;
He should not follow his corrupt passions and, thus, disgrace deserve.
The purpose of man's creation hath ever been to worship God;
O son of man! To follow divine laws every human is bound.
Every being can bring forth fruit only to its predestined degree;
Lo! All created things are arranged according to divine decree.
So, there is a level and a limit for every created thing;
And every creature is satisfied with its own constraint and standing.

Every created thing, with satisfaction, hath its given grade accepted;
None of them hath complained about their limit or their rank
  repudiated.

Hereafter, we are at the stage of the seventh level of the journey;
With a resolute heart I will describe the details of the next Valley.

The Seventh Valley
The Valley of True Poverty and Absolute Nothingness

Now, raise thou thy voice to define the Valley of True Poverty;
Thou art well-familiar with the wayfarer's most arduous journey.
After tarrying in the Valley of Wonderment for but a moment,
The wayfarer starts on the path to sheer nothingness and self-effacement.

Make haste now for we stand at the entrance to the seventh Valley;
Around these seven stars the revolving universe doth dally.
Praise be to the loving-kindness of the All-Glorious Sovereign;
That the sun of the seventh Valley hath dawned on the horizon.
In this valley whose title sings the song of Self-annihilation,
The seeker dies to self and forever finds in God his habitation.

All created things that are visible or apparent;
Are but weak, poor and needy; one and all are suppliant.
Understand: whatever is in the world of creation
Is in the state of utter need and total privation.
Whatever is in the realm of God is wealth and free of neediness;
It is entirely filled with love, effulgent lights and radiant brightness.

If a lover hath attained the stage of union—thus to see the Face of God;
It indicates that his self is totally effaced and that he lives in God.
When, by Divine assistance, he is in reunion with the Beloved,
He is, by the light radiating from God's Face, entirely illumined.
He sees nothing save his Heart's Desire with that luminous Countenance;
Thus he circles round the abode of his Beloved like a compass.

Nothing remains in his heart save the visage of his Beloved;
That is the ultimate goal of the wayfaring life he hath led.
The dazzling light of God illuminates his being entire;
To see God in His full splendour with ardent zeal doth him inspire.
He will burn away all limiting veils that are him enveloping;
And, thus, he will be filled with the light of the Sovereign of Being.
Anything other than the thought of his Heart's Desire
Will be consumed, from its skin to its marrow in that fire.

When all his egoistic qualities are razed in the flame;
God will, then, crown his head with immortality's diadem.
Annihilation in God is the ultimate goal of the wayfarer;
For only God is the Everlasting and everything else will expire!

II THE REPOSITORY OF MYSTERIES: TRANSLATED TEXT

O reader! When the wayfarer hath finally attained to such a station;
His inner self is annihilated in God. Herewith, a valediction!
That is the true meaning of the compulsion of utter submission;
That is the highest stage the mystics achieve, and their consummation.
The wayfarer is now totally free, detached in a preeminent way
From whatever could be an attachment to the world and the earthly
    life's sway.

Therefore, those who have attained to re-union with God,
Possessed of no limited earthly things of this world,
Being entirely set free from all the things of creation,
Thus, to the transient outer world, they pay no attention.
In the ocean of reunion with God they are all immersed;
Filled with the lights of the All-Glorious to the core of their hearts.
No idle fancy or vain imagining do they entertain;
They are not confined to a limited life on this earthly plane.
Sanctified from any sort of egoistic thought, they do not cherish
Any desire to amass wealth and earthly goods that can but perish.
They are free of any idle fancy and vain imagination;
They are brimming over with glory's effulgent illumination.

Whatever he had of existence he risked on the dice that he tossed;
In the battle arena of love, he gambled it all and he lost.
When, for the sake of love, he sacrificed his very existence,
Into the field of love he entered with courage and persistence.

While the bazaar of love thrives and prospers with all of the
    wayfarer's losses;
The dervish's life remains lonely to the end of the route that it crosses.
This is an arena that will bear no allusion or mention;
It cannot be hinted, imagined or grasped by any notion.
Being placeless and timeless, it is beyond all conception;
It is beyond argument; there is no room for discussion.
There is no harbour here for the outer world's limitations;
There is no haven for transient worldly associations.

Thou must bear in mind that the entire world of creation
Must disappear, as the star fades before the rising sun.
O son of man! Whatever the people of world possess
In forms and figures, all are within their set parameters.
O noble one! Whatever exists in the Presence of God
Is sanctified and free from being described by any word.
One must meditate deeply over this delicate matter;
To unravel its meaning and its import to discover.

It is narrated that there are four streams flowing in Eden;
Those are the cause of intoxication in that walled garden.

The Valley of True Poverty and Absolute Nothingness

Nectar, honey, camphor and wine flow in these four rivers;
And these four streams are to the entire world the life-givers.
Nectar symbolizeth love and wine is symbolic of enthusiasm;
Honey meaneth the ecstasy when, of God's Face, there is a vision.
As regards camphor, the inner meaning
Is to the Holy Spirit referring.

In fact, the Holy Spirit is on the highest sphere.
Now to the story about the phoenix give thou ear.
When her age reaches to one thousand years, the phoenix
In despair, piles around her a heap of twigs and sticks.
Perched on the firewood pile, she bemoans and bewails;
As, with grief, the sad story of her life she tells.
She remembers all her actions and the conduct of her existence;
She recollects her past and her present, and of her future she thinks.
Being immersed in her desires, she is filled with regret;
Then, from her wings, a spark flashes and the fire is set.
When totally burnt up is her existence,
Out of love, she lays an egg in the cinders.
She sees herself unchanged and exactly just as she hath ever been;
The reality of her being doth still the same as ever seem.
She is, as from time immemorial, she hath ever been—quite
    undamaged;
Not the slightest particle of her being hath been reduced or ravaged.

This is a mystery, which those who are with God in reunion
Know of; for them the oyster shell of the secret pearl is open.
Love performs miracles without use of the tongue;
When thou art old, it transformeth thee—thou art now young!

Every created thing becomes apparent, having come into being,
Visible in the lights from the Beloved Bahá's Face emanating.
The lover's zeal renders him nimble and vigorous;
He soareth high; the seven heavens he traverses.
Thus, the true goal of wayfaring apparent becometh;
Like the morn in the light of the sun of God, it dawneth.
The wayfarer followeth the path faithfully in his quest for God;
To the vale of poverty and self-annihilation he hath trod.
That was the reason that the Sultan of humanity,[1]
Referring to this stage, said: "Poverty is my glory."

There is much glory in poverty; He was of this mystery aware,
Being, Himself, so close to God at the distance of two bows or nearer.[2]
This is the realm where the inner meaning of the Word:

---

[1] Muḥammad
[2] Qur'án, Súra an-Najm, 53:9

II The Repository of Mysteries: Translated text

"All on the earth shall pass away, but the face of thy Lord"[1]
All these meanings are uncovered, becoming manifest and self-evident
By the light radiating from the Face of the Most Glorious Beloved.

When Bahá removed the veil that covered His resplendent
    Countenance;
The entire universe came into view by Its lights luminescence.
"The veil will be removed" became apparent, and its meaning known
When the beauty of the Loved One's charming Face was unveiled and
    shown.
The secret of creation was unveiled and became apparent
In the effulgent lights of that enchanting, rose-faced Beloved.
When that Lord of loving-favour undraped His radiant Countenance;
All creatures came into being in their visible existence.
As His beauty manifested in its beaming emanation,
The brightness shining from His Face brought all things into creation.

Now the blessing grace of God floodeth not the hearts' terrain
Save in the spiritual springtime, as April clouds bring rain.
Though the grace of the All-Bounteous doth not altogether cease—
For how would life be possible without His energizing grace!
Nonetheless, to every age and people a certain portion is allotted;
It is in a preordained measure by the King of destiny dictated.
God, the Paramount Provider of sustenance for every age and era,
Hath singled out for each of us a certain share of His Celestial manna.
Thus, predetermined flows His grace, premeasured and apportioned;
His grace He showers upon all without being petitioned.
The sustenance is sent down according to the time's exigency;
He allocates for that time from what He holds within His treasury.
Whatever doth exist cometh from the treasure-house of God;
And what hath been created, in its possession, holdeth naught.

O thou trusted one! From the Beloved's cloud of mercy doth but fall
His showering rain only on the soil of the garden of the soul.
Thus, in the spiritual springtime, doth His grace pour in a deluge
Most bounteously upon the souls and hearts, at the start of each new
    age.
No other season has such a share of this most great bounty;
At no other time is His grace showered so abundantly.
When a land hath turned into a barren plain, what profit could it gain
To have a share of this plenteous grace that is showering down like
    rain?
How would the salt-marsh benefit from such an outpouring's share?
How could it enjoy the freshness if the rain was falling there?

---

[1] Qur'án, Súra ar-Raḥmán, 55:26–27

The Valley of True Poverty and Absolute Nothingness

O brother! To precious pearls, not every sea gives birth;
Nor nurtures in its depths lustrous pearls of any worth.
Not every tree branch bringeth forth the most delightful bloom
To tempt the nightingale in spring to warble there its tune.

I pray that, by the confirmation of Bahá and His loving-kindness,
We might inhale from the immortal garden immortality's fragrance.
I pray that we might breathe the scent of the true garden of roses,
That each of us the true and celestial Friend, thus, recognizes.
As we imbibe the aroma of love's everlasting garden,
We take delight in the Cup-bearer of love's manifestation.
The lights emanating from His radiant Face we can see;
We shelter in the shade of the tree of immortality.
Thus we conjoin with and become the intimate companions
And faithful friends of the everlasting city's denizens.
So, under the shadow of the tree of the Covenant of God,
We remain forevermore in union with all creation's Lord.

When, by the loving-kindness of the Divine Sovereign, we attain
The sublime and supernal echelon of self-effacement's plane.
We gaze upon the luminous Face of our Hearts' Desire;
Detached from all else, our hearts with the lights of God afire.

What a wonderful state I am in! How ecstatic are my feelings!
My inner eye is free from the bondage of all created beings.
I see nothing else but God whatever I might scrutinize;
The light of Bahá hath given inner vision to my eyes.

This is the conclusion that thou hast been yearning for;
God aided thee to reach thy goal without hard labour.
O seeker! This is the end to which thou didst so ardently aspire;
And, with the assistance of God, thou hast reached the goal of thy
    desire.
Thou didst tread the mystic path to reach the bounteous King;
And thou hast gained the presence of the most loving Friend.

The dazzling lights of His Face blank out His luminous Features;
While, conversely, no veil concealeth His radiant Countenance.
His chosen ones call the dazzling lights a covering veil;
And yet, what would be able to, that shining sun, conceal?
Indeed, save for those dazzling lights, there is no veil His Countenance
    to shroud;
Open thine inner eyes the lustre of His Revelation to behold.
The Chosen One,[1] that Sovereign of utmost stainlessness of character,
Disclosed a mystery of hidden truth to Kumayl,[1] a staunch believer.

---

[1] One of the titles of Muḥammad

II THE REPOSITORY OF MYSTERIES: TRANSLATED TEXT

Whenever that King of the people of ecstasy a point portrayed;
He would disclose a mystery which was like a lustrous pearl displayed.

The light emanating from His Face hath all the sun's magnificence;
The brightness of its blinding light is the veil that hides His
    Countenance.
There is no doubt that He is shining in His fulsome revelation;
O pure in heart! With the most splendid lights came His
    manifestation.

O thou with the clear vision! His manifestation is so effulgent
That to everyone He is visible, observable and evident.
He revealeth Himself in creation's works, so obviously detectible
That He is more visible—more evident—than all else that is visible.
There is no veil covering His Beauty save Its dazzling glory;
His Face is concealed in Its own blinding lights that shine so strongly.
The veil that doth conceal His Face is only His own radiance;
Into a screen have turned the lights that shine forth from His
    Countenance.

He is hidden because of the intensity of His Revelation;
He is unseen because He is shining with such blinding emanation.
He is manifestly evident in His bearing's intensity;
Just open thou thine inner eye to behold His bright irradiancy.
"Even as the sun, bright hath He shone; but, alas,
He hath come to the town of the visionless!"[2]

This Holy Mariner,[3] with the burden of the weighty gift He brought,
Thus became the Anchor of both earth and heaven, which by Him was
    wrought.
Both the heaven and earth became established firmly by His Being,
Eternal nearness to the ultimate Reality acquiring.
His Presence hath become the very purpose of the universe;
He is the Pivot around which the heaven and the earth traverse.
As His own essence had been annihilated and effaced,
By the Attributes of God, His inmost Being was replaced.
Both worlds were stirred and stimulated by His nearness,
Greatly honoured were they to receive His tender, loving-kindness.
All the atoms of the universe were most desirous
Wishing that He should on them cast His glance all-bounteous.
His being became the ultimate purpose of the whole creation;
Both worlds became visible and apparent through His emanation.

---

[1] **Kumayl bin-i-Ziyád an-Nakha'í** (كُميل بن زياد النخعي) was a saintly convert in the time of Muḥammad and later a most loyal companion of Imám 'Alí.
[2] Jalálu'd-Dín Rúmí
[3] The Manifestation of God

The Valley of True Poverty and Absolute Nothingness

The world circleth around Him like a moth around a candle flame;
He is the Mystic Mount that every phoenix wisheth to attain.
He hath become the Axis around which the whole world pivots;
His Being is the pillar that supports the entire cosmos.

His Presence is the Primal Point while but a line all else doth seem;
He is the Ocean fathomless; while all the rest is but a stream.
The people's souls are clearly seen by His inner vision;
Every atom of creation is faithful unto him.
Each one conveys to Him its homage in the language of humility
Kneeling down or in prostration before His overwhelming Majesty.
With high reverence and respect they bow down, wishing to convey
Their homage, love, submission and how greatly Him they glorify.

With great joy and utmost meekness towards Him they approach
From every side, yearning and desiring His abode to reach.
With lowliness, reverence, and rejoicing in the greatest of delight
From everywhere they come to His dwelling, to circle round it
    resolute.
With hearts full of love for Him, to know Whom is to know God,
They are lining up to circumambulate His abode.

From His chalice all the atoms of the cosmos are intoxicated;
With their inner cores magnetized, they can but follow Him
    fascinated.
Mountain range, ocean breeze, thundercloud and lightning,
Up above, down below, east and west; and everything
That has existence and is named in the circles of creation,
In that Beloved's Presence, genuflects in adoration

Yea, yea! In the Presence of Him Who is All-Glorious,
Both the speaker and the listener are left stunned and speechless.
They are willing, even eager to assist Him in His plight;
Although astounded are they all by the power of His might.
In the Best-Beloved's court all creation bows to His command
All entities are in His power's grasp like prayer beads in His hand.

Now this citation from the Qur'án might draw thine interest:
"All shall be brought into our presence". [1] *Do analyze this verse.*
"All shall be brought into our presence" means that perisheth not any
    soul;
To be certain that the souls are immortal, think it over well.
Not a particle of anything created will perish ever;
To one who says it perisheth, thou must answer: "No, it will never!"
So, at this stage, all created things are in attendance before Him;

---

[1] Qur'án, Súra Yá-Sín, 36:53.

II The Repository of Mysteries: Translated Text

All will appear in His presence with no reduction or expansion.

If thou art drawn to peruse a citation from Bahá'í Scripture,
Then, "The Hidden Words" revealed by Bahá'u'lláh will thee enrapture.
Thus He saith: "Beneath the shade of the tree of life ye were all gathered, [1]
Assembled in My presence most attentive to the words I uttered.
When three most holy and sacred words I did express;
Ye listened, awestruck, lost as if in unconsciousness.
If now ye sanctify your souls and purify your hearts,
Purging them from vain imaginings and all defilements,
Ye would then recall that sacred situation
And behold that celestial realm with clear vision.
The truth of My utterance would unto you all be evident;
The mystery of My utterance would be clearly apparent."

Oh! May my life unto those sugar-shedding lips be made a sacrifice!
To people of certitude Thy secret meaning is evident advice.
Thine utterance is as clear for the people of ecstasy and zeal
As the sun is in the sky! Oh! Thy words quicken every withered soul.

O Thou, my Beloved! Thine animating words encompass
Profuse layers of meaning within their inner nucleus.
O Thou, the Forgiver! At dawn, the breeze of Thy favour
Wafts over those who lie on their beds deep in their slumber.
O Thou, the glorious Sovereign! I pray Thee, out of Thy great bounty,
Grant Thy lovers imperishable and everlasting prosperity.

The tongue is given to man to give praise unto Thee;
The heart is given to man to meditate on Thee.
Thy love is the treasure of the peoples of the earth;
Recollection of Thee is brings health to every heart.
The remembrance of Thee is the healer of all ills;
Thy love is the confidant of every heart it fills.
Thy blessed Name is, for all sickness, the best therapy;
Remembrance of Thee for all ailments is the remedy.
Thy Being is the Sheltering Paradise where, in peace, to dwell;
There will never be an end to extoling Thy Beauty. Farewell.

When the wayfarer traverses this valley he hath already passed
All stages; he hath travelled stage by stage with the help of Bahá's lights.
Since the wayfarer through all the stages now hath trod,
He hath gained eternal life in his union with God.

---

[1] Bahá'u'lláh, *The Hidden Words*, Persian Part II, No. 19.

The Valley of True Poverty and Absolute Nothingness

This implies that anything, which hath ever come into existence,
Is now, before his inner eyes, quite apparent and in evidence.
Everything is clearly visible to his spiritual perception;
His soul and inner eyes are illumined by God's confirmation.
He hath left far behind the notion of God as Omnipresence—
Manifest in His creation. He hath passed beyond such concepts!
He attaineth to oneness above and beyond this station;
O noble one! This union is of hallowed consecration.

O dear one! It is beyond the murmur of words and commotion;
To this stage only the people of ecstasy gain promotion.
This state is a sacred realm, a divine level, a blessed space;
It is beyond any utterance; no words can portray this place.
Only rapture is able to encompass this theme's mystery;
It is beyond the sound of words, discussion, or controversy.

Whosoever hath attained this level and doth dwell in that realm;
Can comprehend the mystery though rapture may him overwhelm.
Or anyone, who by the breezes of this spring hath been refreshed,
Will discern this mystery of the mysteries of the Beloved.
He certainly doth recognize to which ecstasy we are referring;
He feeleth the mystery of our rapture and hears what we are saying.

But the wayfarer, who on the spiritual path treadeth,
Should not deviate from the law by even a hair's breadth.
I stress that from divine Law he should not go astray,
For, to reach his final goal, it showeth him the way.

O son! Verily, within religious Laws lies enshrined
The mystery of the Path; consider this and understand.
O dear one! Likewise in Divine Law thou must explore,
Until the 'Truth' thou findest. There thou must search, therefore.

The divine Law is a tree of whose boughs 'Truth' is the fruit;
Look thou through love's inner eye and this thou wilt not refute.
Through all the stages of thy spiritual journey, a firm hold thou must
> *take*
Of the robe of the Divine commandments, thus, of their sweetness to
> *partake.*

Every person in the world is searching for something;
O comrade! They seek to find it, ardently yearning.
Everyone wishes for a desired outcome in the depth of his heart;
Whereas we desire only love to be of our supplication the result.
What is the use of thine efforts if towards no purpose thou dost aspire?
Praying with some object in view helps the wayfarer achieve his
> *desire.*

O thou the Solomon of time! Thou dost know of all birds their tongue;
Sing thy song to match the tone of each bird that thou dost come upon.
To a bird that believes in fatalism, speak thou of fatalism;
While, to a bird that suffers from a broken wing, speak of stoicism.
If a nightingale warbles winsome melodies, do not pluck its plumage!
Do not treat the royal falcon the same way thou might treat a partridge!

Junun was motivated by his zeal to receive the grace of God;
Thus, he began to tread the spiritual pathway in the quest of God.

Appendix

1 Sangsar

After the Islamic revolution, the name of Sangsar was changed to Mahdíshahr (Persian: مهدئ شهر, also Romanized as Mehdishahr) in order to give it a purely Islamic identity. The city is in Semnan Province, and is 175 kilometres east of Teheran. Mahdí or Mehdi was the title of the hidden Imam of Shí'a Islam whose appearance the faithful are awaiting. Shahr is the Persian word for town. So Mahdíshahr literally means town of Mahdí.

2 Other works

A book of Junun's poetry has been published in Persian under the title of *"The Melodies of Junun"*. It contains various styles of Persian poetry and a short account of his life story.

In addition to poetry, there are also manuscripts of Junun's works in prose. Two significant manuscripts are:

1. Treatise that expounds the process of creation, written in response to questions from some mystics.
2. Dissertation that demonstrates and advocates the validity of the new Divine Revelation, the Revelation of Bahá'u'lláh.

3 Dr Davoudi

Dr A. M. Davoudi was the secretary of the National Spiritual Assembly of Persia. He used to take an early morning walk near Junun's house. One morning, after the Islamic regime came to power, Dr Davoudi went to the park for his morning walk but he did not return. He had been kidnapped and was never seen again. We have no information about what happened to him. He had been a great scholar and author, being a Professor of mysticism and philosophy at the Tehran University. He was then a member of the 'Reviewing Committee' that examined *"The Repository of Mysteries"*, prior to its publication. He made the following comment: "We [The Reviewing Committee] only review the format of this book. This is the only book whose inner meanings and content we cannot assess. It is beyond the grasp of our intellectual concepts."

Dr Davoudi was an authority on Rúmí because he used to teach Mathnáví, the monumental work of Rúmí, at Tehran University. He could see a similarity between Rúmí and Junun. We have to bear in mind that Rúmí is a giant in Persian literature. He is Persia's greatest mystic poet, a star shining from the horizon of the East. He was admired by 'Abdu'l-Bahá. Many early Bahá'í teachers and scholars considered the Ma<u>th</u>nàví to be a bridge between Islam and the New Faith. Dr Davoudi expressed his view, "the tone of Junun's poetry is the same as Rúmí's"—many others have testified to this point. Some believe that Junun had an advantage over Rúmí because he had lived in the New Era. Mr 'Abdu'l-'Alí 'Alá'í, an author and scholar, who was then the chairman of the National Reviewing Committee, said, "The station of His Holiness Junun is higher than Rúmí because he probed into the depth of the revelation of the Blessed Beauty."

4 Influence of the Manifestation

Another Bahá'í scholar, Mr B. Farid, who was martyred in recent years, had a deep insight into the Bahá'í Holy Writings. He was one of the few experts on the Writings of the Báb. Then, as a member of the 'Reviewing Committee', Mr B. Farid commented on *"The Repository of Mysteries"*: "Most probably Junun remains incomparable in his profound insight until the next divine revelation." When he expressed this view I did not agree with him. I argued that the Bahá'í Faith is spreading around the world and people with various backgrounds will come under the banner of the Faith. People with great talent will study the Bahá'í writings and uncover the pearls of wisdom and meanings. He said, "The profound insight of Junun is not just the outcome of reading. I have been studying the Bahá'í writings for forty years. It is a divine grace and bounty." He further explained when the Manifestation of God is on the earth, like a magnet, he draws up those believers whose hearts are utterly pure. They reach to a level of wisdom and mystic vision to which it will not be possible for others to soar until the same condition is created by the next Manifestation of God.

Later, I found an utterance by Bahá'u'lláh in which the Blessed Beauty testifies to the fact that at the period when the Manifestation of God lives on the earth, some of the pure in heart will be inspired with a wisdom and true understanding of such a high degree that even if a person studied for a thousand years they could not reach that level of spiritual insight. The views of the great scholars quoted above testify to the fact that, in some aspects of his literary works, Junun will remain incomparable in the coming centuries. He has been, and will remain, a torch holder of a new Revelation for unborn generations. He will shine like a beacon-fire on the mountaintop.

Bibliography

'Abdu'l-Bahá, *Memorials of the Faithful.* Bahá'í Publishing Trust, Wilmette, Ill. 1997.

Bahá'í Prayers, *A Selection of Prayers Revealed by Bahá'u'lláh, The Báb, and 'Abdu'l-Bahá.* Bahá'í Publishing Trust, Wilmette, Ill. 1991.

Bahá'í World Faith: Selected Writings of Bahá'u'lláh and 'Abdu'l-Bahá. Bahá'í Publishing Trust, Wilmette, Ill. 1976.

Bahá'u'lláh. *Gleanings from the Writings of Bahá'u'lláh.* Translated by Shoghi Effendi. Wilmette, Ill.: Bahá'í Publishing Trust, 1983.

Bahá'u'lláh. *Prayers and Meditations by Bahá'u'lláh.* Trans. Shoghi Effendi. Bahá'í Publishing Trust, Wilmette, Ill. 1987.

Bahá'u'lláh. *Tablets of Bahá'u'lláh revealed after the Kitáb-i-Aqdas.* Trans. Habib Taherzadeh et al. Bahá'í Publishing Trust, Wilmette, Ill. 1988.

Bahá'u'lláh. *The Hidden Words.* Trans. Shoghi Effendi. Bahá'í Publishing Trust, Wilmette, Ill. 1939.

Bahá'u'lláh. *The Kitáb-i-Aqdas: The Most Holy Book.* Bahá'í Publishing Trust, Wilmette, Ill. 1993.

Bahá'u'lláh. *The Seven Valleys and The Four Valleys.* Trans. Marzieh Gail. Bahá'í Publishing Trust, Wilmette, Ill. 1986.

Bahá'u'lláh. *The Summons of the Lord of Hosts: Tablets of Bahá'u'lláh.* Bahá'í World Centre, Haifa. 2002.

Clarke, Adam. *The Holy Bible*, vol. II. Thomas Tegg & Son, London. 1836.

Dhukai-i-Baydai, Ni'mat'u'llah. *Tadhkirih-i-Shuara-i-Qarn-i-Avval-i-Baha'i* (Persian) (An Anthology of the Poets of the First Century of Baha'i Era). Mir'at Publications. 2013

Encyclopaedia Iranica, vol. IX, Columbia University, Bibliotheca Persica Press, New York, p. 206–207.

Harvey, Andrew, *The Way of Passion: A Celebration of Rumi.* Jeremy P. Tarcher/Putnam, New York, 1994.

Lights of Guidance: A Bahá'í Reference File. Compiled by Helen Hornby. New Delhi: Bahá'í Publishing Trust, 1994.

Rabbani, Rúḥíyyih Khánum. *The Priceless Pearl.* Bahá'í Publishing Trust, London. 1969.

Shoghi Effendi. *God Passes By.* Bahá'í Publishing Trust, Wilmette, Ill. 1974.

Taherzadeh, Adib. *The Covenant of Bahá'u'lláh.* George Ronald, Oxford. 1992.

The Compilation of Compilations, vol. II, compiled by Research Department of the Universal House of Justice. Bahá'í Publications Australia, Mona Vale. 1991.

www.ingramcontent.com/pod-product-compliance
Lightning Source LLC
Chambersburg PA
CBHW062024220426
43662CB00010B/1460